FINDING JOHN RAE

FINDING
John Rae

ALICE JANE HAMILTON

RONSDALE PRESS

RONSDALE PRESS
3350 West 21st Avenue, Vancouver, B.C. Canada V6S 1G7
www.ronsdalepress.com

Typesetting: Julie Cochrane, in Granjon 11.5 pt on 15
Cover Design: Julie Cochrane
Cover Photo: John Rae, age fifty-one. Courtesy "Images": John Rae.
Paper: Ancient Forest Friendly Silva (FSC), 100% post-consumer waste, totally chlorine-free
   and acid-free.

Ronsdale Press wishes to thank the following for their support of its publishing program: the
Canada Council for the Arts, the Government of Canada through the Canada Book Fund, the
British Columbia Arts Council, and the Province of British Columbia through the British
Columbia Book Publishing Tax Credit program.

Canada Council Conseil des arts
for the Arts   du Canada

Canadä

BRITISH COLUMBIA
ARTS COUNCIL
An agency of the Province of British Columbia

Library and Archives Canada Cataloguing in Publication

Hamilton, Alice Jane, 1950–, author
   Finding John Rae / Alice Jane Hamilton.

Issued in print and electronic formats.
ISBN 978-1-55380-481-9 (softcover)
ISBN 978-1-55380-482-6 (ebook) / ISBN 978-1-55380-483-3 (pdf)

   1. Rae, John, 1813–1893. 2. Rae, John, 1813–1893 — Travel — Arctic regions.
3. Franklin Expedition (1845–1851). 4. Arctic regions — Discovery and
exploration — British. 5. Northwest Passage — Discovery and exploration —
British. 6. Hudson's Bay Company — Biography. 7. Inuit — Canada — Social life
and customs — 19th century. 8. Surgeons — Scotland — Biography. I. Title.

FC3961.1.R33H36 2017   917.1904'1092   C2016-907441-2   C2016-907442-0

At Ronsdale Press we are committed to protecting the environment. To this end we are
working with Canopy and printers to phase out our use of paper produced from ancient
forests. This book is one step towards that goal.

Printed in Canada by Marquis Book Printing, Quebec

To the Inuit,
who knew all along,
but never received the
credit they were due

ACKNOWLEDGEMENTS

I gratefully acknowledge the information provided by the staff of the following archives, museums and institutions: the Hudson's Bay Company, the Royal Anthropological Society of London, Royal British Columbia Museum, National Museums Scotland, the Government of Manitoba, the Hamilton Association for the Advancement of Literature, Science and Art (HAALSA), the John Rae Society, the Orkney Islands Council, the Royal Society, and the Royal Geographical Society.

I deeply appreciate having had access to the works of such respected authors and historians as William Barr, Pierre Berton, Alice den Otter, Ken McGoogan, Peter C. Newman, Rudy Wiebe, John Wilson, and David C. Woodman. John Walker's film *Passage* was also an excellent source of information. John Rae's published Arctic narrative, as well as his letters to newspaper editors after he returned from the Arctic, gave me valuable insight into his character.

I am grateful for the assistance and advice of Inuit elder and statesman Tagak Curley, historians Mary and Bruce Davey, literary advisor Sue Henry, firearms expert Chris Williams, historian, curator and master storyteller Tom Muir, historian and author Bryce Wilson, John Rae Society president and author Andrew Appleby, Arctic scholar and author Russell Potter, Orcadian historian Ingirid Morrison, Stromness Museum curator Kathleen Ireland, and former owners of the Hall of Clestrain, Jean and Ivan Craigie. Many thanks to my editor Ronald Hatch, for expertly and patiently guiding me through, and to my husband Don Cooper, who was always willing to listen, brainstorm, draw maps, and offer advice and encouragement.

PART I

Discovery

[1854]

→ *Boothia Peninsula, Arctic*
[APRIL 1854]

My men and I had been struggling for days, pulling and pushing two heavy sledges across a section of bumpy Arctic terrain on the Boothia Peninsula, half-blinded by blizzard conditions. Around midnight on the fifth day, exhausted, we stopped in the lee of a hill for a rest and food. I had just finished rewrapping my young assistant Jacob Beads' frostbitten toes, when I heard a high-pitched sound and reflexively reached for my rifle. Moments later, a team of barking dogs emerged from behind a curtain of snow, pulling a man on a sled. I relaxed and lowered my gun.

The Esquimaux driving the dogs appeared to be travelling alone. As he came closer, I noticed something shiny affixed to his sealskin cap. It was a gold band, a sight familiar to me but it looked completely out of place on the clothing of an Arctic native. The gold strip was identical to the bands worn on the caps of British naval officers, and I was immediately curious to learn where he had acquired it. I stepped forward smiling, following the customary native greeting of showing teeth. I had somehow managed to retain all of mine thus far, which is more than could be said of our visitor. I extended a hand toward him, laid the other upon my breast and said, "John Rae."

He responded in kind and announced that his name was In-nook-poo-zhee-jook, but that I could call him In-nook for short. This suited me because I would certainly have botched any attempts to pronounce it properly. Even after living in the Arctic for more than twenty years, I struggled to master the language, and I relied on translators for in-depth communication with the local people. When I recorded Esquimaux names in my notebooks, I tried to spell them out in letters that matched the way they sounded to my untrained ears.

I instructed my interpreter, William Ouligback Junior, to invite the newcomer to join us. Our visitor readily accepted the offer, to which we cheerfully added gifts of pemmican for his dog team. The man's friendly demeanour was engaging, and the conversation soon took on an amiable flow. I noticed that he reached up and touched the band often, as if to reassure himself that it was still there. It was obvious that he was proud of it. I reasoned that, to him, it probably signified a high level of achievement and status.

We shared a meal of roasted caribou meat around a fire prepared by my guide, Thomas Mistegan, and enjoyed conversing about the weather, hunting and other matters. In-nook explained that owing to poor winter sealing conditions many families far in the north, including his own, were very hungry. He and other men from his community were driving their dog teams south, in search of caribou and muskox.

He asked Ouligback about the purpose of our small travelling party. Were we hunting, too? I replied that we were on a journey to learn more about the land. We had begun with a group of twelve men, but various misfortunes had caused us to leave some of them at depots along the way. Our number was now reduced to just five, two of whom had fallen ill and were unable to walk much at all.

I identified myself as a man of medicine, a healer, first. Then I explained my tasks as the overseer of the fur trade in the region, representing the Hudson's Bay Company. He confirmed his knowledge of the organization, so I went on to say that I travelled a great deal, making maps for my employers and for the British government, and working on the latter's behalf to build strong trading relations with the people of the Arctic. We were making more than maps, of course. We were involved in an ambitious British push to open the Great White North of the American continent and use it for access to the Orient. What a paradox that Britain was attempting to conquer massive mountains of ice in the West, in search of faster routes to the riches of the East!

It was complicated for me to describe to anyone my many professional roles at the time: surgeon trained in Scotland, chief factor for the Hudson's Bay Company's fur trade enterprise in the Mackenzie District of the Arctic, certified land surveyor, scientist, naturalist and explorer who was periodically seconded to the British Admiralty under special circumstances. My duties were many and varied, so I usually told people I worked for the Hudson's Bay Company, and just left it at that.

In this instance, however, I felt that some further explanation was necessary, because our new Esquimaux companion was wearing an item which could prove to be of great interest to thousands of British citizens. I suspected there was a chance that In-nook knew something about the fate of the missing Franklin Expedition, which was last spotted by whalers off the southeast coast of Greenland in August 1845. I did not add that for the past seven years, I had been actively engaged in the massive search for the two lost ships and men. I hoped he would mention the gold band during the course of our conversation so as to reveal something about where it had come from.

I did not bother to mention my other mandate: creating detailed records of the region's flora and fauna for various scientific institutions in England, since that information would have been of little interest to him. It was a certainty that In-nook and his people knew more about what crawled, walked, flew and swam in his territory than any foreign observer could ever learn.

In-nook was an enthusiastic listener and conversationalist; I could see that we would get along well. I explained to him that our plan was to rest for several hours, then pack up our supplies and continue our westward journey to the coast of the Boothia Peninsula. Would he care to join us for a day or two? Our stock of food provisions was plentiful, and we would be pleased to have his company. He agreed to travel with us for a while, after which he would take his leave to continue hunting. Would he be willing to sell us a dog to help us on our journey? I asked. Alas, he was unable to do this because he needed the full team to move the large amount of meat he hoped to acquire for his people.

He assisted us, though, by carrying our infirm men on his sled, and I was grateful for his kindness and cheerful company. I was growing more worried about our young fellows, Jacob Beads and James Johnston, who were in poor condition. I had lost only one man in all my years of leading expeditions in the Arctic: Albert One-Eye's senseless drowning five years earlier in the rapids of the Coppermine River still haunted me. I was doing my best to treat Beads' frostbite and Johnston's loss of strength during this journey, but it was obvious they were struggling and needed rest. With In-nook's help we made better progress; the two young men were able to stay off their feet while we travelled together.

On the second night, after we finished our supper, In-nook enjoyed a smoke with my men by the fire. Our bellies were full and the mood was relaxed. According to my timepiece, it was almost two o'clock in the morning; the sun would be fully above the horizon in less than an hour. I decided it was as good a time as any to inquire about the gold capband.

I referred to William Ouligback by his nickname. "Mar-ko, I wish to pay a compliment to our companion about the shiny band he is wearing on his hat. It is most impressive." In-nook smiled when he heard the translation; he reached up and touched it, clearly flattered.

"Where did he acquire such an interesting ornament?" I asked.

Ouligback translated my question, and then In-nook embarked upon a tale which caused the interpreter to sit up straight, his eyes widening with growing surprise. I listened closely as the slow process of storytelling and translation took shape.

"He says the shiny band came from a man who was seen marching in a group of many, many Kabloonans — white men — dragging a boat on a sledge. They looked cold, tired and hungry. It is said that all of the men perished on their journey across the ice."

A shadow suddenly crossed my heart. *Dear God. A group of white people that large in number must have come from Sir John Franklin's travelling party.* I envisioned starving, ill-dressed and ill-equipped British naval men, stumbling across the frozen landscape in a desperate search for a rescue that never happened, doomed to die ahead of their time in a windswept, icy-cold and barren hell. *Did the Esquimaux have the answers to the nine-year mystery of what happened to Sir John Franklin, his ships and crew?*

My mind leapt towards an obvious question: *Why didn't the Esquimaux people help the poor travellers?* I almost blurted out my thoughts but restrained myself because I did not want to insult our guest. I hoped the answer would be revealed without prompting, so I looked down at my hands and held my tongue. I didn't dare risk losing an opportunity to gain information about the mysterious marching group. I carefully chose the words of my next question: "How did In-nook come to be in possession of the shiny band?"

"He says his cousin gave it to him. His cousin saw the men."

I filed this startling information away in my memory for further investigation. Did In-nook's cousin steal the band from a white man marching to his death? Had there been some kind of confrontation? That notion was doubtful. I respected the generous nature of the Esquimaux in that region, so I set aside any thoughts of native violence against the weakened white men. There had been rumours about the Royal Navy's occasional ill treatment of the Esquimaux, but it would have been imprudent to speculate about what may or may not have occurred between the two groups.

"Does our friend know in which direction the Kabloonans were travelling?"

In-nook pointed towards the south, and Ouligback translated his reply: "It is said they were dragging a boat filled with objects on a sledge and marching towards the mouth of a large river, that they were seen about twelve long days' journey to the southwest of where we are now."

I knew of an infamous river that flowed northward from deep in the mainland and emptied into the Polar Sea, in the general region to which he referred. The Great Fish River was widely feared because of its dangerous rocks and innumerable rapids, but sections of its swirling waters were open and teeming with fish throughout the year. Earlier explorers such as Sir George Back had charted it on British maps of the Arctic when he, John Franklin, John Richardson and a large party of men were searching for a route from the mainland to the Northwest Passage to the Polar Sea. The river was later renamed Back's Fish River by the British government, in honour of the admiral who produced a great number of meticulous, delicate sketches and paintings of the region. I wondered if the group of men In-nook's people observed had been marching in search of the river, which would have led them south to possible rescue. Its waters would have provided them with continuous sustenance as they journeyed, thus increasing their chances of survival. If good fortune had been with them, they would have eventually met up with British parties on the lookout for them. It grieved me to think that their courageous march had not lasted long enough to save them.

"Did you personally see any of the men, In-nook? Talk to them?"

"No," he answered through Ouligback. "But many of my own people did."

I knew from experience that Arctic natives rarely made errors when they passed along information from one to another, and another and so on. Because of the absence of writing materials in their homeland, the stories of the Esquimaux were generally verbatim and accurate. In the snowy and windswept north, even a message inscribed upon a rock in blood could vanish within minutes. The lives of the people depended upon meticulous oral record-keeping. I had to find a way of documenting his people's accounts of what they witnessed. "May I meet with your countrymen who saw them? In case there are some Kabloonans who may still be alive."

"I can send a message to the others."

I looked up at the sky. The snow clouds had moved on, which bode well for the next leg of our journey. The waning April moon was barely visible, a slender fingernail of light in a sea of stars. Darkness was brief in the Arctic at this time of year, thus extending our ability to cover long distances if the weather was reasonable. I hoped our new acquaintance and his people would be willing to help us solve the mystery of the missing ships and crews.

I pointed to the moon. "Mar-ko, give In-nook directions to our Hudson's Bay Company depot at Pelly Bay, and tell him we would like to meet with witnesses there after a full moon's time. Advise him that our countrymen are looking for the Kabloonans they saw, that they have been missing for a long, long time. Their families are distressed, anxious to know of their fates. We will trade gifts for information," I added.

Rewards in the form of foreign tools, buttons and cloth were highly valued amongst the Esquimaux; I never travelled without a good supply of these precious items. In-nook nodded gravely as he listened to Ouligback. He agreed to send out my request as soon as he could.

During our fireside conversation, In-nook revealed more of what he understood to be true. It was said that people who saw the marching white men told of how frightening they looked, with spirit-dark faces and rolling eyes. The natives were reluctant to approach them and risk being infected with a fatal disease, or harmed in some other way. He pointed to our rifles, which we always kept close at hand. He said the marching men carried dangerous tools like ours. His people feared these objects that made sharp, loud noises and ejected clouds of smoke; perhaps they carried a poison of some kind. That information answered my question as to why the Esquimaux did not attempt to engage with the marching Kabloonans and offer them assistance.

Through Ouligback, I described my heavy rifle's function and purpose: for hunting and protection against unwelcome advances by predators. I told him the story of when I had been alone in a clearing during a solitary hunting excursion some years earlier. Silently, a band of wolves, more than a dozen of them, emerged from a cluster of bushes, and trotted — as if they were one body — directly towards me, then suddenly stopped, forming a silent, semi-circular formation around me. The largest one had slowly advanced, evaluating the prospects of bringing me to ground for a meal. I remained still, knowing there was no chance of surviving an attempted run for it. I slowly dropped to one knee and raised my rifle, praying that I would be able take the huge beast down with one well-aimed shot. Pulling the trigger with a shaking finger, I fired. The wolf let out a yelp, and jumped sideways. My heart sank when I realized that I had merely grazed him. I thought of grabbing the large knife in my pocket if the confrontation came down to a full-on battle. The knife was a last resource, but I would fight to the bitter end.

There was no time for me to perform the impossible task of reloading the rifle and pulling the trigger again. I had my knife at the ready in case the pack became more aggressive, but before I could reach for it, a miracle occurred. Instead of springing forward and running me down, the pack turned around and trotted off in the direction of the bushes, followed by the wounded male. The sharp report of the gun and the clipping of the lead wolf must have caused them to change their minds about attacking me.

In-nook listened to my story with keen interest. We laughed when I explained that even with such a powerful weapon as a rifle and my extensive experience with knives, I was aware that I would have stood little chance against twelve wolves. I confessed that my entire body shook from head to toe for what felt like a long time after the wolves' sudden departure.

I picked up my rifle, explaining to In-nook that it was the same weapon which had grazed the wolf and changed the pack's notion of attacking me. I emptied the barrel of powder and lead before holding it out to him. At first he drew back, but I could see that he was curious to know how it worked. He held it for a few moments, moving his fingers along the grooves in the polished oak stock, feeling the smooth, metal barrel, curling his index finger around the crescent of the trigger. He rolled the ammunition around in the palm of his hand, assessing the weight and shape of it, while I explained through Ouligback how the firing mechanism caused a small amount of gunpowder in the pan to ignite, which in turn caused the powder in the barrel to ignite. In-nook was intrigued to hear that these two sequential explosions resulted in the bullet being shot out of the barrel at a high rate of velocity.

"If In-nook wishes to fire off a few test shots with the rifle, I will show him how to use it," I offered. Our guest smiled. Yes, he would like to do that. We returned to the discussion at hand. While Ouligback translated, In-nook resumed his story about the marching Kabloonans. I felt almost hypnotized as I watched the flames rising from the campfire and listened to the soft, rhythmic sound of our companion's voice. In that setting, it seemed to me as though I was dreaming the news of the naval men's suffering, or hearing the conversation from a distance. Finally, after what seemed like hours, I turned to Ouligback.

"Mar-ko, we must ask two more questions." I held up two fingers for In-nook to see.

"One, can he tell me approximately when these Kabloonans were seen?"

In-nook gestured and replied: "Four winters past."

I was further taken aback to hear that if the marching men were, indeed, from the Franklin Expedition, a group of them had still been alive as recently as 1850, while search parties were scattered everywhere looking for them. When the expedition left England in 1845, the British Admiralty declared the ships were equipped to sustain life for three years, perhaps four if it became necessary to impose severe rations upon the crews. I wondered when the men had made the decision to abandon at least one of the ships, and how any of them could have survived for up to five long years in one of the harshest climates on earth.

"Two, would In-nook be willing to trade his shiny cap-band for one of my tools, so I may show it to the families of the men who died?"

There was a long pause while our visitor considered this proposal. It was abundantly clear from his melancholy expression that he was very attached to it and feeling conflicted about giving it up. Finally he gave Ouligback his answer.

"Our guest is disappointed to part with the band, but he has agreed to trade with you for it. For the families of the men who died."

I was relieved to have in my possession an object which had probably belonged to a British naval officer, as evidence that a group of men very likely from the *Erebus* or *Terror* was seen in an area southwest of Boothia Peninsula. I assured In-nook that his unselfish gesture would mean a great deal to the loved ones of the Kabloonans who had lost their lives in his homeland, so far away from their own homes.

The next day I kept my promise about showing In-nook how to use my rifle. He was a good student, and after several enthusiastic attempts to hit a target at fifty yards, he was able to relax, take aim and complete his shots with accuracy. He was impressed enough with the weapon to attempt some sort of trade for it, but of course I could not grant his wish. It was essential for Mistegan, Ouligback and me to carry one rifle each, for hunting and safety reasons.

→ *Boothia Peninsula*
[APRIL 1854]

We bade farewell to In-nook-poo-zhee-jook, he with one of our axes lashed to his sled, and I with the gold cap-band pressed between the pages of my notebook. We continued our westward journey across the peninsula, through foggy spring air and sticky snow, frequently meeting with rocky obstacles which forced us to reposition our equipment and alter our course. Complicating matters further was the worsening health of our two youngest men. In addition to these physical challenges, there was the near certainty, from what we had just learned, that Britain's two remaining search ships, piloted by Sir Edward Belcher aboard the HMS *Resolute* and Captain Richard Collinson with the HMS *Enterprise*, in addition to another party from America, were looking only for ghosts, not men. It was time for those search parties to find their way home.

I wrestled with making a decision about proceeding west at all, now that we had acquired such important information and our own travelling power was so diminished. By nature, I have always had a strong aversion to abandoning even the smallest of tasks. Even when great obstacles were presented to me, I was known for being determined to finish every undertaking I had set out to do.

I had charted the eastern coast of the Boothia Peninsula during an 1846 and 1847 expedition, when I ascertained that it was not an island as previously thought, and therefore unlikely to offer any link from the Gulf of Boothia to points west. Was I being stubborn and selfish, risking the lives of those two young men in my charge by persisting in trying to reach the western coast of the Boothia Peninsula at this time? What was I hoping to find there? I had a hunch; that was all. I asked God to grant me the wisdom and power to reach the edge of the Polar Sea and then return our two infirm men to their families, alive.

Ouligback and Mistegan never complained, but it soon became clear that we three were exhausted from hauling overburdened sledges across difficult terrain, especially when it blew a complete storm of ice and snow. My forty-one-year-old knees were growing stiff from the exertion, and my shoulders and arms were tight and aching. I had always been able to fall into a deep sleep for short periods of time and awaken feeling refreshed, but now that we had met In-nook and heard his story, my thoughts were racing and cluttered. A quiet mind eluded me.

During the few times we stopped on this troubled leg of the journey, I drifted into an uneasy half-sleep and experienced disturbing dreams. In one haunting image, I was lying face down on an ice floe in choppy waters, attempting to hold on to the slippery edges with frozen fingers. I saw images of men floating nearby, their vacant eyes open and their faces ghostly white. They were upright and bobbing about on the surface of the water, like tin bath toys. I awoke to the sound of nearby groaning. It was coming from Beads.

I knew that the two weakened young men in our party would fare better with a few days of absolute rest. I concluded that this could be accomplished if we built a good shelter and left them there with food, warm coverings and other provisions while we travelled only as far as the coast and then returned for them. Based upon previous surveys of the North American coastline and according to my calculations, it would take Ouligback, Mistegan and me two days to get there. Each man expressed relief when we discussed the plan. The boys could rest for a while and we could keep moving. We constructed a small snow hut to house Beads and Johnston, and I promised we would see them again in four days' time. I intended to keep that promise, no matter what we encountered when we reached the shores of the Polar Sea.

Our group of three pushed ahead on our snowshoes at a brisk walk, taking turns pulling my scientific equipment on one sledge. Not a minute was to be wasted. We consumed dried pemmican as we moved, pausing only briefly to rest. On the second day, the two guides suddenly stopped in their tracks and lifted their faces to the air.

"What is it, Mar-ko?" I asked.

"A little bit of a salty smell, Ablooka," he replied, using his Esquimaux name for me. He then said something to Mistegan, who nodded in agreement. "The coast is not far away."

A white veil of spring fog obscured our vision, making it difficult to ascertain our exact position, but according to my compass we were still on course and the coast should, in theory, lie due west and ahead of us. I sent Mistegan forward. He returned less than an hour later, reporting that visibility was poor, but the salty smell grew stronger, convincing him that we were close to our destination. He led us to where he had marked a spot with a pile of small rocks. We dropped the ropes of the sledge and sat down to rest. Now I could smell salt in the air as well. I pulled out my notebook and summarized the previous week's events, including our chance meeting with In-nook and his proffered information about the fate of the Franklin Expedition.

I was disappointed that our mission to map the west coast of the Boothia Peninsula would not be completed this year, but all was not lost. According to the custom of explorers in these northern regions, we constructed a cairn of rocks to mark our location, and cached some provisions within it. To this, I added a piece of paper with the date, my name and a description of the dual purpose of our expedition.

Once the cairn was sealed, something remarkable happened, and our sagging spirits were lifted. A sharp wind suddenly arose from the east and drove the fog away, revealing an excellent view to the west, all the way across the Arctic tundra. I sent Mistegan a few miles north in search of game, while Ouligback collected moss to build a cooking fire on the rocks.

With visibility improved, I was able to observe the area and take proper readings with my surveyor's instruments. I stood up and stretched. "Mar-ko, I am going to take a walk, climb that hill and see what's out there."

"All right, Ablooka. Fire looks good."

I picked up my telescope, rifle and shot bag. The wind was freshening; I tugged my sealskin cap down over my ears. When I reached the crest of the hill, I discovered that we were on a cape, jutting westward from the land and curling inward again. We were many hundreds of miles above the tree line; land elevations similar to this one appeared to be randomly strewn, as far as the unaided eye could see.

During a survey expedition a few years earlier, I had ascertained that King William Land was not attached to the North American continent, and was therefore a large island. I wondered what kind of channel existed between the two masses of land. Would it be completely blocked by centuries-old pack ice, that glacial colossus constructed of compressed layers of snow, ice and sediment? Pack ice descends and retreats with the changes of the polar seasons, but it never truly melts.

My heart skipped a beat when I looked down from my vantage point and noticed a long white strip separating two coastlines. A wide ribbon of ice snaked from the south and far out of sight, trending northward.

I dropped my things and scrambled down the hillside onto the rocks. Fresh snow covered everything. When I reached the shore and wiped some of it away, I saw that the ice was rough, fragile and young, the age of one winter season. This was indeed a channel, and its wind-driven waves had been frozen in a heartbeat of time with their crests still in place. The ice squeaked and muttered as the slow spring thaw broke the crystal bonds holding it together; I could see that its tenuous grasp on the rocky shoreline was giving way to water burbling up from beneath.

How far north was this channel's reach? Could Franklin's *Erebus* and *Terror* have come close to this area? Were they on the floor of the Polar Sea somewhere out there, or beset in pack ice and still visible? I had heard of the British government's recent decision to officially declare all of the men dead, but it came as no surprise to hear that Lady Franklin and her many supporters refused to believe it was true. In a letter from my sister Marion, I learned that upon hearing the announcement Lady Franklin donned gay, colourful clothing and declared that there was no reasonable basis upon which to make such a dreadful assumption. Word had it that Lady Franklin and Sir John's niece, Sophia Cracroft, appealed tirelessly to public sentiment to exert pressure on the Admiralty and prolong the search. They also raised funds to support a private expedition to ascertain what had really happened to Sir John Franklin and his men.

I climbed the hill again and took up my telescope. To the north, at a distance of around thirty miles, I saw a high mound of land jutting into the channel, dwarfing everything else in view. The map depicted the mass as part of the mainland, but I suspected this was not the case. If my hypothesis was correct, the land mass was in fact a large island. Its crescent shape and bulk acted as a sentinel and barrier, protecting the channel from the invasion of descending pack ice, thus explaining why the ice lying before us had been recently formed. A notion concerning the general location of a navigable link in the Northwest Passage began to take shape in my mind.

Excited, I returned to the temporary camp where a kettle of snow water was coming to a boil on Ouligback's fire. Mistegan had arrived from his hunting expedition with six adult Arctic hares for skinning and cooking.

"I'm sorry, Ablooka. No caribou."

I approached the men, waving my hands. Our tea and food would have to wait while I showed the men my remarkable discovery. "The hares will make a fine meal for us, Thomas. Men, come with me!" They followed me to the top of the hill; I pointed to what lay beyond.

"What do you think of this?" I asked, trying not to sound too enthusiastic. There was a moment of silence, a brief discussion between the two men in Cree, and then Ouligback replied.

"This ice is young, Ablooka. It travels from north to south, and it looks to go far. When it is warmer and the birds have arrived, maybe winds and currents can move a boat on its waters, to join with the rest of the Polar Sea."

My laughter erupted and spilled down the cliff onto the rocks below.

"By God in Heaven, it *is* young ice, fellows!" I cried, clapping them both on the back. "There is a very good chance that this is the waterway the British Navy has been trying to discover for over a hundred years. I suspect this may be part of the missing link in the Northwest Passage!"

I knew my discovery could not be verified until the channel was ice-free and fully navigated by a ship, next year at the earliest. I would have to be patient. In the excitement of the moment I wondered if my employers and the Admiralty would agree to equip me, so I could organize a two-pronged expedition to navigate the channel — both overland and by sea — to map the western Boothia coastline, and continue the search for the missing *Erebus* and *Terror*. I wondered again if the ships or at least some remains could still be found, and if by some miraculous twist of fate, any living British souls remained in the area. Was it possible that a sympathetic Esquimaux group had taken in some wandering Kabloonans? Perhaps we would find more answers at Pelly and Repulse Bays if In-nook was successful in finding people who were willing to come and speak with us.

"Mar-ko, explain to Mistegan that we must eat soon, take a short rest, pack up and retrace our route from the east. We should have about sixteen hours of daylight ahead of us. The wind may slow us down, but we've got to get back to Beads and Johnston. I will take readings now and make notes, while you prepare our meal and Thomas reloads the sledge."

As we worked I realized that with all the excitement of a fresh discovery, I had forgotten to give the cape a name. First, I logged the coordinates of the location in my notebook: Latitude 68°57'72" N, Longitude 94°32'58" W. I took temperature, wind and barometric pressure readings and so forth. Then I sketched my closest approximation of the elevations, contours and surroundings into my book so I would have my own copy when I produced the maps for the Hudson's Bay Company and the Admiralty in London. I pondered what a suitable name might be for the hill and the promontory adjacent to it.

"Point de la Guiche," I said to no one, recalling a fellow I had met on a train a few years earlier when I had been travelling from Hamilton in Canada West, to Detroit and New York. The strange little man wore smart-looking clothes and looked aristocratic enough, or so I thought at the time. Holding a monocle to one eye, he had introduced himself as Count de la Guiche. The journey had passed quickly because he turned out to be an amusing travelling companion, but I soon suspected that he was not a count at all. I am still not sure why I named that important place after such a frivolous person. Perhaps it was because the moment of discovery reminded me that things are not always as they first appear to be.

While we consumed our meal, we had a brief conversation about the fact that we had changed our travel plans because of Beads and Johnston. Mistegan shook his head, disappointed that we would be unable to continue our northward journey along the Boothia coast.

"Too bad those two boys came with us. I could tell they wouldn't make it. They were never strong enough. They aren't even full-blood Cree or Ojibwa. It's the blood that matters," he muttered. Ouligback translated and I replied:

"Whatever their blood is or is not, Thomas, it is our obligation to return them to their families alive."

→ *Pelly Bay*

[MAY 1854]

We arrived at the Hudson's Bay Company depot and settlement by the shore of Pelly Bay on the northern coast of the mainland, with Beads

and Johnston alive and in tow on the sledges. We had been able to purchase a dog from a passing native along the way; we were also lighter on
provisions, which helped us move more efficiently during the return leg
of our journey. I was encouraged to see a group of Esquimaux men,
women and children cheerfully encamped next to our own people, and
waiting for us. More were arriving with dogs and sleds. The speed of
communication amongst the Arctic natives over vast distances never
failed to impress me. It was not surprising that the news of our request
for information had spread quickly.

While my equipment was being unloaded, Hudson's Bay Company
men erected a tent for our meetings and stocked it with chairs and tables,
paper and pencils and so on. I was pleased to see that our native visitors
assisted them with good humour and energy, which bode well for collecting helpful intelligence from them. Before we retired to our respective buildings, tents and encampments, Company food was offered to all,
and pleasantries were exchanged. Early the next morning, I positioned
myself at a writing table in the interviewing tent. Two Company men
stood at the entrance to organize the flow of visitors, Ouligback settled
beside me to translate, and we began the interviewing process.

"Kabloonans. Many of them. Walking, falling down. They looked so
thin, like skeletons. Some had no strength to get up again and just lay
where they fell. Others tried to help them to their feet."

"Mar-ko, ask them to describe what the men were wearing."

"They say the men were poorly dressed for the weather conditions,
Ablooka. They were wearing light coverings, unfit for the winter cold,
with small caps and some kind of cloth wrapped around their heads and
necks. Their hands were barely covered with thin, stitched material that
was wrapped around each finger. These coverings were full of holes."

I scribbled notes as quickly as I could while he spoke, not wanting to
miss anything. "What was on their feet?"

"Their foot coverings looked worn and ragged too; the men moved
as if their feet were feeling much pain."

I winced. Frostbite. "Is it true that they were dragging a boat?" I
asked.

"Yes. The boat was on a sledge, which became stuck on the ice, again
and again."

"What was in the boat?"

"The people were nervous about coming too close to the Kabloonans, but it appeared as though the boat had many objects in it. It looked very heavy. It became stuck on pressure ridges rising out of the ice, and some of the men cried out as they tried to haul it up and over the icy mountains." I thought of the boat being filled with equipment such as scientific instruments, weapons and ammunition, kettles for cooking, bedding, extra clothing, oil lamps, medicine, personal belongings, and so on. It must have weighed well over a thousand pounds.

"Mar-ko, did the witnesses observe if anyone was in charge of the travelling party?"

"A big Kabloonan was leading the march." I wondered who the man was.

"Was there any communication between the natives and the British sailors?" I inquired.

"Not much," Ouligback replied. "They say the Kabloonans were frightening." I recalled that In-nook had mentioned similar remarks made by his people.

"How was that so?"

"The men were shouting things and making sounds that were unfamiliar, strange." Ouligback went on to explain that to the ears of the Esquimaux, the sounds were more like angry spirit noises than human voices.

"The local people were worried about the objects some of the men had strapped to their bodies. Long, hard sticks that looked as though they might be used as weapons of some kind. They had never seen people like this before, never seen the things that hung from their backs and shoulders."

Ouligback turned towards me, squinting. "I understand why the spectacle of the marching men, their rifles, and the strange sounds they made caused my people to be afraid," he whispered. "We must try to explain to them who the men were, Ablooka, what they were carrying, and why they were crying out like that."

I put down my pencil and looked at him. "Of course, Mar-ko. Take all the time you need." The exhaustive work we did together periodically caused me to overlook my interpreter's strong connections to these Esquimaux people, some of whom could well have been his relatives. I felt a twinge of regret, along with pity for the natives and the confusion they must have experienced when they saw spectres of white men, marching and uttering words in an unfamiliar tongue, shouting wildly, carrying objects that made no sense to the observers, dragging a boat with mysterious contents. It is within the nature of all human beings to fear things we do not understand.

—

We had been conducting the interviews for a week, when Ouligback brought to my attention that there were other Esquimaux who knew more about what happened to the marching men, and who had apparently acquired many objects from them. I listened to this news with great interest, and decided that it would be wise for us to conclude these Pelly Bay interviews and move on to our Repulse Bay headquarters. Repulse Bay had better facilities for treating our ailing young men, and we would be able to accommodate more Esquimaux visitors with food and payments for additional information.

"Mar-ko, please tell these people that they are very brave to travel so far from the North and pass along this important information to us. We will pack up and move on to the Hudson's Bay Company settlement in Repulse Bay, where more food and supplies will be available. Tell them how to get there. Explain that we invite all of their countrymen to come and meet with us for sustenance and information, that we want to hear more, and that we will pay well for any items they may have collected from the Kabloonans. Tell them these objects have important spiritual meaning for us."

→ *Repulse Bay*
[JUNE AND JULY 1854]

We left the dog and one sledge behind at the Pelly Bay depot, which was just as well because the temperatures had climbed above freezing during our journey to Repulse Bay. Most of the snow on the ground had disappeared, and we frequently became bogged down in mud. Swarms of black flies and mosquitoes harassed us along the way; it was an unpleasant journey, and our patience was hanging by a thread by the time we arrived at our destination. My spirits lifted, though, when I saw that an even greater number of Esquimaux were arriving to meet with us. They brought many items of British origin with them, including engraved silver cutlery and plates, badges, lengths of gold braid, compasses, watches, telescopes, pieces of firearms and a tattered *Student's Handbook*, proof that there had indeed been contact between the natives and the men from the doomed Franklin Expedition. I thought of our interviews with the visiting natives at Pelly Bay, of their insistence that there had been little to no communication with the marching Kabloonans. I wondered how they had acquired all the objects they presented to us. From the dead, perhaps?

As the weeks went on and more relics appeared at the table, it became apparent that the handbook was the only piece of written material among so many different kinds of items. I wondered how it had survived alone when no other papers were in evidence. Of course, if the Esquimaux found books amongst the men's possessions, they would have had no use for them except as fuel. What had happened to the ships' logs, notebooks and 2,900 books from their two libraries? What fate had befallen the works of Shakespeare, Milton, Donne, and even books published under the name of the expedition's commander, Sir John Franklin? Had those cherished writings given the doomed British men any comfort while they waited for rescue?

I traded tools for every object our visitors brought to the table. They expressed appreciation for the items I gave them in exchange for the British sailors' belongings. In my view, they gave us something of immeasurable value: tangible evidence and straightforward answers to difficult questions.

For two months — the duration of the fleeting Arctic summer — I conducted meticulous and methodical cross-examinations of every person who brought relics and information. With Ouligback's help, I spoke with them in groups, as individuals and in various combinations, looking for common threads and checking for possible inconsistencies in their stories. An increasingly alarming picture emerged as men, women and older children added more details to the stories we had heard from In-nook and the natives we met with at Pelly Bay.

"Two large ships were stuck, far apart, in the sea ice. They were there for many winters. Kabloonans came off the ships, sometimes in small groups and, at other times, in large ones."

"The smaller groups had one boat with them, and the larger ones had two, which they had to drag and push across the ice on sledges. The boats were heavy, full of things, and they got stuck a lot." This testimony concurred with what we had heard from the previous group.

People pointed to the canvas walls of the interview tent. "The men put up sleeping places like this one, made of materials they brought from the ships." The natives from whom we were now collecting testimony had learned of much more than the others we interviewed in Pelly Bay. They had seen not just marching men dragging boats, but places where the sailors had set up tents for shelter and rest. I wondered how many other natives caught sight of the ships as they carried on with their own nomadic lives, moving from place to place in search of sustenance.

The fact that the men of the Royal Navy and the travelling Esquimaux had little contact with each other was disappointing. My own survival in the Arctic had often depended upon my interactions with the natives. They had taught me their methods of fishing, hunting and how to clothe myself in animal skins. Why had no native interpreters and guides been hired by the Royal Navy to join Franklin's two parties, in case the ships became trapped? Such an arrangement could have been made possible with my assistance, because I was living in the Arctic and well acquainted with some natives who had good translation skills. How tragic, I thought. We gently encouraged our visitors to continue with their stories.

"Some of our people were brave. They went close to a group of men who were walking, like this . . ." A woman lifted up her knees and stamped her feet, to imitate marching. She placed her hands on her stomach and groaned as if she were in pain. Others spoke of a brief attempt at communication between one of the men and a few natives.

"They say that the man who seemed to be the leader of the Kabloon-ans tried to describe what had happened to a ship, by raising his arms and making gestures." The interviewees told of how the man drew his arms and hands together, as if they were crushing something, after which he pointed to the ice and made the gestures again.

"He must have been referring to the ships, Mar-ko. Are they saying that a ship was crushed, maybe both?"

"They think he meant that a ship was crushed, but they are not certain of it. They heard that a second ship sank in one piece after a mysterious explosion happened on board, but these people aren't sure about that, either."

"Did the white men ever ask for help?"

"No, not for help, but the Kabloonan leader — the biggest man in the group — bought a small piece of seal meat from our people to share with his men. It was all they could spare, because food was scarce at that time, for everyone."

I urged them to continue telling their stories. My neck was sore from being hunched over a small table recording the testimony of every person who spoke, later cross-checking and reviewing it all in my quarters. There was no doubt, however, that the information they brought to us created a dramatic picture of the sightings of the missing men.

Ouligback continued translating. "The people who saw the marching men did not feel safe, and the big Kabloonan seemed to want nothing more than meat from them, so both groups moved away from each other as quickly as possible."

"Were the Kabloonans ever seen again?" I inquired.

"No, but after that winter season, the natives heard loud, cracking noises in the air. They didn't now what to make of those sounds. A short time later, they found the remains of a Kabloonan settlement on the shore of a large island somewhere to the south."

I tried to imagine the terrible condition they were in as they continued their 1850 death march, in a futile search for rescue. I was surprised to hear that any of them had enough strength to set up camp at all.

"Can you describe the scene where they died?"

"Many men's bodies, Ablooka. Fresh bones and the feathers of geese on the ground near the bodies. Barrels with black powder in them. Objects my people had never seen before, items made of materials other than bones and rocks." Metal, I thought.

"It is said that a boat was turned over on the shore of the island. The body of a large man was underneath. He was lying on his stomach."

"Did the body look like the big man who was marching with the others when the natives saw them earlier?"

"No one is certain of that."

I shuddered and wondered about the identity of the man, and whether he had been a British naval officer, the owner of the gold cap-band I had purchased from In-nook. My telescope was resting on a table in the interview tent. A man pointed to it. "A tool like that was tied to him with a strap. An object was sticking out from under the body, too. From the way this man is describing the tool under the body," Oulig-back said, "it sounds as though it may have been some kind of gun."

An officer, I thought. "Mar-ko, I am going to gather some of our own weapons and display them on this table. Ask these people to wait for a few moments."

I went to a nearby building where racks holding different kinds of guns belonging to the Hudson's Bay Company were stored under lock and key. A staff member let me in. After picking up a variety of rifles and shotguns, I returned to the tent and set them down in front of the group I was interviewing. I collected some pieces of the guns they had brought to us as relics belonging to the dead Kabloonans, and placed them alongside our own weapons. The natives' eyes widened as they scanned the table full of objects. They murmured amongst themselves and pointed to the shotguns and rifles.

"Ask them if they think our weapons resemble the objects the marching men carried and what was later seen at the encampment, Mar-ko." As he relayed my question to his people, I could see from their reactions that they believed there were many similarities. "Yes, especially this one, Ablooka." He pointed to a double-barrelled shotgun, and our visitors nodded in agreement.

"Is it the same kind of object the people saw tied to the big man's body, beneath the overturned boat?" I asked.

"Yes, Ablooka. They say it looks the same."

I then fully understood why the natives had broken apart the guns they found with the bodies. Like In-nook, they did not understand the operation and function of guns, Kabloonan killing tools. They had ignored the kegs of gunpowder they found at the dead men's encampment, figuring correctly that the strange material was of no use to them.

"Please tell me more, as much as can be remembered about the boat and the people."

"Some of the dead Kabloonans were wearing many items of clothing. Other bodies had been stripped of flesh with sharp objects, probably knives. Missing hands, arms, feet, legs, heads. Bones lay in boxes, in piles, and some were scattered around the camp. The bones had been broken and the contents sucked out of them, like we do when we eat meat, Ablooka. We boil the animal bones and suck out the softened marrow, or scoop it off the top of boiling liquid and swallow it. It sounds as though the Kabloonans did the same thing with human bones."

The strain of what he was hearing from these people — his people — was showing on poor Ouligback's face. My stomach turned over several times, and I fought back nausea. Despite the fact that I had witnessed many gruesome sights during my years as a doctor and explorer, and even though I had killed and eaten thousands of birds and animals, the mental images of men dismembering their dead companions and sucking on pieces of their remains caused me physical discomfort.

I swallowed and drew a deep breath. It would not do to show the others how I felt. "I know, Mar-ko," I whispered. "Bone marrow is rich in nutrients." So this was how they had the strength to keep moving, I thought. *Dear Lord*. Those poor, godforsaken, miserable men. How dreadful it must have been for them when they were on their death marches, dragging their belongings, kettles and cooking fuel, along with the severed joints, bones and other parts of their deceased comrades in boats on sledges across mountains of ice.

A woman looked away while she spoke. "Pots for cooking flesh and bones. Pots with boiled bones inside them." I asked how she knew the kettles to which she referred contained human flesh, and not the meat and bones of some kind of bird or animal.

"Hair. Teeth. Pieces of white Kabloonan skin. Kabloonan bones. Many cut marks on bones. Bones cracked open."

"Boiled skulls with big holes. No flesh inside skulls. Flesh scooped out."

"Pieces of brains in white men's cooking pots. Kabloonan flesh and bones like some kind of soup inside white men's boots."

I swallowed hard. "Mar-ko, why would there be cooked flesh inside leather boots? Could this be how the men shared their food?" He shrugged his shoulders and nodded, his expression pained. The idea of it seemed unthinkable, but no other explanation came to mind. The remains must have been boiled with melting ice in some kind of vessel over a fire, then poured into the dead men's boots. I blinked my eyes to banish the bizarre image of leather footwear filled with liquid and floating matter. As a physician, I was aware that a starving body feeds upon itself until the heart ceases to function. As an explorer who had occasionally suffered from want of food, I was no stranger to persistent hunger pangs. As a human being, I felt great compassion for the poor men who had been forced to adopt such extreme measures in a failed bid to survive.

Ouligback looked at me and then looked away. His expression spoke of pity, disgust and fear. "Ablooka, do you know the Esquimaux word for what we call this . . . strange practice?"

"I think so," I replied. "*Quaq*?" I winced when I spoke the ugly word, because I knew that within the belief system of the Esquimaux, any sign of cannibalism was considered to be the mark of a great threat, a malevolent creature of chaos, the collapse of unity within a group, a good spirit gone bad. There would be no place for the offending soul among the stars, where all the others dwelled. There would be no visits with departed relatives via meteors shooting through the aurora borealis — just complete and utter banishment.

Ouligback looked down at his hands and nodded.

"Mar-ko . . ."

"Yes, Ablooka. All of them are saying the same thing."

I slumped in my chair. We had heard enough. There was only one more question to ask. "Were any living Kabloonans seen again?"

"No."

→ *Repulse Bay*
[AUGUST 1854]

We concluded the interviews with our Esquimaux visitors, and after hosting a feast for all, we bade them farewell. During a long period of exhaustive meetings, I had collected enough testimony to prepare a formal report for both the Secretary of the British Admiralty and for my employer, Sir George Simpson, Governor-in-Chief of the Hudson's Bay Company.

The report contained descriptions of what the Esquimaux had witnessed near and on the west and south coasts of what they referred to as a large island — in all likelihood King William Island — during the winter of 1849 and the spring of 1850. There was a reference to kegs filled with black powder, which I assumed to be ammunition, along with a large quantity of what sounded like ball and shot, as well as goose bones and feathers strewn about the cooking site. Some of the bodies had been buried in shallow graves, probably while the remaining men had enough strength to do so. Others were in tents and a few lay under the overturned boat, including the body of the mystery officer with the telescope and double-barrelled shotgun. The Esquimaux who visited the men's final encampment collected compasses, guns, watches and other pieces of equipment, not knowing what the objects were used for but believing that they were interesting and perhaps even of some value.

My report included the grim evidence of cannibalism at the dying men's final encampment, along with a reference to the mutilated state of the corpses and the human remains in the kettles. I wrote that "our countrymen had been driven to the last resource — cannibalism — as a means of prolonging existence." I drew a sketch of some of the relics the natives brought to me, including the crests on the silver forks and spoons found with the men's bodies, for the Council to review. I concluded the report with an added note about how my party had fared during the winter months, explaining that we "passed the winter in snow houses in comparative comfort, the skins of deer shot affording abundant warm clothing and bedding," to provide contrast to the appalling conditions the Royal Navy men had endured. This comment may have been awkward for the officials to read, but I hoped it would wake them up to the fact that this sort of tragedy should never have happened at all.

On completion of the investigation, I reached the only conclusion which made sense to me: there were no wandering survivors, and all members of the Franklin Expedition had indeed perished. I finished my report in early August, and affixed my signature to it:

"I have, &c., John Rae, Chief Factor, Commanding Hudson's Bay Company's Arctic Expedition."

Then I prepared a second document, itemizing the list of relics I had acquired from the Esquimaux, feeling confident that descriptions of the objects and their markings, along with my own sketches in the report, would end any lingering doubt about the fate of Sir John Franklin's lost expedition. I wrote "Urgent" and "Personal and Confidential" in large letters on both sides of each envelope. I wrote a letter to my sister Marion, telling her that all was well with me, and advising her that I would travel to Orkney as soon as I had completed my business in London. The full report and accompanying list, along with my letter to Marion, were immediately dispatched in a locked box to York Factory, where a Hudson's Bay Company ship filled with furs was waiting to set sail for London.

I also composed a letter to the editors of the *London Times*, intentionally omitting any mention of cannibalism, to spare the dead men's families and loved ones from knowing what had happened to many of the bodies. I simply stated that local people had seen the bodies, and that as far as we knew from their testimony, the Royal Navy men had died from starvation. I sealed the envelope, and tucked it into my personal writing chest for later dispatch to London.

After I completed these writing tasks, I retreated to my Repulse Bay quarters and scrubbed every inch of my body with hot water. I stood in front of a mirror, shaving blade in hand. I had not seen my own image for many months. I never shaved during expeditions, because thick facial hair provides protection from insects, wind burn and frostbite. I am not sure why, but I decided not to remove the bulk of beard growth just yet. Maybe I wasn't quite ready to make the transition to gentrification. Too much unfinished business, perhaps.

I slowly ran a hairbrush across my head, through curls that used to be shiny and reddish brown, but which were now in the process of dulling to an unappealing brownish grey. Deep lines fanned out from the skin around my eyes. It should not have surprised me to see how the effects of age and more than twenty years of living in such a harsh climate had taken a toll on my youthful appearance, yet I felt disappointed with the image in the mirror. The changes were an unwelcome reminder that I was no longer a young man, that the time would soon come when I would be less suited to the challenges of living and journeying in the frozen spaces of the Arctic. The notion of taking a fair and good woman as my wife and mother of our children had been entering my thoughts more frequently as the years marched along. If I waited too long to return home and settle down, I would be too old and long in the tooth to find a mate.

A number of capable men who worked for me at our Repulse Bay headquarters volunteered to winter over and prepare for another journey in the spring. They had discussed the idea amongst themselves, and surmised that it might be possible to mount another expedition in 1855, to find more evidence, bodies, and perhaps one or both of the ships. While I appreciated their enthusiasm, I countered that we simply did not have enough time to make proper preparations for another journey so soon. A responsible explorer tries to eliminate as much guesswork as he can when planning an expedition, and I took my duties as both a leader and a scientist seriously. The weather and an abundance of animals to kill were always unpredictable, but reliable equipment and an adequate stock of dried food supplies could mean the difference between life and death. If we did not have enough pemmican to last us through times of deprivation while we travelled, the consequences would be disastrous.

Furthermore, I explained that it was necessary for me to take the objects I had collected from the Esquimaux and return to London with them before the Arctic winter set in. I also figured that seeing the relics with their own eyes would surely convince the authorities to look harder for the two remaining British search vessels and the American ship and crew searching the region. It was essential that they be advised of my findings.

As I packed the Franklin Expedition artifacts into a trunk for my journey to York Factory and England, I asked God to bless the souls of all the unfortunates who had lost their lives in the failed search for the Northwest Passage. I prayed for the doomed men's families and loved ones, who would soon be informed that unless some sort of miracle had occurred, any remaining hope of finding even one survivor was lost.

→ *Hudson Bay, North Atlantic and England*
[AUGUST–OCTOBER 1854]

I arrived in York Factory to the news that my mother had suffered a stroke at her home in Stromness, Orkney. My sister Marion and her husband John were taking good care of her, I was confident about that, but I was impatient to get to London and then back to Stromness. When I closed my eyes, I tried not to picture the lively spirit of my dear mam being trapped inside a prison of disability.

There was much business for me to complete before my own early September departure for England aboard the SS *Prince Rupert*. I turned my attention to overseeing the secure storage of Company boats and equipment in preparation for the long Arctic winter. After that, I was busy with administrative matters, such as performing the final calculations of wages the Hudson's Bay Company owed to the men who had served with me on the Boothia expedition. In early spring, we had begun our expedition from Repulse Bay with a party of twelve men from the Arctic region. It quickly became clear that seven of them were unsuited to the harsh overland travel conditions, and I had been forced to send them back to our headquarters. On reflection, I was surprised that Ouligback, Mistegan and I managed to make it even as far as the western coast of the Boothia Peninsula, given our greatly diminished capacity for efficient travel.

The men from our original travelling party arrived at York Factory to collect their wages. There were grumblings about the meagre sums received by those who had been dismissed, but it was very simple, of course: one should only be paid for work completed, unless there are other mitigating circumstances. Beads and Johnston were given full payment for the time they had spent preparing and travelling, despite the infirmities they suffered along the way. A bonus for the two grateful young men was the fact that we carried them with us — sometimes on our own backs — and did everything we could to bring them home alive.

Jacob Beads lost three toes to frostbite, but he was fortunate; he could have fared far worse. James Johnston was improving as well, gaining much-needed weight and growing stronger. He declared that the life of an explorer was not for him; I shook his hand, and agreed wholeheartedly. Words such as "explorer" and "expedition" may sound romantic to some young and energetic minds — including my own, as a free-spirited child in Orkney and ship's surgeon at the age of twenty — but months and years of deprivation and hardship wear heavily on even the strongest bodies and spirits. In truth, few men are physically and mentally suited to that wild sort of life.

I told Ouligback and Mistegan that after meeting with the authorities in London, I would do my best to inform them about any plans for further exploration. If the Admiralty accepted the geographical coordinates and information I had collected on this journey, perhaps the Hudson's Bay Company would consider seconding me again as the leader of another search expedition. There was also the matter of completing a survey of the North American coastline, including the rest of the Boothia Peninsula. I was still employed as chief factor of the Mackenzie River District, but I was beginning to wonder just how long I wished to continue working for my employers. I had a sense that a new chapter in my life would unfold before long.

At York Factory, Ouligback, Mistegan and I shook hands and, with a heavy heart, I bade my interpreter and guide farewell. When an expedition ends, it is always difficult to say goodbye to one's trusted companions, and this time was no exception. I had worked closely with the highly regarded Esquimaux interpreter William Ouligback Senior, Mar-ko's father. I had great respect for him. With the exception of one odd but brief estrangement between myself and his son William Junior on our journey, we had functioned together as if we were each an extension of the other. Now I was alone again, with a hollow feeling in the pit of my stomach.

As poor luck would have it, the departure of the *Prince Rupert* from York Factory was delayed by two weeks of infuriating, early-season freezing in the northern regions of Hudson Bay. Now that the news about the fate of the Franklin Expedition had been dispatched to the Admiralty and to my employer Sir George Simpson, I was impatient to set sail for England. There would be questions about my report. I was prepared to answer them, and then return to Orkney as soon as possible to see my ailing mother.

God must have listened to my prayers, because just when it seemed as though the *Prince Rupert* would be stuck at York Factory until the following spring, whalers sent good news from the north. Rising temperatures and winds from the southeast had moved the ice blocking our exit. The captain received clearance to set sail immediately.

The hazards of storms at sea are very similar to the dangers on land: fierce winds, paralyzing cold, blindness, the loss of balance and disorientation place all living beings in great peril. In many ways, part of the voyage home to Britain was no less diminishing than dragging a heavy sledge through a blinding blizzard for days on end. Our North Atlantic crossing was gruelling, and there were times when the conditions at sea were dangerous to the point where I wondered if we would make it home to London at all. A voyage which should have taken twenty-one days stretched to more than thirty due to violent, persistent storms which almost sank us. Four of the *Prince Rupert*'s mainsails were ripped to shreds. A lifeboat was knocked loose from its fittings and very nearly washed away; crew members tasked with mending the sails were sometimes thrown from their high perches, landing with a sickening thud on the ice-lashed decks. One poor young fellow was tossed into the sea when the ship listed heavily to starboard. The crew frantically cast ropes to the lad, but saving him was impossible because the frigid, turbulent water quickly exhausted him. He did not have the strength even to grab the knotted end of a rope.

Every man aboard a ship feels a terrible sense of grief when a soul is lost at sea, but in the midst of a raging storm there is no time to think, let alone reflect on a tragedy. We said a prayer — each man in his own way — for the lost sailor, regretting that he could not be given a proper sea burial. We were all busy, focused on emerging on the other side of the storms relatively intact. I was fully occupied in the infirmary, tending to the injured and sick and not immune to queasiness in my own stomach either, sometimes retching into a bucket while I stitched wounds and bound broken limbs. It was a great relief for all of us when the ship finally approached the southwest coast of England. A Royal Mail vessel pulled up alongside the *Prince Rupert*, and I handed the agent the letter I had composed for the editors of the *Times*. *Tara Gott*, I thought. An old Orcadian phrase for *it is done*. As soon as my letter was published, the news would quickly spread throughout the public domain.

PART II

Under Attack

[1854]

→ *Southeast England*
[OCTOBER 22, 1854]

We limped into port at Deal early in the morning on Sunday, October 22nd. The moment the *Prince Rupert*'s anchors were set, a tender approached the ship and a message marked "Urgent" was delivered to me: "Proceed to Admiralty House in Whitehall immediately upon arrival, to meet with First Lord Sir James Graham and members of the Arctic Council." I was not surprised to be summoned to such a meeting straightaway. No doubt the Council members had been anxiously awaiting my arrival with the full testimony and the Franklin party relics.

The carriage journey along the dirt roadway from Deal to London felt as though it lasted forever. While we rumbled and bounced through the quiet villages of Kent, impatience — my lifelong companion — overtook me. I had no appetite for enjoying the gentle countryside and the beauty of the view because, by then all I could think about was the news and objects I had brought with me from the Arctic, and the discussions which lay ahead in the meeting at Admiralty House. I was relieved to be the only passenger, for I was exhausted and in no mood for engaging in light conversation.

The relics I had procured from the Esquimaux were carefully packed inside the large satchel on the seat beside me, alongside my bag and the case containing my violin. I examined the list of the satchel's contents, wondering for the hundredth time what had gone through the minds of those poor sailors during their long, wretched search for a rescue party that never arrived. As a scientist and physician, I am not generally given to thoughts of the supernatural, but I found it difficult to shake the feeling that I had intruded upon the spirits of others, that I was invading their privacy. Perhaps it was the other way around.

I had managed to identify some of the markings on the items. I had seen a list of the officers and crew of the *Erebus* and *Terror* a few years earlier, but few of the names remained in my memory. I wondered if the Royal Guelphic Order of the Hanover Crest bearing the motto *"Nec aspera terrent*, G.K. III., MDCCCXV"* was the property of the expedition commander, Rear Admiral Sir John Franklin, since the award was usually conferred upon officers of the highest ranking. Sir John was a celebrated explorer, author and veteran of the Napoleonic wars. There could be no doubt that a circular plate bearing the name Sir John Franklin and the initials "K.C.B.", Knight Commander of Britain, belonged to him.

I surmised that a silver fork engraved with the initials "H.D.S.G." might have belonged to Harry Goodsir, the assistant surgeon aboard the *Erebus* but, of course, I could not be certain of this. A silver tablespoon with a crest and the initials "F.R.M.C." caught my eye, because I was familiar with the name of *Terror* Captain Francis Rawdon Moira Crozier. He was known to be a man of great sturdiness, determination and grit, a veteran of expeditions to both the Arctic and Antarctic. I imagined that he would have waged a fierce and stubborn battle against the elements. There was also an assortment of officers' silverware, some bearing crests and other initials I could not decipher.

I was intrigued by the remnants of what had once been the *Student's Manual*. Who had brought the *Student's Manual* aboard one of the ships? What was he studying? Was he as young as I had been during my early days as a medical student at the University of Edinburgh? My heart was heavy at the thought of his being prevented from completing his course and living his life.

Men had warmed these objects with their living hands. They had extracted a good deal of information from the watches, compasses and telescopes. They were now dead and forever silenced, unable to tell the stories of their discoveries, hardships and inglorious demise. No matter how hard I tried, I could not dispel the terrible thought that some of Franklin's men had consumed the flesh of fallen sailors using these fine silver utensils. I hoped I understood — if only from the limited perspective of a survivor — the suffering and madness they endured. I had experienced near starvation during an Arctic expedition in 1847, but we managed to drag ourselves to headquarters before it was too late. I shook my head, trying to banish unsettling images.

I forced my thoughts towards a cheerier scene concerning the departure of the ships for the Arctic. My sister Marion and her husband John Hamilton told an entertaining story about Sir John Franklin and a chosen few of the ships' officers who enjoyed a farewell supper at their home in the Orcadian port town of Stromness. The date of the gathering was the 24th of May, 1845, the eve of the great expedition's final departure for the Arctic. Sir John spent the night there, while the *Erebus* and *Terror* drew fresh water for the voyage from Login's Well. Marion told amusing stories of much merriment in the Hamilton home that evening. The aging rear admiral, who by that year had grown quite florid in the face, bald of pate and broadened about the girth, stood up after the meal and danced a lively jig to Orcadian sea shanties, played with great exuberance by the Logie Brothers on their fiddles. He was suffering from a head cold at the time, but the good food and music soon distracted him from his discomfort.

Marion said the finest port was served to Sir John following his impromptu dance, after which he — normally a tea drinker — duly fell asleep in an armchair by the fire. She covered him with a woollen Hudson's Bay Company blanket, blew out the candles and left him to dream of the great adventures to come. According to her report, he was bursting with energy in the morning and, after a hearty breakfast of fresh eggs and lamb sausage, he bade a jovial farewell to his hosts.

Little wonder the commander of the most costly and elaborate of all British naval expeditions was in high spirits that night! The *Erebus* and *Terror* were setting off on a sensational voyage of discovery, with all the advantages of the newest marine technology in their favour: steam engines, screw propellers for manoeuvring the ships through narrow spaces, angled wooden planks especially designed to withstand extreme weather conditions, heavy iron bow reinforcements, heated living quarters below decks, and so on. John Franklin was certainly no stranger to the dark side of the Arctic, but if he had any misgivings about the inherently dangerous project he was about to undertake, he certainly showed no public signs of it.

Although I had seen many paintings and sketches of those two mighty bomb vessels, Marion, John, their children and my mother were fortunate to stand at the water's edge beside the Stromness kirkyard where our father is buried and watch the magnificent, newly outfitted *Erebus* and *Terror* under full sail, being borne away through Hoy Sound with the outgoing tide. Union Jacks were flapping in the wind; 134 officers and men were assembled on deck in full naval uniforms, arms raised and bent in formal salute. The ships' bellies carried years' worth of reading materials, an impressive collection of musical instruments for on-board entertainment, pickled and sealed food provisions, and the finest china and linens for the officers. It must have been a grand sight, indeed.

A wave of sadness interrupted my pleasant daydream, and I found myself wishing that I had been there for the beginning, not bringing home grim news about the end. As the carriage drew nearer to the city, more horse and pedestrian traffic appeared on the road. The bucolic southeast countryside was being replaced by increasing sound and movement, which briefly distracted me from growing discomfort about the meeting ahead and the constant intrusion of melancholy thoughts.

⟿ *Admiralty House, Whitehall, London*
[OCTOBER 22, 1854]

An adjutant escorted me up the winding staircase and showed me into the office of Sir James Graham, first lord of the Admiralty. I had met him briefly two years earlier at a Royal Geographical Society event. We had exchanged a few polite words that evening, but we did not engage in any meaningful conversation, and I doubted we made a lasting impression upon each other.

The first lord stood stiff and tall behind a large desk, his expression cool. He did not offer his hand to me in greeting. Despite our being only acquaintances, I was taken aback by such a frosty reception. He stretched out his arm, showing me to a chair. I took a seat, placed my hands upon my knees and learned towards him, eager for the conversation to begin. He placed two glasses on his desk, poured whisky from a crystal decanter into both, took a long draught from his glass and sat down across from me. I do not drink spirits, so I took a small courtesy sip and put the glass down.

"Doctor Rae, I hear your North Atlantic journey from York Factory was quite arduous."

"Yes, Sir James. We did indeed experience a challenging crossing."

The first lord lifted his brows and inclined his head towards the door. "We will meet with members of the Council after this." He wasted no time in coming right to the point: "You advised us, in writing, that you have obtained information concerning the fate of Commander Franklin, his men and his ships."

"That is correct, Sir. I dispatched my report to your secretary at the end of July." He sipped the whisky, and slowly licked his lips. He had, of course, read my grim account of cannibalism amongst the last group of survivors. I assumed that the first lord and members of the naval council would personally want to review the testimony and discuss the details with me.

"You wrote that you have acquired relics which you believe came from the missing expedition."

"Yes, Sir."

"And you have these articles with you now?"

"I do." I lifted my heavy satchel off the floor, undid the fastenings, withdrew the relics and carefully set them on the desk until most of the surface was covered with assorted metals, pieces of guns and scientific instruments, utensils and other items. The first lord affixed a monocular lens to one eye and closely observed the items one at a time, taking care to avoid touching them.

"Why would the men have brought cutlery with them when they left the ships?" he wondered aloud.

"Sir," I replied, "the utensils are quite light in weight, especially when compared to the other items. Altogether, I think they weigh no more than five pounds. I suspect they were objects of personal importance to the men, because they have been embellished with crests, initials and so on." I pointed to various items. His eyes followed my gestures, as he examined the remnants of Britain's greatest naval mystery.

"As you can see, Sir James, many of these relics are damaged and broken. Here are timepieces, a length of gold braid, brass buttons. Here, we have pieces of guns, a compass, a chronometer and other instruments used in navigation. And here, silver cutlery embellished with the Franklin crest, a star-shaped Order of Merit, and a silver plate bearing Sir John Franklin's initials. Over there, a silver spoon bearing a crest and the initials F.R.M.C."

The first lord pursed his lips. "Francis Rawdon Moira Crozier, Captain of the *Terror*," he whispered. It occurred to me in that moment, when he said the name, that he was seeing the relics as more than pieces of metal, brass, and fragments of material. The artifacts were suddenly coming alive for him, just as they had for me. They had been the property of men with names, families, loved ones. I thought of how he would have personally wished the men farewell and Godspeed before their initial departure from the docks at Greenhithe, London, on May 19, 1845.

His eyes remained on the spoon when he spoke. "Tell me exactly how you came into possession of these, Doctor Rae."

"I purchased them directly from the many Esquimaux who came to meet me at Repulse Bay in June and July of this year, Sir."

He frowned. Nine years after the last sighting of the *Erebus* and *Terror*, the first lord of the Admiralty was looking at the possessions of the officers and crew, the first real evidence of the men's demise. What was going through his mind at that moment?

The relics spoke for themselves, but I knew it could be a challenging task for me to convince the authorities that the information in my report was accurate because its contents relied entirely upon testimony I had acquired from the Esquimaux. The first lord and his colleagues — indeed, most of the British establishment — believed that all natives, whether they lived in the steaming jungles of Africa or in the frozen Arctic, were primitive and uneducated, that God's truth held no meaning for them.

As a Scot who worked for a British company, and as a man who had travelled extensively in the Arctic for more than two decades, I occupied an unusual space somewhere in between the two vastly different cultures. I was in the unique position of being familiar with attitudes and perspectives on both sides of the North Atlantic: the practices and belief systems of the Esquimaux, and matters of importance to the British. I had also heard the rumour that some members of the Admiralty perceived me to be an eccentric and oddball scientist, who consorted with savages while conducting British business in the frozen regions of North America.

The truth is that I could never have survived there without the support and teachings of the Esquimaux; they taught me everything I needed to know to keep my men and myself alive on our journeys. I trusted them and, even more, I enjoyed being in their company. I found their propensity for engaging in play and tomfoolery amusing, endearing and delightful. Yet, when circumstances called for concentration, stamina and a serious attitude, they never let me down. In fact, I preferred to work with the natives, rather than the British. The reasons were simple: the Esquimaux were accustomed to engaging in hard work because their own survival depended upon it. I suppose that my acceptance and approval of Esquimaux ways was confusing to nineteenth-century Britons, who were suspicious of anyone who was not white and Christian.

"Doctor Rae, you documented detailed testimony from native people exclusively, declared it correct, affixed your name to it and passed it along to us. You are surely aware that we — including you — would be ill-advised to assume that Esquimaux truths are equal to our own." Of course, I bristled at his remark but chose my response with care because I knew that if I was disrespectful towards the naval authorities, I would pay the price of ostracism. I wanted them to accept my own faith in the integrity of the Esquimaux, but there was even more to my wish than that. I had worked hard to build my professional reputation on both sides of the Atlantic Ocean. I was proud to be considered an expert in Arctic matters; that distinction meant a great deal to me.

"I appreciate your concerns, Sir James, but if we are meant to solve this great mystery, I encourage you to set aside notions of the Esquimaux as being untrustworthy. Our mutual objective is to examine the facts that have been passed along to us. The evidence of which the natives speak is still where they found it, and probably intact because of climactic conditions. There is no reason to think we will not be able to travel to the area, locate the remains of the sailors and verify the reports of the natives."

He glanced at me and sniffed. I wasn't sure if he was reacting to the suggestion of mounting another costly search for the remains of the expedition, to my reference to a future search party including me, or to both. "Did the natives tell you anything about the commander himself?"

I knew the first lord was under continuous pressure from Lady Franklin and her many supporters to find an explanation for the mystery of her husband's disappearance. "I regret to say that no one seems to have intelligence about Sir John Franklin. Not as of yet, anyway, although I am quite sure the information will be attainable at some point in the future." I was intentionally leaving the door open for discussions about further searching in the areas where the Esquimaux saw the marching men and discovered the gruesome British encampments.

"Why did you not journey onward in search of remains, Dr. Rae? Surely, you had the time before returning to your headquarters. Everyone is aware of the high rates of speed at which you travel in the Arctic." His eyes returned to the map.

"Two of my men's lives were in danger, Sir. They were failing. If we had continued on, they would have perished. I will never take risks with the lives of men under my charge in order to search for the deceased." I could see that he was becoming increasingly uncomfortable as our conversation moved closer to the most distressing elements contained in my report. He wiped his mouth with the back of his hand, stood up and began to pace about the room. After a minute or so, he stopped and turned to me. He cleared his throat and changed the subject.

"I ask you, why the devil do you believe everything these native people tell you?"

"Sir, the Esquimaux in that area have never given me cause to doubt the honesty of their words, nor indeed the accuracy of what they say. I went to great lengths to interview and cross-examine each person, alone and in groups, during a period of two months. I detected no fundamental conflicts in their evidence. They had nothing to gain by inventing stories because I had already purchased the relics from them, as an act of good faith."

"And your interpreter?"

"William Ouligback Junior and his father before him are excellent speakers of the English language. I have faith in their translations." I carefully returned many of the relics to the satchel, retrieved a rolled-up map of the Arctic region from another bag, unfolded the tattered document and laid it upon the desk. Graham squinted into his handheld lens as he watched my finger slide along the surface of the paper.

"Your report refers to a party of many white men who were seen on or near a large island. Where do you think these people came from?" he inquired, his eyes on the map.

"Well, no one is absolutely certain, Sir, but it is believed that they came from two large ships which were beset to the west of King William Island, where there is extensive pack ice." I ran my finger down the map, south from Peel Sound into Victoria Strait, and brought it to rest on an area of the Polar Sea west of the island.

"How did the white men communicate with the natives?" He sniffed again.

"They communicated through gestures," I replied. Graham removed his lens, rubbed his eyes and glared at me.

"Gestures," he repeated.

"They indicated that at least one ship had been sunk by pack ice some time earlier. I do not know exactly when this happened, but apparently it occurred in the autumn, probably during the latter part of 1848.

"The group of marchers was observed by the Esquimaux more than two years later," I added. The first lord cleared his throat, and I wondered if he was taken aback by the suggestion that men from the expedition may still have been alive as recently as 1850, when dozens of British search parties were scattered throughout the region, looking for them. There had been no reported sightings of them or the ships.

"Were these purported eyewitnesses the natives you interviewed at Pelly Bay and at Repulse Bay?"

"No, Sir. I met with their friends and relatives. The information I collected was reliably passed along from person to person. This is the manner in which all information is disseminated in the Arctic — "

He interrupted me, his voice rising. "Why, in God's name, did these eyewitnesses not come and meet with you *themselves?*" he hissed.

Despite its harsh delivery, the question was reasonable enough; only four years had elapsed between the final sightings and the testimony I acquired at Pelly Bay and Repulse Bay. I hastened to explain the eyewitnesses' absence. "Last year, there was a life-threatening lack of food for the northernmost native communities in the Arctic, due to very poor weather conditions and the resulting changes in animal migration patterns. It is also likely that great numbers of animals perished from starvation. Apparently many Esquimaux starved to death, including women and children. The witnesses of whom you speak were actively engaged in hunting while I was conducting interviews at Pelly and Repulse Bays. They were gathering as much meat and provisions as they could, to feed their families during the coming winter." The irony of the fact that we were discussing Esquimaux deaths from starvation against the backdrop of British cannibalism was not lost on me; it was impossible to tell whether the first lord was having the same thought.

Like many of his upper-class contemporaries, the first lord's knowledge of the Arctic did not extend very far beyond his own, well-fed British perspective. He did not understand the day-to-day nature of subsistence living, or that the Esquimaux existed under the constant threat of starvation.

"So, the natives from whom you took testimony concerning Sir John Franklin, his ships and the men under his command, were not even there when these — hungry white men — were encountered? Good Lord, man! This story is becoming ever more preposterous! Have you been living in that godforsaken region for too long?" He sat down and spun his chair around to face the window, his fists clenched.

To say that I was insulted by his outburst would be an understatement. He had attacked my good sense, judgment and professional capabilities. I understood his frustration with circumstances he could not control; nonetheless, he had no right to belittle me. I had come to the meeting with honest, altruistic intentions but he was apparently determined to discredit me and my trust in the natives' reports. I refused to let him see how his outburst bothered me. "I understand your skepticism concerning the veracity of my sources and their testimony, Sir James. From outward appearances, it does seem to be second-hand — "

"I will remind you that it *is* second-hand, Doctor Rae!"

The first lord stood up and stared out the window toward the empty Horse Guards Parade Grounds, his back squarely turned to me. A clock ticking on the mantelpiece was the only sound in the room. The outdoor light was fading, the room was growing dim, and I was beginning to feel claustrophobic from the tension in the stale, musty air.

For some time, I had heard voices in the next room. I assumed they belonged to the men who came together and met as the Arctic Council. Was Sir James' dismissive attitude shared by the others? Would more skepticism and irritation await me on the other side of the door? I began to dread the next round of questions. The first lord glanced at the clock. We had been engaged in this fruitless discussion for almost an hour. He sighed, and turned to face me again.

"Do you, Doctor Rae, have absolute faith in these native accounts about the fates of Franklin's men?"

"I do, Sir." My view on the matter was as simple as that. Nothing — no arguments, fits of temper or criticism — could move me from maintaining my steadfast belief in the truth of their testimony.

Sir James sat down behind his desk again, clasped his hands together, rested his chin upon them and looked at me. This simple gesture made him seem more human, less imperious. I leaned slightly towards him, sensing his growing anguish. The tone of his voice softened.

"Your report states that the white men observed by the Esquimaux looked emaciated, with the exception of one, whom you presume to have been an officer because of his attire, equipment and weapon. You also refer to someone matching that description being seen later at a British encampment, deceased. Am I correct?"

"You are right, Sir. We cannot know with absolute certainty, however, that the marching man the natives first referred to is the one who later perished under the overturned boat."

I was unwilling to engage in conjecture concerning the appearance of an individual I had never seen, although the natives I interviewed at Repulse Bay suggested that the man under the boat looked like the leader of the group of marchers. Was he the commander? A captain? A lieutenant? Was he the man who purchased a piece of seal meat from the natives in 1848? I had a vague notion about who he may have been, but I kept my thoughts to myself. Whoever the man was, he, along with the others, had made a Herculean effort to survive. The names of the men the Esquimaux had seen meant absolutely nothing in the final analysis.

The first lord pointed an unsteady index finger in my direction. "Based upon what you have been told by others, do you personally have any theories concerning the identity of the man with the telescope at his shoulder and a gun under his body, Doctor Rae?"

"I cannot say because I do not know, Sir James. The natives referred to him as *Aglooka*." I did not add that I had once heard of a young British naval officer who had long ago befriended an Esquimaux boy and his family in the region, while his party searched for the elusive Northwest Passage. Apparently, the native boy's grandmother had expressed her affection for the young Kabloonan by bestowing the Esquimaux name upon him. There would likely be speculation in Britain, but it was impossible to know the identity of the officer under the boat without a body to examine. I changed the subject.

"You have read, Sir, that it appeared many of the bodies had been methodically cut and dismembered." It was all in the report.

He nervously glanced over at the fireplace. The wood was hissing and crackling as it burned. "Wild animals, perhaps? Wolves? Foxes? A few moments ago, you mentioned that the natives were starving last year. Is it possible that those hungry people found our men and dismembered them?" His eyes were upon me again.

"Sir, no. Absolutely not. The Esquimaux have strong spiritual reasons for choosing starvation over the alternative of eating human flesh. An Arctic native who indulges in such an act of desperation would be cast out of his group, indeed from all Esquimaux society, and in their view, he would forever be locked out of the spirit world."

"I will remind you, Doctor Rae, that we British hold the same damn beliefs!" It was a defensive, yet revealing statement. I confess that I was pleasantly surprised to hear it.

Aha! I thought. *You have just said it yourself, Sir James. We are not so different from the Esquimaux, after all.*

"I ask you, why *should* we believe what they say?" He banged his fist on the table to emphasize his growing frustration.

"I know the Esquimaux and their values well, Sir James," I said quietly. "And I believe them."

He slumped in his chair as emotion overcame him. His cool, professional mask fell away, and he emitted a surprised gasp as the man, not the first lord, suddenly perceived the horror and tragedy of it all. His eyes filled with tears, and he awkwardly raised a hand to cover his trembling lips. Sir James Graham personally knew every hand-picked officer aboard the *Erebus* and the *Terror*. I resisted an impulse to reach out and place a comforting hand on his arm. Instead, I nodded and sighed in sympathy. For a moment, at least, the tense atmosphere in his office had shifted from skepticism to grief. It was a relief to observe his human reaction to the news he was fighting so hard to discredit.

The painful truth is that the extreme nature of the Arctic climate was consistently hostile to even the most extravagantly fitted British ships. By the mid-nineteenth century, the list of vessels lost in the Arctic had grown long. Sir John Franklin's party had been extraordinarily well equipped according to British standards, but Royal Navy training, clothing, provisions and packaged food were no match for the fundamental tracking, hunting and self-preservation skills required for survival in the region. Even with iron reinforcements to strengthen their hulls and powerful steam engines with propellers to thrust them forward, the grandest of ships could not resist the irrepressible forces of moving Arctic pack ice.

The first lord cleared his throat, wiped at his eyes with a handkerchief and collected himself. "Right. Come with me, Doctor Rae. Members of the Council are waiting to view the relics."

I returned the remaining relics to my satchel, rolled up the map, rose and followed the first lord to the door. As he reached for the handle, I attempted to raise the topic of my promising discovery the previous spring. "There is one more thing, Sir . . . when I was travelling with my two guides on the west coast of the Boothia Peninsula, I am quite certain that we located a section of what might be the missing link in the Northwest Passage. Perhaps you would consider a different approach the next time — "

He interrupted me. "We shall see about that much later, Dr. Rae."

If the meeting with the first lord was uncomfortable, the next one was nothing short of a nightmare. I glanced heavenward and prayed that my good friend and colleague Sir John Richardson would be in the meeting. I had been pleasantly surprised in 1847, when the celebrated scientist and explorer personally chose me to assist him in leading an expedition in search of the lost Franklin ships and men. We had travelled many hundreds of miles together in the Arctic, and during that time we became fast friends. He knew my ways and respected my professional opinion, and I felt the same way about him. I looked for his face as soon as we entered the meeting room, but I was profoundly disappointed to see that he was not in attendance.

"Sir James, I do not see Sir John Richardson in the group."

The first lord leaned in and said, "He was unable to join us. He had plans with his family, and London is too far for him to travel on the Sabbath. By the way, the young man you see over there is a reporter for the *Times*." With that, Sir James Graham left me standing there, alone.

At least a dozen pairs of eyes which had simultaneously watched me come through the doorway were then lowered towards the heavy leather satchel in my hand. The moment was unnerving; it was as if time had stopped. I felt as though I had divested myself of my clothing in the other room and walked through the door naked. The oddest aspect of my entrance was the silence that greeted me. I had expected to be acknowledged and peppered with questions about my journey and experiences, but to my great surprise and embarrassment, none was forthcoming. The men appeared to be curious about the contents of the satchel, but once they had first laid eyes upon me, they seemed to dismiss my presence altogether, as if I were invisible. I recognized a number of them: Sir Francis Beaufort, Sir James Clark Ross, William Parry,

Frederick Beechey, Sir George Back, all survivors of earlier Royal Navy Arctic explorations.

I set about assembling the relics on the large table around which the Council members were gathered. While they were examining them, making sketches and murmuring amongst themselves, the *Times* reporter approached me and introduced himself as Mr. John Barrow. He requested an interview, but given the unsettling fact that the others had yet to even acknowledge my presence, I was reluctant to say anything. What was going through their minds?

Barrow held up a piece of paper. His voice sounded unnecessarily loud in that quiet room. "Doctor Rae, might I ask you to comment on this?" He quoted: "From the mutilated state of many of the corpses and the contents of the kettles . . . a means of prolonging existence . . ." I was taken aback when I heard the very words I had penned in my private report to the Admiralty and my employer, news that I had never intended to be released to the public.

"I beg your pardon?" I was incredulous. "That is confidential information. This is not the report I sent to the *Times*! My report to your newspaper simply states that the men have all perished. You cannot . . ."

I looked around the room at expressionless faces, suddenly understanding what the assembled group already knew: a copy of my *private* report had indeed been given to the press. Why? I wondered. Why would they want such a scandalous story about their own colleagues to be publicized? It didn't make sense to me, and the worst part was that there was absolutely nothing I could do about it. I was the last one to know, and in that moment I felt as though I was being played for a fool. At the best of times I am not a man of many words; I could not think of anything to say, but the reporter was persistent.

"Surely, you wish to make a statement before the news goes to press, Sir. Many of our readers will wonder about the veracity of your shocking announcement, and whether your sources of information can be relied upon at all." It was clear that he had already been counselled about who could not be trusted. All eyes were upon me. I realized that it was essential for me to think on my feet, because there was no time at all to digest what was happening.

I fought to hide the shock I felt about such scandalous information being made public. My heart was pounding. "Very well, then, Mr. Barrow, I will give you a statement. Once I had collected the artifacts you see here today, along with *two hundred hours* of testimony from the Arctic residents, I prepared a *private* report for the Secretary of the Arctic Council and Sir George Simpson of the Hudson's Bay Company. You just quoted a passage from it, Mr. Barrow. I believed that the most sensitive contents contained therein would remain confidential to spare the public and families of the lost men from further anguish. As you are no doubt aware, I sent a shorter report to your editor, excluding those details."

I paused, hoping that at least one man in the room would speak up and lend support to my statement. There was silence. I knew then, beyond a shadow of a doubt, that I was on my own. Realizing I had nothing to lose by speaking my mind, I pressed on: "Wouldn't you agree that confirmation of their deaths is news enough? That the memory of the men who suffered such misery should be honoured, and not tainted with sordid details about their last moments?" The reporter John Barrow did not respond to my question; indeed, the room was quiet, save for the odd cough and clearing of a throat. I picked up the satchel and began to collect the relics.

"Gentlemen . . ." I began. I feared that the Council members would lay claim to the relics and that the objects would disappear, along with what little remained of my credibility. "As you can see, many of these objects are personal. The identifiable ones will be returned to the families of the lost men. I will take them with me today, because they were purchased with Hudson's Bay Company funds, and my employers will wish to examine them as well. They will be made available to you for further viewing, in due course."

Barrow, the reporter, called after me as I prepared to exit the room. "Doctor Rae, why did you return to England now with these relics, instead of remaining there to search for the bodies of Sir John and his men? Are you aware of the £10,000 reward being offered by the British government to the person who ascertains the fate of the Franklin Expedition?" Stung, I could think of nothing further to say. I had simply run out of words.

Dusk was approaching as I descended the steps of Admiralty House, crossed the Horse Guards Parade Grounds, and walked towards St. James's Park. The satchel containing the relics felt even heavier than it had two hours earlier, as though the Royal Navy's decision to make my report public added further weight to its sad contents.

I entered the park and lowered myself onto one of the benches over-looking the pond. I had always enjoyed listening to Sunday evening church bells and street sounds in London, particularly after spending months or years of relative silence in the Arctic, but I felt no joy on this late afternoon. It grieved me to think of mothers, fathers, wives, broth-ers, sisters and children suffering and weeping upon hearing the tragic news of cannibalism among the last survivors. These poor people might wonder forever if their own loved ones had participated in — or been victims of — these final desperate acts to prolong their lives.

I tried to understand why such melancholy tidings would be released in the newspapers, and concluded that there had to be some sort of rea-soning behind it. For an hour or so, I took a scientific approach to exam-ining my confusion by picturing myself in Lord Graham's shoes. Firstly, it was well known that the obsessive British search for a sea link across the North American Arctic had failed time and again. On previous ex-peditions, then-lieutenant John Franklin had succeeded in charting considerable stretches of the North American coastline, but his three separate attempts to locate the Northwest Passage had been fruitless. On one disaster-plagued journey between 1819 and 1822, eleven of his twenty men had perished from starvation and violence. Nonetheless, the romantic Franklin Expedition was enormously popular with the people of Britain because it symbolized ambition, wealth, and indisput-able naval dominance across the globe. After 1848, when it was feared that the *Erebus* and *Terror* were in peril, many British ships and men were subsequently lost in searches for the missing vessels and their crews.

I sifted through the facts as I understood them, and formed my own hypothesis. Nine years after the ships' departure and disappearance, I surmised that the British government wished to let go — once and for all — of its fanciful and wildly expensive quest for completing the Northwest Passage to the Far East. Lord Graham appeared to have little interest when I attempted to tell him that I believed I had located a section of the correct sea link. The authorities wanted to make their past failures disappear from Britain's collective consciousness, and turn the public's heads towards current and future endeavours. They had already issued a proclamation declaring that all of the men had bravely given up their lives, in the name of God, the Queen and their country. Less than seven months after the declaration was made and the subject was ostensibly closed, however, I came along and threw a wrench into the government's efforts to make the story go away quietly. The missing men were dead all right, but they had become desperate enough to eat each other!

I remained on that bench for a long time, brooding. Queen Victoria and her advisors closely followed the news, of course, so they would have been aware of my report and the Admiralty's decision to publish it. Whatever the public reaction, I suspected that the notion of finding a sea passage across the roof of the North American continent would soon die in the hearts and minds of the British public.

I also considered the fact that Britain and France had recently become engaged in a war between Turkey and Russia, an event forged by tricky alliances, power, politics and mutual concerns about Russian expansionism on the continent. Such a complex land and sea enterprise required great numbers of men, weapons, horses, ships and expensive equipment to battle the Russian Bear, along with a measure of goodwill from the public. Nine years ago, the government had enjoyed the support of the British people when the *Erebus* and *Terror* had set sail in search of the Northwest Passage. Now the authorities needed the public to let go of its failed Arctic dream, and somehow believe in the necessity of Great Britain's engagement in the Crimean conflict.

Perhaps the Admiralty hoped that my scandalous report would provide the government with benefits on two major fronts: a wave of shock would run through the minds of the British public, but the news would not directly reflect on their storied institution. Instead, I would be the recipient of distrust, derision and ridicule for believing the words of the Esquimaux. I would play the unfortunate role of scapegoat, a distraction which would likely keep Lady Franklin busy for some time to come. She had been constantly pestering the Admiralty to find her lost husband, even after the official announcement of his death. Were they banking on Lady Franklin leaving them alone, and turning her attentions towards discrediting me?

It had pained me terribly when the *Times* reporter asked me about my motive for travelling to England instead of organizing another expedition and pushing west to collect more proof. His reference to my return to London as soon as I could because of the reward money was insulting, to say the least.

The air became damp, so I finally gathered my things and set out in the direction of the Covent Garden Hotel where I sometimes lodged when I was visiting London. In the morning when the dreadful news took the country by storm, I would quietly go to the Hudson's Bay Company offices and book the earliest available passage home to Orkney.

→ *London, England*
[OCTOBER 23, 1854]

I awoke with a start the next morning, my mind in a fog. Where was I? At sea? In the Arctic? In England? Scotland? It took me a few moments to realize that I was staying at the Covent Garden Hotel, and that it was almost daylight. Even though I had lodged at the hotel previously, the surroundings felt strangely unfamiliar, as if I had never before occupied this comfortable space. I had tossed and turned throughout the night, slipping in and out of disturbing dreams. Now raindrops tapped steadily at the window. I briefly considered rolling over and going back to sleep.

Suddenly I sat bolt upright in bed as my mind cleared and it struck me that this would be no ordinary day. Far from it. While London slept under a blanket of mist and darkness, the *Times* was busy printing copies of the morning paper containing the gruesome news about Sir John Franklin and his men. It was certain that other newspapers would be following suit, so the story would soon — if not already — be circulating throughout the city and beyond.

I washed at the nightstand and dressed for the day. A maid knocked at the door and set a breakfast tray on the table, along with the morning edition of the *Times*. I turned the paper face down, not wishing to see the news before I had consumed at least some of the meal. I managed to get through a cup of tea, a boiled egg and half a sausage before curiosity got the better of me. I took a deep breath and flipped the paper over.

As usual, the first several pages of the *Times* were crowded with notices, advertisements, excerpts from speeches, financial information, and so on. I slowly turned over pages one, two, three, four and five, then page six. There was nothing of note on any of them. I gingerly turned another page and there it was, occupying two half-columns in the uppermost section of page seven:

THE ARCTIC EXPEDITION

Intelligence which may be fairly considered decisive has at last reached this country of the sad fate of Sir John Franklin and his brave companions.

Dr. Rae, whose previous exploits as an Arctic Traveller have already so highly distinguished him, landed at Deal yesterday, and immediately proceeded to the Admiralty, and laid before Sir James Graham the melancholy evidence on which his report is founded.

I was relieved to see that the tone of the article was dry and neutral, which gave me some hope that the Arctic Council members had further discussed the matter, considered my argument against publication and made an effort to tone down the grim elements of the story. I read on.

Dr. Rae was not employed in searching for John Franklin, but in completing his survey of the coast of the Boothia Peninsula.

He justly thought, however, that the information he had obtained greatly outweighed the importance of the survey, and he has hurried home to satisfy the "public anxiety" as to the fate of the long-lost expedition, and to prevent the risk of the loss of further life.

So far, this is quite satisfactory, I thought. When I read more, however, a jolt of disappointment ran through me. The newspaper had inserted a direct quotation from my private report.

> From the mutilated contents of the kettles, it is evident that our wretched countrymen had been driven to the last recourse — cannibalism — as a means of prolonging existence.

The *Times* added that according to my report, some of the corpses

> had been sadly mutilated, and had been stripped by those who had the misery to survive them, and who were wrapped in two or three suits of clothes.

The word "cannibalism" leapt off the page and my heart sank. My private report had indeed been published in the most widely read newspaper in Britain. The article went on to quote from my writing that a few of the unfortunate men must have survived until just after the arrival of migrating wild fowl, probably around the end of May 1850.

I covered the breakfast meal with a napkin and left the hotel clutching the heavy satchel containing the relics in one hand and an umbrella in the other, my footsteps quickening as I dashed past screeching newspaper boys frantically waving copies of the morning paper above their heads. I threaded my way through a maze of umbrella-covered pedestrians, and blinkered, high-stepping horses splashing through puddles, pulling carriages filled with all manner of humans and cargo. The odours of the city seemed stronger, rendered particularly foul by the dampness. I felt oddly exposed and threatened, despite the fact that I was just another body among hundreds of people who were busily going about their weekday lives.

I made my way to Hudson Bay House, the home of the Company's headquarters in Fenchurch Street, in search of my employer, Sir George Simpson. Along with yesterday's absence of Sir John Richardson at Admiralty House, that of Sir George had caught me by surprise. I thought the Company's governor, with whom I had been well acquainted for more than twenty years, and who had been actively involved in the mat-

ter of finding the missing expedition, would surely have been in attendance if he had any notion of what awaited me in that council meeting
room. I had sent him a copy of my private report. Was he not invited to
the meeting? Perhaps he, too, had no idea that the cannibalism testimony had been placed in the hands of the press.

I rushed inside the office in Fenchurch clutching the satchel, and inquired if the governor was present. My question — indeed, my very
presence in the reception area — seemed to cause some measure of discomfort among the clerks, and of course, I understood why. They would
have been aware of the morning's news about the fate of Sir John
Franklin and his men. Sir George came out of his office. I must say that
he was a welcome sight. I had not seen him in three years. He had lost
more hair and his bushy sideburns had changed from silvery grey to
white, but in his sixties he still looked strong and physically fit. We
shook hands and he led me into his office. I noticed that a copy of the
Times was lying on his desk, open at page 7.

"It is good to see you, my boy." He had always called me "my boy,"
which I did not mind at all, since he was some twenty-five years my
senior, and he had been my mentor ever since I was hired by the Hudson's Bay Company at the tender age of twenty. He had taken me under
his wing when I first arrived in the Arctic, probably because I reminded
him of his younger self: curious, adventurous and strong. My own father passed away a year later, and I suppose Sir George became a sort of
father substitute for me when I was so young and far away from my
family.

Many people did not care for him, though. He was known to be impatient, arrogant, dictatorial and sharp of tongue. He was, however, an
astute man of enterprise, and he was well respected for that. There had
been times when I was angry with Sir George for expecting too much of
me after I was appointed chief factor for the Mackenzie River District.
Occasionally, when I was exhausted and in need of respite, I wrote to
him and asked for periods of leave to return home and rest. He had ignored those letters altogether. Despite my grievances concerning his
lack of sympathy for others, I admired his wit and business sense. When
we spent time together, I enjoyed his company.

We sat down and, at Sir George's request, I laid out the artifacts upon the vast surface of his polished ebony desk. He examined them with great interest, picking up pieces of broken watches, compasses, silverware, and so on.

"This collection is quite astonishing, isn't it, John?" He weighed the silver plate in both hands, looked closely at the assorted sets of initials on the smaller items through a magnifying glass, felt the gold braid between his fingers.

I nodded. "The remaining objects will be delivered to you, Sir George, so your staff can go about the task of recording them in a Company catalogue, and return the appropriate pieces to the owners' families. With your approval, however, I would like to keep some of the broken instruments and a few pieces of cutlery for my own interest."

"I think you have earned that privilege." He sat back in his chair and looked at me. "John, I know you well enough to respect your painstaking work in interviewing and cross-examining the Esquimaux. I have no doubt concerning the veracity of the information you have obtained."

I described the lengthy and melancholy task of recording the evidence about the starving men's demise and its aftermath. George Simpson and I were like-minded on the subject of the natives in that polar region: they were not given to violence against others. He was personally familiar with Esquimaux traditions of record-keeping and sharing information with others. He also understood why the natives would have been fearful of the strange white men, marching in grim processions towards their own deaths. It was a relief for me to discuss the situation with someone who had personal experience with the Esquimaux — a man with authority — thus lending credence to my account.

Sir George said it was most unfortunate, but he was not surprised to learn that I had been treated poorly during the meetings at Admiralty House. He told me that I had provided far more information than anyone in the British government wanted to hear. Despite his own requests for an audience, no member of the Arctic Council was willing to discuss the report with him and no, he was not invited to yesterday's meeting.

"I expect they all knew I would support you and accept the testimony, my boy," he said. "It's easier to ignore one voice than two." Then he rubbed his hands together and leaned forward. Observing these gestures, I knew a question was coming.

"John, I understand that this is a difficult time for you, but I must ask you something important. Why *did* you include the story of cannibalism in your report to the Admiralty? Would it not have been better if it had never been mentioned at all?" He held up his hands. "I confess that I am quite curious about that."

It was a reasonable question, and I thought carefully before replying. "Sir, those of us who have lived and worked in the regions around Hudson Bay know that the Franklin Expedition was over-supplied and woefully under-equipped for the momentous task at hand. There were no skilled hunters aboard, nor had interpreters been hired. It seems that no one on either ship was trained in Arctic survival."

He placed his palms on the table between us. "Aye, from what I understand, that is true enough."

"In my opinion, the men's lives were in peril the moment the ships reached the other side of the Atlantic Ocean. I gave the situation careful thought before making the decision to return to London. I came to the conclusion that if the authorities were to receive tangible evidence of cannibalism in the future, I would have been heavily criticized for hiding what I had learned from the Esquimaux at Pelly Bay and Repulse Bay. It was never my intention to make that tragic truth available to the public. And as you know, Sir, I have always had a tendency to report the facts as I see them."

"Or hear of them, from sources you trust." He smiled. "Aye, you have been doing just that — in great detail — since we first met, my boy, and I admire you for it. We could always count on you for reliable information. Who can say if the Admiralty will learn a lesson from this tragedy? Somehow, I rather doubt it but I also can't imagine them undertaking such a massive enterprise again." He shook his head and folded his arms across his chest. "Much too costly in lives and equipment."

I sighed. "I thought I was doing something useful. It never occurred to me that those in authority would set me up as the whipping boy for public resentment. I can be a bit naïve sometimes, I'll admit."

"Both you and I are well aware that the British government is intent upon keeping up the front that the Royal Navy is indestructible, even when pitted against the forces of nature, my boy. Even when there are failures," he added. He lifted his hand to his temple. "Rule Britannia!" he cried, with a mock salute. "We know better, but business is business, and they saw their venture as the holy grail of global enterprise. Let it all settle down. Great Britain is engaged in yet another war, and facing an ugly series of battles we will probably lose. The general public has other problems to think about right now. By the way, have you heard about the Asiatic cholera epidemic here in London? What a nasty affair. Take care of yourself, and remember that the Hudson's Bay Company needs you more than ever in the Arctic."

"I am requesting a period of leave from my duties in the Arctic, Sir. My mother has had a stroke. I wish to book passage to Stromness aboard the *Prince of Wales II*, on the next date of departure."

He raised his eyebrows. "Oh. I'm sorry to hear about Margaret. Of course, go home for a while to see her, get some rest and we will continue this discussion in the new year. The next sailing will be on November 3rd. Let's speak to the clerk and make arrangements for you."

I was not surprised to hear that my pragmatic employer's primary interest was in getting on with business. I understood his reasons for wanting the Company's massive fur trade operations to continue without interruption, but the more I thought about the strain of attending to business at so many distant depots and offices, of constantly being on the move in harsh polar conditions while growing older, the less inclined I felt to continue my employment as a chief factor.

I bade Sir George farewell and, as I left his office, a clerk handed me an envelope which had just been delivered, addressed to me. Who knew I was at Hudson Bay House that morning? The handwriting was unfamiliar and distinctively feminine. I tucked it into my pocket and proceeded on foot to the Royal Society for Improving Natural Knowledge at Somerset House on the Strand, of which I was a member in good standing. I hoped to find a quiet place in one of the reading rooms so I could read the letter and collect my thoughts in privacy. When I arrived at Somerset House Square, I was surprised to see a small crowd milling about the entrance to the Society. I had spent a good deal of time at the

Royal Society when I was visiting London, so it should have occurred to me that someone would have anticipated my presence there, once the dreadful news began to spread around the city. I lowered my head and tipped my hat forward to conceal my face, glancing around for an alter--native door to the building. I considered leaving the square, but to my chagrin, someone with paper and pencil in hand recognized me.

"Doctor Rae! I should like to have a word with you! Why do you believe the stories of savages?" Heads turned and a dozen pairs of eyes were suddenly upon me. I inched towards the entrance, wishing I had shaved away more of my heavy beard so I would be less recognizable.

"Over here, Doctor Rae! Why did you not stay in the Arctic and search for the bodies? Why did you come home so soon?"

"What about the reward? Is that why you came home? Is it?"

"I shall not answer that question, or any others at this — "

A large hand gripped my elbow. I was swiftly ushered up the steps and into the building, with the eager crowd close at heel. The bolting of a door muted the sound of excited voices. I was relieved to find myself suddenly inside the Royal Society offices, with a fellow Scotsman and member I recognized: Gerald McIntosh. The older man guided me up the staircase, past the portraits of scientists and explorers, and escorted me into an empty reading room. I put down my bag and stared at my unexpected saviour with gratitude. "Thank you, good sir, for rescuing me. I am most grateful."

"Not at all, Dr. Rae. I am quite certain that you would do the same for me, if I were being hounded by a mob of pesky journalists and curiosity seekers."

The spacious room was a welcome sight. It had the pleasant, familiar smell of wood and old books: hundreds of volumes filled shelves that soared upwards to the finely carved oak ceiling. Faded carpets, wooden desks and creaky floorboards suggested many years of purposeful use, whilst small groupings of polished leather armchairs lent an intimate air to the surroundings. I walked towards the window. The news that I was in the building must have been spreading, though, because in just a few short minutes, I could hear the crowd growing more vocal. I sank heavily into the soft seat of a chair and let out a long sigh. My legs were restless; I placed my hands on my knees in an attempt to settle them down.

Gerald McIntosh, an avuncular, big-boned man with a generous helping of extra flesh on his body, slowly lowered his bulk into an armchair across from me and leaned forward. "Shall I order some tea for us, Doctor Rae?" I nodded. He rang for a servant.

He was a well-respected mathematician and instructor at King's College, a senior academic with a solid reputation, and a Scot. On this turbulent morning, he became more than an esteemed fellow member, he became a friend.

"Gerald, I presume that you have read this morning's news about the Franklin party in the papers?"

"Aye, I have." McIntosh nodded and leaned back in his chair, while reaching into his jacket pocket to retrieve a pipe, along with a packet of tobacco.

"Do you have your pipe with you, John?"

"I do not smoke."

"Ah, will you mind if I do, good doctor?"

"Not at all." A servant carrying a tea tray slipped silently into the room. "Cummins, please ensure that our privacy is strictly maintained while we are here."

"Very good, Sir."

Gerald rose when the servant left, locked the door and sank back into his armchair. He tapped the stale contents of his pipe into a small dish on the table beside him, stuffed fresh tobacco into the polished wooden bowl, and tamped it down. He lit it slowly and drew the flame inward, until the burn was established. My breathing began to slow as I observed him performing these simple acts. I experienced a moment of melancholy, because his actions reminded me of my men in the Arctic, engaging in the same calm ritual around a blazing fire, their carved pipes in hand and our company's presents of tobacco in the bowls.

My new companion squinted at me through a haze of blue-grey smoke. "Aye, John. I am aware of your report. We do not know each other well, but I have admired your achievements as a scientist and Arctic expert for some time. I am sorry to see that all your years of good, sensible work have come to this . . . nonsense." He waved a hand towards the window. Shouts could be heard, now, as the crowd grew more restless. Agitated, I approached the window again, stood to one side of it so no one would be able to see me, and peered out.

"You are a practising physician, explorer, surveyor, manager and naturalist, am I correct?" he called out, trying to distract me from observing the activity in the square.

"Aye." I took a seat again.

"And you are a Scot, an Orkneyman." He continued. "Of course, I, too, am a Scot, but I am from the mainland, the Kincardineshire region. We mainland Scots are unique in our own right." He chuckled and puffed on his pipe. "Our English neighbours fervently believe us to be half-savage hairy beasts, possessed of impulsive character and vastly limited brain function!

"In fact," he continued, "it thoroughly delights me to see a fellow Scot exceed English expectations in the arts and sciences. The English can be quite a foolish lot. Full of their own importance, in my opinion. You were the recipient of the Royal Geographic Society Founder's Gold Medal in 1852, is that correct?"

"Yes. I surveyed and charted a stretch of the North American coastline."

McIntosh grinned. "The gossips reported that although you were in Great Britain when the award was bestowed, you absented yourself from the ceremony."

"Aye, that is true," I replied, surprised that he knew such a trifling detail. "I was at home in Orkney with my family, and on a fishing excursion with a small group there, actually. To be honest, being awarded the medal was a great honour, but I have a tendency to feel somewhat awkward at formal occasions. I find the atmosphere a bit on the fussy side, and London was a long way to go for an hour-long ceremony." We both smiled at that remark. I sipped the tea slowly, breathing in the soothing vapours.

"One more thing, if you don't think me too nosy," he said. "I heard that McGill University in Montreal, Canada, conferred an Honorary Doctor of Medicine degree upon you last year."

I nodded, embarrassed now.

"Congratulations, Sir," he said. "Tell me, were you able to be present for that ceremony?"

"It, too, was a great honour, but I was travelling in the Arctic at the time." I felt sheepish. Thus far, my record for turning up at special occasions was less than impressive.

"John, you are a level-headed man with an enviable reputation. I trust that the terrible news you learned from the Esquimaux is, in fact, true. I will wager that you never intended for it to become public knowledge."

"Thank you, Gerald, for your confidence in me. I tried to prevent the news from being released — "

He interrupted me, displeasure clouding his cheerful expression. "The Arctic Council and Parliament have made a mess of it all, John. They never really understood what they were up against in the Arctic. Such a shame. So many lives lost to no purpose."

"I wholeheartedly agree, Sir."

I have spent more time in solitude with my own thoughts than in easy conversation with others and, sensing this, Gerald led our discussion with enthusiasm. No doubt he was feeling quite energized by the notion of harbouring an unexpected fugitive from public scrutiny. The story, as he may have perceived it, was a jolly good one but I could also see that he possessed an empathetic character and that along with being a bit too earnest, he was well-meaning.

"As you know all too well, John, Lady Franklin has fostered nothing short of a public frenzy about the mystery of the missing Franklin Expedition. She is quite simply driving everyone mad with her obsession. Of course, the loss of the ships and men is tragic, and I do sympathize with her, but now that your Arctic findings are being released, I fear she will try and turn the situation around to her own advantage. She would certainly not be above casting suspicion on your report about cannibalism by questioning your professional credibility as a man who consorts with natives, not to mention the integrity of your sources. Her priority will be to clear her husband's good name and consign him to the annals of British exploration history as the best there ever was. And who knows what other mischief she will get up to? My unsolicited advice to you is to ignore her, if you possibly can." He cleared his throat and sipped his tea.

I put my teacup and saucer on the table, rose again and began to pace, pausing at the window. The image of my body hanging from a hastily constructed gallows flashed across my mind. I silently admonished myself for momentarily entertaining such a ridiculous and dramatic thought.

I turned to face him. "For years I have sympathized with Lady Franklin's plight, but the Admiralty and the politicians weren't the only ones she pestered over the years. She wouldn't leave me alone either." I paused, uncertain about the wisdom of making a disparaging comment about her to someone I did not know well, or indeed, to anyone at all.

I reached into my pocket and felt the edges of the envelope, anxious to open it privately somewhere, wondering if it contained a letter from her. "I won't be surprised if I hear from Lady Franklin soon," I said. "She will not have pleasant words for me. To be honest, it has been difficult for me to remain patient in my dealings with her . . ." I hesitated about saying anything more to my companion.

"Whatever you say in this room today remains here, John. Your words will go no further than these four walls."

"Well," I offered, "Jane Franklin never seemed to notice that as a chief factor for the Hudson's Bay Company, I was tasked with many other responsibilities, including overseeing the fur trade business in the Arctic. Planning, mounting and leading every survey expedition took at least a year, which she felt was far too long. Why, in 1848, she even tried to join Sir John Richardson and me on a long search expedition to find the missing men, but to my great relief, my colleague dissuaded her from coming with us."

"How extraordinary!" Gerald exclaimed. "We've got to at least give the woman credit for being fearless! Can you imagine what it would have been like to climb icy mountains with her? How very awkward!" he shuddered.

"You know," I said, "Jane Franklin went as far as to visit my elderly mother in Stromness three years ago, although I am quite certain that she had little interest in my family. I am convinced it was an attempt to gain attention from the press, the public and from the authorities in London."

Gerald looked amused. "No doubt most Orcadians were none too pleased with her arrival! Such a persistent and nervous disposition. Tell me, was her omnipresent companion Sophia Cracroft with her?"

"Yes, she was."

"Oh, my." Gerald frowned, and drew from his pipe. "Your poor mother."

"Aye, my poor mother. The two women probably think of Orcadians as primitive, simple creatures. Hardly the equals of the sophisticated circle of people with whom they surround themselves," I added.

"Orkneymen are made of superior stock. Just consider their strong Viking roots. They are a proud, unsinkable lot, in my opinion."

I took measured steps back and forth across the room, because walking had always felt more natural to me than sitting. My nerves were frayed, so I felt an even stronger impulse to keep moving. I stroked my beard and attempted a half-joke: "I suppose in the eyes of Lady Franklin and her London society crowd, I am not just a half-savage Scot, like you, Gerald. I am a two-thirds savage Scot who 'went native' in the Arctic, and became a fully-fledged hairy beast at that!"

He chuckled at the notion.

"John, have you heard the story about Lady Franklin and the ghost?"

"I beg your pardon?"

"Apparently Lady Franklin and her niece were visited by a retired sea captain here in London, who claims that the ghost of his deceased daughter appeared before her living siblings one night with the news that Sir John is alive and trapped in sea ice near Victoria Island. The apparition declared that she had seen him and the missing ships."

"Good God! If I weren't a scientist, I should shiver at that one!" Jane Franklin hadn't a clue about what a real ghost is. I had seen far too many of them in my Arctic travels as a physician, fur trader and explorer: the cold, the hungry and the dying. Their stricken faces and dull, sunken eyes would be forever etched in my memory.

My restlessness was building. This thoughtful companion meant well, but I felt too unsettled to remain in the room and engage in conversation with the crowds calling my name below. It was time for me to leave the Royal Society, although I had no idea of how to escape unnoticed.

"Thank you very much, Gerald, for your kindness and hospitality, but I must really take my leave now and disappear somewhere in this crowded city. I will need time to collect my thoughts, and . . ."

A brief shadow of disappointment swept across Gerald's face, but he quickly recovered his countenance of good cheer, and he was gracious about my abrupt announcement. He rose and waved a hand towards the locked door. "Of course, I do understand your discomfort, John. You have weathered a terrible gale during your recent sea crossing, and I fear you have been dropped into a tempest at home."

We shook hands. "Come with me," he said. "I will call for my carriage so you may be swiftly delivered to a destination of your choice. No one will know where the driver has taken you."

"Good sir, I can walk. My bags are at a hotel in Covent Garden. I think I will move to another place of lodging today. Travelling on foot is no hardship — "

"I will not hear of it, John. My driver will help you pick up your things in Covent Garden and take you wherever you wish to go. That blasted crowd is not going to disperse anytime soon. Come, make your exit from the rear of this building, away from prying eyes. I shall personally escort you."

He unlocked the reading-room door and requested the immediate delivery of his carriage to the rear. We stood together beside the window for a moment, out of the crowd's sight. Shouts and chattering rose from below; I winced as I heard my name being called. We used the servants' staircase to reach the exit. Gerald's driver was waiting, reins in hand, as instructed. The sky remained a dark, leaden grey, but the rain had stopped, at least for now. Gerald paused before closing the carriage door, looked me directly in the eye and offered a broad smile of reassurance.

"I have not seen you on this day, John."

"Good day to you, Gerald, and God bless you for this."

The driver snapped the reins and we disappeared, unnoticed, into the crowded streets of London. We picked up my things from the Covent Garden Hotel and proceeded in the direction of another hotel, in the Russell Square area. Once we were on our way, I retrieved the mystery envelope from my pocket, curious to see whom the feminine handwriting belonged to, and what message it held. I was not surprised to discover who had authored it:

Lady Franklin
4 Spring Gardens, London

Dr. John Rae:

Lady Franklin requests that you join her for tea at her rooms in Park Gardens, on Tuesday, October 24th, at four o'clock p.m.

Please reply to this invitation at your earliest convenience.

Sincerely,
Sophia Cracroft

The last two people on earth I wished to see were the widow of Sir John Franklin and her husband's niece, Sophia Cracroft, but it would have been unfair to ignore them altogether, and it was an appropriate gesture for me to personally offer my sympathies. It was highly doubtful but I hoped Jane Franklin would grant me just a few moments to explain my belief in the Esquimaux testimony, and that she would somehow accept that I had never intended for the report to be published. I knew, however, that the chances of her believing the words of the Esquimaux, or listening to my side of the story, were slim at best. Nevertheless, I decided that as soon as I reached my new lodgings, I would dispatch a reply to Miss Cracroft, accepting Lady Franklin's invitation. For the most part, it is wiser to stand your ground and defend your position in the face of criticism than to run away from it.

Gerald McIntosh's carriage driver delivered me to a spot behind the university, next to the rear entrance of the hotel. I was in no mood to pause at the hotel pub for a meal and visit with Sam the pubmaster, as was my usual custom. The staff at the Tavistock knew me well; I was a quiet guest, and I always paid a good reward in exchange for discretion and privacy. I greeted Neil, the manager, at the reception desk, and asked him if we could speak in private. He led me into his office and closed the door.

He looked uncomfortable, embarrassed. Like many others, he was surely shocked and dismayed to hear that a number of Franklin's starving men had been forced to resort to such desperate measures in an attempt to prolong their lives. He probably wondered — although he would never ask it directly of me — if the story were really true. He was a good fellow, but I had neither the energy nor the desire to discuss the matter with him or anyone else at that time. Perhaps he felt the same way. Rather than pretend that this was a morning like any other, I decided to make a brief reference to the awkward subject and end it right there.

I looked down at him; he was almost a foot shorter than me. "Neil, I presume you have read the news about the fate of the Franklin Expedition in this morning's papers?"

He lowered his eyes to the desk and nodded. "Yes, Sir, I have."

"You see," I continued, "the most distressing elements of the report were supposed to remain private. It is deeply unfortunate that they have become public knowledge." He nodded in agreement.

"Neil, I wish to stay here anonymously for at least ten nights, and with this morning's news, I am sure you can understand why. Would you please record my name as William Hamilton on your list of lodgers?"

"Certainly. Will you be taking your meals in your room then, Mr. Hamilton?"

"Yes. I should like a room on the top floor, with a view to the Square, and a 'Do Not Disturb' sign on the door. And one more thing. Please bring me hot water, extra soap and drying cloths."

I had decided to use the surname Hamilton, because my sister Marion was married to John Hamilton of Hoy, Orkney, and the name was hardly uncommon in London. I chose the name William for a personal reason. Nine years earlier, while I was busy working in the Arctic and just months before the *Erebus* and *Terror* sailed out of Stromness, my beloved older brother, William Glen Rae, shot himself through the head with his rifle. He had not been much of a correspondent, but I had heard that he seemed to have settled in well with his wife and four children at his newly established Hudson's Bay Company depot in Yerba Buena, California, a Spanish settlement which became known as San Francisco two years after his death. Will was four years my senior, a giant of a fellow who could make me dissolve in tears of laughter anytime he pleased. As a boy, I followed him everywhere, sometimes to his chagrin. I could never understand why William, my hero, would take his life — all because he had been unfaithful to his wife. Was there more to the story than we had been told? I would always mourn the loss of Will. I wanted to feel him near me, even if only in name.

Neil excused himself for a few moments, and returned with a key. "It is done, Sir. I shall personally assist you with your bags, if you will follow me."

I clutched the satchel as I followed the manager up the stairway. Neil had said, "It is done." The simple phrase struck me at that moment, and I thought of Orkney.

"*Tara Gott*," I said.

Neil turned around. "I beg your pardon, Sir?"

"Just a little catch in my throat."

Once I was alone, I removed my hat, overcoat and boots, opened the window to admit the cool late-October air and poured kettles of steaming water, delivered by Neil, into the tub. I vigorously scrubbed my skin until it was pink, as if to remove the stains of my humiliation. Afterwards, I reclined on the bed and closed my burning eyes.

I had invested more than twenty years of my life in the service of the Hudson's Bay Company and the Crown, forging new trails and lining the pockets of my employers and countrymen. By and large, I believed I had conducted my business with integrity and respect for others, on both sides of the Atlantic Ocean. It was no secret that the Company and the British government had their petty differences of opinion about how to administer their expanding interests in North America. It was natural for governments and private enterprises to disagree on matters of land holdings, profits, leadership and so on. I had never been much concerned about these sorts of things, but now that the Admiralty had turned its back on me, I did not know who I could trust in high places, other than Sir George. I turned onto my side, drew my knees to my chest, and wept bitter tears of anger and injury, the first I had shed since William's untimely death. I tried in vain to shut off repetitive thoughts and let sleep take over, but my mind refused to be still.

Members of the Arctic Council had scarcely met my eyes at Admiralty House, as if an unpleasant odour clung to my clothes. It was well known that a number of them had come perilously close to starving to death during their own Arctic expeditions. Had they simply forgotten about the terrible pain and confusion which accompany extreme cold and hunger? Or that it can drive a person mad? A perfectly rational man can lose his mind as starvation robs him of his flesh, his organs, his thoughts. Sir John Franklin himself, the brave Arctic hero praised by Englishmen as "the man who ate his boots," had published a book describing his own experience of extreme deprivation in 1821 near the Coppermine River, and his miraculous rescue by the Yellowknife natives.

In my view, there was a critical difference between the members of the Arctic Council and the unfortunate men of the *Erebus* and *Terror*: no one I met with at Admiralty House had, in fact, reached the final stage of starvation. This good fortune applied to me as well. On one journey when an early winter had set in and there was no wildlife to be trapped, shot or caught for food, I experienced the pain of my body consuming its own fat and muscle tissue before I was able to reach a Hudson's Bay Company depot. After that episode, I returned to Orkney for a rest. I will never forget the shocked look on my mother's face when she gazed upon my altered form. She clenched her teeth, and announced to our family and neighbours that I was thereafter not permitted to set even one foot in the Arctic ever again! Mam was a wise woman and a wonderful mother, but her five sons were never very good at listening to her admonitions.

Had my own deprivation gone on longer, I would have perhaps known first-hand the panic that settles in after a long period of being cold, lost and wasting away. Could any of my countrymen — regardless of their education, religion or beliefs — be absolutely certain that they would never resort to extreme measures in order to prolong their lives? Rescue could, in fact, be just moments away. For the surviving men of the Franklin party, there had been months and years of prayers but no rescue or release from the agonies of certain starvation.

As I lay on the hotel bed, I fretted about the absence of my friend Sir John Richardson at the meeting. Was he really too busy with his family to miss such an important gathering of the Arctic Council? It stung that he had not made an effort to meet with me on my return from the Arctic, since we had spent a good deal of time together searching for the missing Franklin party.

Then suddenly, I recalled that he had been unknowingly exposed — first-hand — to the last recourse, during the terrible 1819 to 1821 overland expedition along the shores of the Coppermine River to the Polar Sea. In that moment, I understood why he had avoided the meeting.

Dr. John Richardson, among others in the British travelling party under the command of Lieutenant John Franklin, had been tricked into consuming considerable amounts of human flesh by a murderous native, Michel Terrohaute, when food provisions were depleted. John Richardson, a gentle and pious man, had been forced to execute Terrohaute when no one else intervened. He never spoke of it to me, but I suspected that the memory of those two dreadful experiences surely haunted him. It stood to reason that the fresh news about members of John Franklin's party consuming the flesh of their fallen must have driven him into a terrible state of melancholy. My own feeling of having been rebuffed by him was quickly replaced by a wave of sympathy for my friend.

As the hours passed and autumn darkness set over London, I thought of the earlier discussion with my employer, Sir George Simpson. There were things I wished to talk to him about at this difficult juncture in my career with the Hudson's Bay Company, but he was right: I needed to take some time away from it all. While I was in the Arctic, I had managed to save a decent sum from my salary because there was nothing of interest to spend it on over there. Perhaps in the new year I would have a clearer perspective on where I wanted to be and how I wished to proceed, both personally and professionally.

After several hours of reflection in the Tavistock Hotel room, I was too exhausted to bother with lighting the lamp and reading. My thoughts shifted from the immediate past to the near future: getting the nasty business with Lady Franklin out of the way the next day, walking the streets of London in the evenings for exercise and peace of mind, reading in quiet corners of the university library, and then sailing home to Orkney. After much thought and reflection, I was finally able to drift off to sleep.

→ *Spring Gardens, London*
[OCTOBER 24, 1854]

After taking a late lunch in my room, I exited the Tavistock Hotel and stepped into the cold glow of London's late October light, when the sun hangs low in the sky and casts long, dark shadows across the city. I had taken extra time to bathe and donned somewhat formal attire, in an effort to appear citified for the meeting with Lady Franklin. I was certain my efforts would not be enough to her liking, but what did it matter when she was probably angry with me anyway?

The morning newspapers had published new articles and editorials about yesterday's scandalous news. I was relieved to ascertain that my own character was not under attack; the so-called savages of the north, however, fared poorly in the opinions of the writers.

It grieved me to read about the unreliability of native peoples. How could anyone presume to judge the hearts and minds of others when they do not know them, have not passed even one day in their company? On the other hand, it was every newspaper editor's job to attract readers to current news, stories and debates. Londoners certainly enjoyed their gossip, and there could be no doubt that my return from the Arctic with such unsettling news was giving people much to discuss.

I left Russell Square and walked along Bedford Place, past the stately home of Sir John and Lady Franklin. The mistress of the house was not in residence, because she preferred to oversee the business of searching for her lost husband from her rented Spring Gardens apartments, in full view of Admiralty House. Her move to that location with her husband's niece Sophia could not have been coincidental. The two women were well positioned for keeping an eye on the daily comings and goings of their neighbours. It may bear repeating that I was not looking forward to this meeting with John Franklin's widow. Despite her feminine appearance and demeanour, I had always been aware of something fierce in her, and I felt with certainty that she would not hesitate to cast aside any obstacle which blocked her chosen path.

A tall, expressionless butler opened the door to her apartments. He took my coat and hat. I had left what remained of the relics in a trunk locked in my room at the hotel. I followed the man along a wide hallway to the library where tall, multi-paned windows overlooked tired, late-season gardens. Despite the dreary time of year, however, the room was filled with light. I recalled being in this room with Lady Franklin in 1852, discussing the details of my next expedition for the Hudson's Bay Company and search for the missing ships. Sir John Richardson had been there as well, along with Miss Cracroft. The two women were curiously inseparable; they seemed to function as one person, which made me feel somewhat befuddled when a conversation was underway. It was difficult to understand who I was really speaking to, whom I should address, with whose eyes I should make contact.

The library was quite cluttered this time. As the years passed and the great mystery remained unsolved, the room itself seemed to have become a more frantic space. Maps, open books and documents covered every table surface, even portions of the floor. Perhaps Lady Franklin intended for me to observe the room in that condition to emphasize the fact that despite the British government's earlier declaration that all Franklin Expedition members had perished, and regardless of the physical evidence I had brought home from the Arctic, she still believed that if the search were to continue unabated, her husband could be found alive.

A small writing table beside the window was piled high with papers. A scuffed-looking pen and inkwell were in place, ready for the next volley of letters Jane Franklin would probably fire off to her long list of targets in her quest to find her husband. I wondered if there was any truth in the rumours that Jane herself had penned the words to the ballad "Lady Franklin's Lament."

I admired the rhythm and sentiment; the poem reminded me of shanties sung by the fishermen I liked to follow around when I was a boy in Orphir:

> With a hundred seamen he sailed away
> To the frozen ocean in the month of May
> To seek a passage around the pole
> Where we poor sailors do sometimes go.
>
> Through cruel hardships they vainly strove
> Their ships on mountains of ice were drove . . .

I was taken aback when Lady Franklin's petite, aging figure swept into the room wearing full mourning attire. It was widely known that she had refused to dress in mourning clothes after the British government officially declared all of the men dead. Sophia Cracroft came in behind her. I was even more surprised to see Sir John Richardson, who was so conspicuously absent at Sunday's meeting, enter close behind them, followed by one of the servants carrying a tea tray. I rose from the chair and performed a bow in the direction of the ladies. Lady Franklin did not offer me her hand. I briefly caught Sir John's eye but he looked away.

"Lady Franklin," I began, "I wish to extend my deepest condolences for the tragic loss of your husband and his men. Sir John Franklin was a courageous man." She stared at me in reply. I nodded at the niece and addressed Sir John:

"It is good to see you today, Sir. I trust you are well."

"I am well enough, Dr. Rae."

Gone were the amiable smile, the easy manner and familiarity, the feeling of rapport between the two of us. This was the man who had sent a book containing the sonnets of Shakespeare to me from London, to help drive away times of mental boredom when I was wintering in the Arctic. I am certain that we were both aware of each other's dismay at meeting under such uncomfortable circumstances. When we were all seated, Lady Franklin turned to face me. Her white crepe head covering emphasized the melancholy expression on her face; her appearance confirmed that she had finally recognized her husband was deceased.

"Dr. Rae, I shall not mince words with you this time." *This time? When did you and Miss Cracroft ever mince words with anyone, Lady Franklin?*

Her niece added, "You have returned from the Arctic with an appalling report."

"I have," I agreed, addressing her aunt. "The news is indeed distressing. It was never intended to reach public ears, I can assure you — "

Lady Franklin's grey eyes lit up with anger. "Do not speak to me about what should or should not have happened! You have taken to heart the useless words of savages and declared them to be truths! In the eyes of God and your countrymen, your allegations are false and unpardonable!"

Sophia Cracroft attended to serving tea, carefully pouring cups for all present and leaving mine to the last. I glanced at Sir John, who sipped from his cup, staring into the middle distance. It struck me as ironic that John Franklin's niece was seated in a chair positioned under a wall-mounted map of Van Diemen's Land, where Sir John had been appointed as Lieutenant-Governor of a large British penal colony over a decade earlier. Franklin's six-year tenure in that strange land had ended without warning, when he had been replaced and called home to Britain. There had been rumours of disagreements with the local government, and of overspending during the Franklins' time of service in the colony. Something about the erection of numerous statues, arguments over administrative matters, along with the creation of elaborate and expensive social programs for female convicts. There had been murmurings about Lady Franklin and her husband's niece undertaking costly expeditions to climb mountains and so forth. Of course, it was all hearsay.

Lady Franklin continued: "I have held vigil for my husband for nine long years. I know him better than anyone on God's earth. Even *you* are aware of his impeccable record and moral superiority during times of great hardship. He would never, ever, stoop to such depravity." She glanced at her niece, who added: "Nor would he ever allow his men to do the same."

"You have lost your mind," Lady Franklin declared. "Even if you publicly admit to your foolish belief in the words of savages, it is too late now. The damage has been done, and you alone must be held accountable for all of this nonsense."

"Lady Franklin, I understand the depth of your sorrow — "

She leapt from her chair, a furious blush washing over her pale face, her fists balled at her sides. "You — Doctor Rae — understand nothing! You have been living among those natives for too long. You have always been an outsider here in London. How dare you presume to know realities beyond your own primitive Scottish borders, or anything about how devout and educated Englishmen think?"

"Dr. Rae, who can say with certainty that your Esquimaux friends didn't murder our men, steal their property and then sell it to you?" hissed the niece.

I shook my head. "I am disappointed to hear those harsh and shameful thoughts coming from seasoned travellers such as you, Lady Franklin, and you, Miss Cracroft," I retorted.

I had come to the meeting expecting a challenge, but I bristled at this personal attack on my Orcadian origins. Not so long ago, Jane Franklin and Sophia Cracroft had showered me with flattery, hoping I would set aside my many other responsibilities and devote all of my time to searching for the lost expedition. Now I was being accused of uncivilized and, even worse, untrustworthy conduct.

At that moment I realized it was futile for me to remain in that hostile room, attempting to defend myself against such vicious attacks. I placed my hands upon my knees, preparing to rise. "I stand by my report. It is most unfortunate that the authorities have inexplicably chosen to disseminate confidential information to the British public.

"To be honest," I continued, surprised that despite my usual reticence about engaging in confrontations, a spirited rebuttal came to me so readily, "this circus of accusations is quite regrettable, a terrible disservice to the great numbers of courageous Royal Navy men who have perished in the Arctic. The Esquimaux and I have reported the truth. I too am deeply concerned that the information has been released to the public." I glanced again at Sophia Cracroft, who sat motionless and frowning, teacup in one hand and saucer in the other, with her generous skirts arranged perfectly around her. "I suggest that you consider questioning the motives of the authorities. Ask them why they passed along my private report to the *Times*. To divert public attention from other, pressing British military activities abroad, perhaps." I clasped my hands together. "The current war in the Crimean Peninsula comes to mind . . ."

Sir John Richardson cleared his throat, placed his teacup and saucer on the table and stood up, making it clear that he wanted to be somewhere else — anywhere, at this time. He bowed to Lady Franklin and her niece, briefly nodded in my direction and, wordless, he left the room. As I watched him leaving, it occurred to me that his swift exit was a clear enough message that he was taking the Admiralty's dismissive side in the conflict. As much as he was turning his back on me, though, he wasn't offering a helping hand to Lady Franklin in that tense moment. Her scowl followed him.

Just as Sir John left, another man entered. His long, intelligent-looking face, curly brown hair, sharp eyes and wide brow were familiar, but in the heat of the moment I could not think of his name. He removed his tall hat and took Richardson's empty chair in response to a flustered, welcoming gesture from Lady Franklin. She collected herself, straightened her skirts, and offered a weak smile to the new arrival.

"Dr. Rae, meet the celebrated novelist and champion of British social justice, Mr. Charles Dickens." There was no handshake, no greeting, just a vague nod of heads.

Dickens stood and stepped towards me, his expression serious. "Dr. Rae, my dear friend Lady Franklin has requested my presence here today. She believes it is important for me to meet you personally and advise you of her — of our — concern about the veracity of your very damning, public report."

I wondered just how long these two people had been close friends, and if there were some kind of mutual plan afoot. I could not resist asking an impudent question: "Mr. Dickens, have you been following this story for the last nine years? I have been unaware of your involvement in discussions about the mystery."

His reply was crisp. "Dr. Rae, I believe you have been far away in an alien land for a very long time. I should be surprised if you were kept abreast of anything of much consequence in this country. I can assure you that I have remained well informed by Lady Franklin and numerous sources over the years."

Lady Franklin interrupted: "Charles dear, Dr. Rae shall not be staying for very long today, so rather than stretch this into an historical discussion, perhaps we should address our immediate concerns."

"Very well." Dickens approached the window, his hands clasped behind his back. He leaned forward and peered outside, as if he were inspecting something of interest in the dying gardens below. He turned around and faced me: "My good man, you should know that I have taken the plight of poor Lady Franklin and her fellow sufferers very much to heart. I must do what I can to question your sources of information in this mysterious, so-called private, report." He cleared his throat. "As a result of spending so much time in such a remote part of the world, it is unlikely that you have heard of my popular weekly journal, *Household Words*."

My back stiffened at the mention of his journal, realizing that the dissemination of widespread publicity against the Esquimaux and me was on the minds of Lady Franklin, Miss Cracroft and Mr. Dickens. "Of course I have! Correct me if I am wrong, Mr. Dickens, but is it not the one featuring gossip and matters pertaining to the management of domestic staff, in addition to the analysis of the social misdeeds of British citizens?" It is not in my nature to be sarcastic, but I could not help myself.

Dickens' eyes widened. He glanced at Lady Franklin, who in turn looked to Miss Cracroft, at a loss for words. Dickens' rebuttal was swift. "I am insulted, Dr. Rae! My weekly journal is much, much more than you imply! *Household Words* has a conscience, for heaven's sake! We publish writing of exceptional quality. We explore essential human matters concerning health, education, welfare and social justice. It is a widely read and highly respected publication. By coincidence, I have last week's issue here . . ." He reached for his bag. I raised my hands, to stop him from extracting a copy of the periodical and giving it to me. "Not just now, thank you. I have enough books and papers at this time."

Jane Franklin's voice suddenly became something approaching a shriek. "Dr. Rae! Mr. Dickens and I remain unconvinced about the reliability of the native testimony you documented about my husband, his ships and his men. Will you at least have the courtesy of responding to Mr. Dickens' concern about your report?"

"Lady Franklin, I should point out that there was no mention of names in the Esquimaux testimony because, naturally, the natives did not know the identities of any of the men they saw. No one knows when or how your husband died. I have made my position on the whole matter clear to Sir James Graham and the members of the Arctic Council. Yes, I do trust my sources. The Esquimaux have never given me a reason to doubt the intelligence they pass along to me. I will always stand by the veracity of my report, every word of it. To say I am disappointed that its contents have been made public knowledge is an understatement."

No one responded to what I had just said, so I moved towards the door. "Good day, Lady Franklin. Good day, Mr. Dickens. Miss Cracroft." Sophia appeared at my side as I reached for the door handle. She glowered at me and spoke through clenched teeth.

"You will pay for this folly, Dr. Rae. I promise you will pay dearly."

"Wait a moment!" Jane Franklin had leapt from her chair. She took up her black skirts and rushed towards me. Her eyes looked startled, panic-filled. "Where are my husband's belongings? His award, his crest, his plate, his . . ." she paused, shaking, ". . . his silver cutlery. Where are our things? Do you have them?" She saw that I carried no satchel, and she lifted a trembling hand to her lips. In that moment, when she dropped her mask of anger and defiance and revealed her grief, I felt sympathy for her.

"Lady Franklin, I have placed your husband's possessions — indeed, all of the relics I acquired from the Esquimaux — in safe keeping. As soon as the examination and official log of the items have been completed, the Hudson's Bay Company will ensure that all identifiable objects are swiftly returned to the families of the lost men."

She looked at the floor and nodded, no longer able to hold back her tears. She turned away and fell into the embrace of her husband's niece, sobbing. There was nothing more to say, so with a heavy heart and no small measure of relief, I quietly took my leave from Spring Gardens. I was saddened by the fact that it had ended like this, with so many lives lost in the Arctic and countless numbers of hearts broken at home.

The dramatic events which had unfolded after that chance meeting with In-nook on the Boothia Peninsula seemed to have gathered the momentum of an avalanche. At this point, I had no control over public opinion, but as I exited Lady Franklin's building that afternoon, I vowed to pick up my pen often and use it in defence of the Esquimaux and their testimony. I needed time to think about this strange turn of events, to form a strategy for landing on my feet once the furor subsided. With these thoughts swirling about in my mind, I kept my head down with my hat low on my brow, and made my way back to the hotel.

Shortly after I had settled into an armchair in my room, there was a knock at the door. Who knew I was staying here? I wondered, concerned that someone from the press had followed me from Spring Gardens. I was relieved to see that it was Neil, with an envelope addressed to me. My name was printed in large letters, as if to disguise the author's own handwriting. I broke the unidentifiable seal, curious to see the contents of the envelope.

24 October, 1854

My Dear Friend:

Your evaluation of the situation at Whitehall is quite correct, and most concerned parties are aware of this.

I beg you to draw from the great well of strength within you and be patient.

God is watching over you and He knows your faithfulness to the truth. In time, you will be highly praised for your integrity and your unimpeachable judgment of human character.

I do not ask you to forgive me for my silence during your time of need, but I shall always pray that you will.

With deepest respect, from a Fellow Traveller.

I put the letter on the table, seated myself, picked it up and read it again. These seemed to be the words of a devout Christian, and the author appeared to be struggling with a guilty conscience. Who wrote it? The "fellow traveller" who came immediately to mind was Sir John Richardson. He was familiar with the oral system by which the Esquimaux shared and preserved information. His absence from Sunday's meeting and his silence in Lady Franklin's library were out of character for the man I thought I knew so well, yet I was now beginning to see the difficulty of his position on the matter. He was nearing the age of retirement, and I surmised that he feared the ruin of his good reputation. It was clear that whoever wrote the letter believed he had much to lose by stepping forward as a supporter of me, even though he had faith in the testimony I had acquired.

Whether or not it was Sir John who wrote the letter, it troubled me to think that our friendship had faltered. Some twenty years my senior, John Richardson had also studied medicine at Edinburgh University. We had much in common: a mutual passion for exploration and studies in naturalism, even a shared love of English literature. When two like-minded men spend days, weeks and months together, it is inevitable that their conversations turn to more personal matters, and our friendship was no exception. He told me about his close relationship with John Franklin, and of his fondness for Franklin's first wife Eleanor, who died at home in 1825 while her husband was embarking on an Arctic exploration journey out of the Port of Penetanguishene in Upper Canada.

One day, after we had eaten a meal of roasted caribou meat and we were resting by the fire, John Richardson spoke of John Franklin's second wife, Jane. "She is a complex woman, John," he said. "Very intelligent, energetic, nervous. Her sense of curiosity seems to know no bounds. She is passionate about engaging in adventure and travel, for example."

"D'you think she fancies the idea of being an explorer?" I inquired.

"I wouldn't be surprised." He paused. "Keep this entirely to yourself, John," he said. "Since Jane Franklin is a woman and as such not eligible to join the Navy or officially explore uncharted territories, I have sometimes wondered if she married John Franklin not so much for the man he is, but rather for his connection to the British Admiralty."

I thought about it. "It is no secret that she pushed the Admiralty to choose her husband as commander of this expedition."

Richardson sighed. "He had a good deal of hesitation about going, you know."

"Good Lord! He went against his will? Did she force him into it?"

He was silent for a moment. "No, I would not go as far as to say she forced him, but she certainly badgered him until he gave in. John Franklin was in his sixtieth year when the *Erebus* and *Terror* left for the Arctic. He confided to me that what he really wanted was to complete the remainder of his career as a consultant for the Admiralty in London."

I tucked the letter into the envelope and put it away with my other papers, wondering if the author would write to me again in the future. Would hearing from him alter the distressing course of events which were unfolding in London and beyond? I doubted it. There was no point in making further suppositions concerning the thoughts, beliefs or actions of others. I had experienced enough mental exertions that day, and tomorrow would come soon enough.

→ *London*

[OCTOBER–NOVEMBER 1854]

I was still in no mood to seek out companionship with friends and acquaintances while I waited at the hotel for departure day to arrive. I spent a good deal of time in my room and in the quiet spaces of the university library, reading newspapers and making notes, thinking about how to get rid of the albatross tied around my neck. I regularly took my exercise after dark, often walking the streets through much of the night, my footsteps fast and purposeful, as if I were forging a new route far away, searching for something. I walked many miles for the purpose of maintaining good health, but walking also offered an escape from tossing and turning as I tried in vain to sleep.

The *Times* published a letter from a brother of one of the missing men:

"Dr. Rae should have kept silence altogether, rather than give us a story which pains the feelings of many." He added, "A number of people still cling to hope of finding the men alive. I don't, but others do . . ."

I could not begrudge the poor, bereaved man his opinion. If I had been in his shoes, I would have felt the same way and would probably have penned a similar letter, wanting others to know of my feelings about the horrible details being made public. I wrote to the editor of the newspaper: "I think of the families, as well. I, too, am pained."

Another letter appeared in the *Times*. "Why hasn't Rae verified his report? It is deeply reprehensible that he has not done so. It weakens his information."

And another one, the next day. "Why would the men bring utensils with them if they were abandoning the ships? This makes no sense. Silver cutlery would be a burden and useless on a survival march."

I responded to this challenge by writing to the editor right away. "I have reflected on the gentleman's question about verifying my report," I replied. "I believe I have done so, through an exhaustive interrogation of the Esquimaux and diligently documenting their testimony."

The *Times* also published a letter from New Zealand, written by Royal Navy Captain Thomas Collinson. The captain suggested that the Admiralty place me in charge of organizing a two-pronged Arctic expedition to search for more evidence. Whilst I appreciated his faith in my abilities, I had made the decision to never, ever work with the Royal Navy again, and I highly doubted that they would have any wish to work with me.

There was, however, one important piece of business to get out of the way before I considered my own plans for the future. I wrote a letter to the British Admiralty, claiming my right to the £10,000 reward money being offered to the person or persons who had ascertained the fate of the Franklin party. I had not thought about the money when I made the decision to return to London with the relics, but it was true that I was the first person to shed any light on the mystery. Based on the frosty reception I received from the first lord, I anticipated some opposition from members of the Arctic Council. On the other hand, there was nothing to be lost by applying for the reward, because I was already in an extremely uncomfortable position concerning the British government and public. I had been humiliated enough already.

The newspaper then reported that the Admiralty had decided to defer its decision about assigning the reward to anyone, until the return of Captain Collinson's brother Richard from a five-year absence at sea aboard the HMS *Enterprise* in search of the missing expedition. Apparently, the younger Collinson had acquired some important intelligence concerning the fates of Sir John and his men. Where on God's earth had Richard Collinson been all these years? All I could do was wait and hope the decision — whenever it came about — would be in my favour.

I also wondered if I was not yet finished with the mystery of the missing men and ships, and whether I could privately undertake further investigation. While I waited for the departure of the *Prince of Wales II*, I gave thought to the idea of organizing my own search party. Given the information I already possessed, I surmised that there might be a good chance of locating the Franklin encampments, collecting specific evidence, and thus being in a position to prove the veracity of the Esquimaux testimony. Perhaps I could revisit the channel I suspected to be the missing link in the Northwest Passage. These two objectives were not so farfetched, and achieving them would give me a great deal of personal and professional satisfaction.

– PART III –

Home:
The Orkneys

[1854]

→ London to Stromness, Orkney
[NOVEMBER 1854]

The evening before our departure for Stromness, I received a message from the shipping office of the Hudson's Bay Company, informing me that the scheduled ship's surgeon had suddenly taken ill. Would I be willing to take his place on the voyage? I was more than willing. The surgeon's cabin aboard the *Prince of Wales II* was well appointed and comfortable, and I hoped that if all was well during the journey, there might be some spare time for reading and making notes, helping the crew on deck, and strolling for exercise.

In the morning, I stood on the deck of the *Prince of Wales II*, waiting for the barque's holds to be loaded so we could begin our eastward journey down the Thames to the North Sea. The morning air was damp, cool and cloudy, with a light southwesterly breeze. If wind conditions were favourable, it would take a little more than a week to travel up the eastern coastlines of England and Scotland to the northern isles of Orkney.

The east London docks used by Hudson's Bay Company's ships stood at the waterside of Lower Thames Street near the Custom House. They were often awash with mud, dung and all manner of effluvia, simmering as if the area was just on the verge of a boil. The scene on the morning of the *Prince of Wales II*'s departure was loud and chaotic, with foremen yelling into vast crowds of desperate, impoverished men pushing and shouting, seeking a day's labour. Tethered animals bleated their distress, hooves slipping and sliding on their own urine and feces, their eyes wide with fear and confusion. Hundreds of wooden boxes and crates of all sizes teetered this way and that, as cursing workers hauled them up and into the ships' yawning holds.

I looked back at the city, admiring the great dome of St. Paul's Cathedral rising majestically above the dark pall of coal-fire smoke that was constantly being belched into the city air from thousands of chimney pots perched upon rooftops. The River Thames was a steady means of conveyance — through London, beyond and back again with the tides — for such flotsam as planks of wood, empty bottles and packing crates, branches, rubbish, body parts, offal, human and animal waste, and a vast assortment of unidentifiable objects. When the Celts settled along its banks twenty centuries earlier, they had named the river *Tamesas*, meaning "Bright Water." Expanding populations, animals, agriculture, and then the filth of waste materials created by machines and industry had forever altered the pure nature of the river's waters. A heavy price was being paid in the name of progress. Sometimes I thought about the cost of the white man's great push to open up the polar regions of North America, and experienced my own misgivings about being a participant in an enterprise which had the power to destroy everything in its path, except when nature held up its heavy hand and brought human progress to a halt.

The crew took their posts at the ship's stations, some of the sails were hoisted, and the vessel was released from the dock. I drew deeper breaths as the *Prince of Wales II* slowly moved eastward on the river, past Greenhithe pier — where the Franklin Expedition had first set off from England in a blaze of glory more than nine years ago — past the Isle of Dogs and Gravesend and eventually into fresh air, where the jaws of the snake opened and the Thames merged with the cleaner waters of the North Sea. The remaining sails rose up in quick succession, flapping furiously in the wind until each one was filled with air and secured in the appropriate position.

Once we had left London behind, I took pleasure in listening to the familiar creaks and groans of a ship under sail, as she rose and fell with the waves. There was a fresh breeze on this November morning, and I was reminded of sailing our beloved 18-foot yole *Brenda* in the waters around the Orkney Isles with my brothers, the wind beating at our faces and my brother William shouting orders from the helm.

We would be making a brief stop at Aberdeen, where some of the ship's cargo would be offloaded and more supplies picked up. Commander Herd would then set her course northward for Stromness to deliver goods for the winter. Later she would make the return voyage to London, loaded with furs from the Arctic, Orcadian whiskies, various assortments of dried fish and woollen goods. I was invited to take my evening meals with the commander and the ships' officers.

I was apprehensive about the prospect of dining at the captain's table. I did not wish to be questioned about the events of the last six months or the recent outcry in London, but I resigned myself to the likelihood of having to say a few words at some point. At eight o'clock, a steward showed me to my chair. There were four officers including the commander. We remained standing until he was comfortably settled.

"Good evening, gentlemen," he said, "and welcome aboard, Dr. Rae."

Commander Herd and I knew one another from previous voyages back and forth between London and Stromness. He was a stocky, round-faced and fair-haired fellow with a pleasant disposition. He was also a sensible man. I liked the way he ran his ship, with good discipline and a fair hand.

"Good evening, Sir, and thank you."

"I trust your accommodation is comfortable enough, Dr. Rae."

"Indeed, it is."

A fine meal of roasted lamb was served; the table soon came alive with good-natured banter. Some of the men had been on shore leave or assigned to other ships, and they had not seen each other in a while. Commander Herd turned to me while they were chatting among themselves.

"Dr. Rae, I should think you are looking forward to being at home in Orkney and seeing your family. Tell me, how is your dear mother, Margaret?"

"She is not well just now, Mr. Herd. She recently suffered a stroke, which has apparently left her with some paralysis. My sister Marion and her husband John live next door to her in Stromness. John is a physician and he attends to our mother several times each day."

The commander sighed. "Ah yes. Old age is an affliction we will all face one day, if we survive long enough to experience it. My own mother is now under full-time care in Portsmouth. She had a series of spells last year, and one can readily see that she is failing." He paused, and put his fork and knife down on his plate. "It doesn't seem so long ago that she was bright and full of energy."

The robust conversations around the table began to fade. The others were straining to listen in, but trying to hide their curiosity. I assumed the men were counting on the subject of John Franklin arising at some point because it was inevitable, given my presence at the table. Commander Herd opened the conversation, before one of his men had time to make a clumsy remark.

"Dr. Rae, please forgive me for being so forthright. I must confess that I — we all, of course — are most disheartened to learn that any hope of finding survivors from the *Erebus* and *Terror* is lost. Such a tragedy. Although the men were officially declared dead by the government last winter after nine years without a sighting, I suppose humans, by nature, have a tendency to hold on to some sliver of hope . . ."

I leaned back in my chair, my hands gripping its arms, keenly aware that the first words I uttered would be remembered. "It is indeed a great tragedy, all of it, Sir. It is most unfortunate that we cannot change what is true, despite our fervent desire to do so."

One of the younger fellows was unable to hold his tongue. "But surely it cannot be true that British naval men resorted to consuming the flesh of their companions," he blurted. "Our nation is the most civilized society in the world. We are well educated. We believe in *God*, for heaven's sake!"

The commander swiftly intervened. "Wellington, you ought to learn to manage your words, to think carefully before you speak. We cannot pretend to know what those poor wretched souls went through, because neither you nor any of us were there. You mustn't be so arrogant as to presume that you personally understand the situation."

I was grateful for Commander Herd's wise response, but I felt warmth creeping into my cheeks. I was disappointed but not surprised that my report was again under critical scrutiny, and that I, the bearer of bad news, was under pressure to explain and defend something infinitely complex and confounding to most people. In truth, I did not have the stomach for engaging in a debate about morality, education, or devotion to the rules of the church. The younger man adopted a softer tone but persisted.

"Since there were no Englishmen present to witness the events, Sir, would you agree that it is impossible to know with absolute certainty what really *did* happen?"

An older officer joined in. "Dr. Rae, surely you cannot argue with Mr. Wellington's point. How can one possibly trust the testimony of savages? For years, I travelled far and wide with the British navy. I have seen with my own eyes the vast differences between God-fearing Englishmen and primitive peoples. How can we believe the stories of ignorant pagans, of people who can neither read nor write? Who would sooner burn a book as fuel for their fires than take meaning from its leaves?"

Wellington chimed in. "How is it that you, an educated and well-travelled man, are willing to accept such horrible stories as truths?"

Commander Herd probably enjoyed a good debate as much as anyone, but his eyes narrowed and he brought a firm, authoritative hand down upon the table, the sudden smack catching us all by surprise. This discussion was an ambush in the making, and it was clear that he did not like it one bit.

"Enough, gentlemen!" he shouted. "It is inappropriate to harass Dr. Rae with such questions. This is neither the time nor place for an inquisition. As commander of this ship, I am ordering you to change the subject immediately." The men exchanged glances and looked down at their plates, subdued. I placed my hands on the table, and looked the two impudent men directly in the eyes.

"The commander has made a sensible decision, gentlemen," I said. "This may not be the time and place for such a controversial discussion. It will take time for the dust to settle, and I hope that in the future, more detailed information will be discovered and made available to all."

"But the bloodthirsty natives . . . everyone knows about *them*!"

I bristled. "Do they? Do *you*? You hear rumours, read stories and so on, but do you and the others really know the hearts and minds of the Esquimaux? Look, I am a strong supporter of education, and I suspect it would serve you well to fortify yours before you pass judgment upon others." My appetite had vanished, but I remained seated at the commander's table, consuming some of the meal and half-heartedly participating in light conversation. I was damned if I would let on that the men's words had stung me.

The remainder of the voyage passed without incident, although the order to be silent on the topic of the Franklin tragedy and cannibalism did not prevent some of the men from casting dark glances my way. I tended to the occasional case of seasickness and mild injury, but kept mostly to myself, with books and note-making to keep me occupied. The solitude suited me well because I knew I would soon see members of my family, and there would be much to discuss.

→ *Aberdeen*
[NOVEMBER 1854]

The *Prince of Wales II* sailed into the port of Aberdeen in mid-morning. By the time the anchors were set, we were surrounded by numerous skiffs and yoles, and the noisy exchange of goods began to take place. The harbourmaster and a Hudson's Bay Company representative boarded the ship to deal with documentation and bills of lading. I tidied up the infirmary and then stood on deck, watching boxes and items being removed from the hold and replaced by goods bound for Orkney.

Since I was a small child growing up by the shores of Clestrain Sound on Main Isle in the Orkneys, I had never tired of watching the comings and goings of sailing vessels and fishing boats. This morning was no exception; the weather was as fine as could be expected for the northeast coast of Scotland in November. I picked up my telescope and looked closely at the shipyards, curious to see what was being built. My eye came to rest upon an almost-finished brigantine resting on a crib, with her two masts anchored in place. She was crawling with builders and gleaming with a fresh coat of varnish. What a lovely sight she was! I had always admired brigs because of their speed and manoeuvrability. They were relatively small, no-nonsense ships, designed to outrun just about any other vessel when all seven sails were hoisted, to dance circles around the larger, heavier, clumsier ones.

A thought came to mind as I slowly looked her over through the lens, and my heart began beating a little faster. I pulled my notebook out of my pocket right then and there and sketched her. Then I made notes as the idea began to take more shape. The more I wrote, the more enthused I became, thinking about the possibilities, ignoring everything around me.

→ *North Sea, approaching the Orkney Isles*
[NOVEMBER 1854]

I leaned against a rail on the foredeck of *Prince of Wales II*, telescope in hand, as she rose and fell on the waves, heading with the tides in the direction of Orkney's Main Isle. The day was fine, crisp and cool. I indulged in one of my favourite pastimes, observing migrating birds and recording their approximate numbers in my notebook. I would later add the Latin names to each item on the list, according to G.R. Gray's official system of bird species classification.

A fresh gust from the northeast filled the sails and pushed the great ship towards home. Excited, I searched for the islands marking the entrance to Hoy Sound, the southern gateway to the Orkney archipelago. Finally, the majestic Hills of Hoy hove into view, and I felt my pulse quicken at the first sight of the land I loved.

→ *Stromness*
[NOVEMBER 1854]

I had written to Marion from London, telling her that I would sail with the Company's *Prince of Wales II* on her next voyage to Stromness. Sure enough, a large family party awaited my arrival at the town docks: my mother Margaret Glen Rae, her nurse Marion, my brother-in-law Dr. John Hamilton, Marion and John's children and the housekeeper, Bessie. The faint, high-pitched sound of children's shouts joined a chorus of seagull cries as our ship made her approach. Fishing boats moved out of our path, the ship slowly came about in the waters of Hamnavoe, the sails were let down, and we dropped anchor.

Our mam, once a handsome and robust woman, appeared to have shrunk in the two years since I had last seen her. Her tiny figure was now bundled in a blanket and confined to a wheelchair. The eldest Hamilton son, Gavin, a tall young man of nineteen, knelt beside her, extended his arm and pointed a finger in my direction. So much had changed since the glory days of our life at the Hall of Clestrain on the other side of the sound. Our family was much diminished and changed by this time, through emigration, births and deaths. I was eager to put my arms around Mam, around all of them. Excited, I waved to them — the Arctic, London, brigantines and migrating birds all forgotten for the time being.

The children were held back until I stepped onto the wharf with my things. Once they were released, they descended upon me, one or two of the older ones grabbing at my arms, the little ones my trouser legs and the ones in between, my overcoat. Marion and John stood quietly until the children's greetings subsided, and Mam's nurse had wheeled her to where she could, with one slender arm, reach out and touch me. I bent down and kissed her cheek, then crouched to embrace her, tightening the Hudson's Bay Company blanket around her small shoulders. Holding onto her hand, I rose and greeted my sister and her husband.

Our group retired to The Haven on the Plainstones beside the harbour, once the Hudson's Bay Company offices my father had overseen in Stromness, and now Mam's home. It felt good to have my feet on the ground in Orkney again. In the absence of the usual fog or rain, the view from The Haven's kitchen window was perfectly clear that day. As I peered through it, I was able to see the outline of our former family home across the waters of Clestrain Sound, and a melancholy feeling washed over me.

Even though the Hall of Clestrain was now in the hands of a new factor and his family, to me it would always be our home. Most of the time, mist and rain rolled in like curtains, obscuring the view across the water, which almost made it simpler to accept not living there anymore.

When the Hall was hidden by fog or rain, I was able to look ahead and imagine new possibilities, instead of being reminded of the idyllic life that I had believed was mine as a child.

→ *The Haven, Stromness*
[NOVEMBER 1854]

The others left my mother and me alone for a little while in The Haven's kitchen. At first, I observed her through the eyes of a physician, and then as a son. Her paralyzed arm was tucked in at her side under the blanket. I saw the warmth in her eyes; I could tell that her spirit was still there but she was fragile. I was afraid to hold her too tightly for fear of breaking her.

I kept my emotions in check. "Mam, it is good to be home again."

Tears filled her eyes. She could not reply, although the words were probably formed and well organized in her mind. I sat at the kitchen table with my mother in her wheelchair close beside me. As I talked, I stroked her hands and spoke about life in the Arctic as if I were reading aloud from one of the many letters I had written to her during the years I was away.

"This latest journey in the Arctic was challenging, Mam. The weather was more fickle than usual. Sometimes it was fine in the morning but blowing a nasty gale in the afternoons. When the blizzards came, we had to stop and wait for them to pass because we could no longer see where we were going."

She blinked several times, to let me know that she was listening.

"It was difficult to spot our hunting quarry in those conditions, and of course we were always on the lookout for sources of victuals when our supplies grew low. We got along well enough on the pemmican recipe I had learned from the natives, although the mixture of dried venison, berries and salt quickly becomes a rather tiresome diet. Our daily fare was not as meagre as it was in 1847, though. Will you ever forget when I returned home from that one? My belt was around my knees! You forcibly fed me for weeks despite the fact that I was a fully grown adult!" I chuckled at the memory of her hovering over me like a hawk. I detected a sparkle in her eyes, and that little discovery made me smile.

"Oh, and on warmer days when the snow melted into pools of water, the midges and mosquitoes bred faster than rabbits! Dark clouds of them rose as one from the water's surface, and their assaults were relentless! Dragging sixty pounds of instruments on a sledge through swarms of biting insects across the Boothia Peninsula was quite a challenge for this forty-one-year-old body." I patted my knees and wiggled them for her as if I were a child spending time with his mother, regaling her with stories after a day of youthful activities.

"Living in a snow house is cozy, of course," I continued, "but it can drive you to distraction if you don't get out and about for a few hours a day, even in the foulest weather. You spend two hours building it and then you are all wedged in together, wrapped in deerskins, and you have no choice but to bundle up in little groups to sleep, much as we did when we were children living right over there at the Hall. One man would turn over and the others were forced to do the same or face each other, wretched breath and all. Someone would pass wind and we would all join in. We called it 'The Last Piper'!"

I chuckled at the memory. "Before long, I began to build separate, smaller snow houses for my sleeping quarters, because the men all enjoyed smoking tobacco, and I slept poorly in the smoke-filled space." Mam already knew the stories, but she had never discouraged me from telling them again. I wondered if she was feeling too tired to hear more tales of the Arctic but I pressed on, regretting that our conversation could only be one-sided.

"I felt responsible for the men's mental well-being as much as their physical condition. When the wind was blowing snow and visibility was almost nil, it was every man for himself when we played football, because the point was to stay warm and alert. We behaved like schoolboys, diving for the ball like gulls on a floating fish! In the warmth of a snow house, I often unpacked my fiddle and played a simple melody, with all of us trying to move around in a squatting position, pretending to dance a jig or two. There was much laughter and merriment in those silly moments!"

Remembering her fondness for watching migrating birds, I took

Mam's hands into my own and recited the names of birds I encountered in the Arctic spring and summer, many of which wintered each year in Orkney: golden plovers, bar-tailed godwits, red-necked grebes, white-billed divers and bonxies.

Although I had described it to her before, I knew that Mam never tired of hearing about the aurora borealis — *aksarnerk* in the natives' language — dancing green curtains shooting upwards, streaking blue, violet and red across the clear Arctic night sky. Her pale eyes twinkled when I spoke of shooting stars, spirits of the dead visiting each other in the *qilak* — living air — the native equivalent of what we called the heavens.

After a while, Mam began to show signs of fatigue, so I lifted her from the chair and carried her to bed. "Rest now, Mam. I'll look in on you later."

I stepped outside and stood on the stone beach at the edge of the water, telescope in hand, looking across the sound towards the Hall of Clestrain. Even from a distance, the great height of that Palladian mansion never failed to surprise me; there was such a grand quality to the steep roof and dramatic form, its twin chimneys rising upward as if they could touch the heavens. The building overlooked hundreds of acres of the many small holdings of tenant farmers, their low stone houses thatched with straw, heather or turf to shield the dwellers from the savage wind and rains which swept in so often from the sea. I decided to pay the resident Mackay family a visit at the Hall the next day.

During supper next door at the Hamilton home, I told the children stories of the Arctic and distributed little presents of feathers and stones among them. I played a couple of tunes on my fiddle and some of them danced, much to everyone's delight. When they were settled into bed, if not all yet asleep, I lingered at the dining table with Marion and John. The compassion on Marion's pretty face was just visible in the candle-light.

"Johnny, you must be tired after all your travels and your time in London. Of course, it's your decision whether you wish to tell us any of it this evening, or if ever."

I rubbed at my beard and moustaches, which had begun filling in again now that I was away from the city. "Let's talk about other things, and then I will retire next door. I don't want to think too much about the people and events in London, not tonight, anyway."

She placed a gentle hand on my arm. "The change of scene and a rest will do you the world of good," she said, "and I'm so glad to know you'll be spending some time with Mam."

"She has changed so much since I last saw her two years ago. Why, she barely ate any supper. Stuffed grouse was always one of her favourites." I shook my head. "I foolishly thought my return might pick up her appetite a little bit."

"How long will you be with us this time?" As I observed Marion's face more closely in the lamplight, I noticed signs of strain and fatigue.

"I'll stay for a while. See in the New Year here in Stromness, and return to London for Company meetings in January. I will come home at a moment's notice if I am needed."

Marion met her husband's eyes and then turned to me. "John and I are thinking about immigrating to Canada West, when the time is right." She didn't mention our mother, but we all knew that her death was not far away. "We think John will be able to open a medical practice in Hamilton, where Richard and Tom live, and close enough to Jessie and her family."

Our brothers were now living in the port city of Hamilton on Lake Ontario, running Rae Brothers & Company. Our sister Jessie and her husband Hector had moved to the area in 1840. We lost William in America, and a younger brother had died in infancy. Our eldest brother James, a sea captain, had perished off the west coast of Africa in 1832. If Marion and John moved away, there would be no members of the Rae family living in Orkney. The notion of everyone leaving the Orkneys behind shouldn't have bothered me so much, but it did.

I shook my head. Scots were emigrating from their homeland by the hundreds, because the colonial government was offering them better land and living conditions in North America. The Raes were among the few lucky ones because our family had never been poor. I had naïvely assumed that future generations of Rae children would be raised in Orkney, just as my siblings and I had been. It seemed not so long ago when our young bellies had been full, our parents were nearby, the cook was busy in the pantry, and true bedtime stories of pirates made us shiver in our beds. I had followed my own adventurous heart and lived in the Arctic since the age of twenty. It never occurred to me that Marion would consider leaving the Orkneys.

Marion spoke softly. "We cannot go back, you know. It's time to begin looking ahead, Johnny. Don't you think a new life in Hamilton, close to Tom and Jessie's children and to Dick, with good schools nearby for our children and better professional opportunities for John, would make sense for us?"

"Not if it means that no Raes live here." As soon as the impulsive remark was out of my mouth, I wished I could take it back. Marion's spine stiffened and she spoke in slow, measured words through clenched teeth. "I have remained here faithfully in Orkney with John and our children to look after Mam and stay close to her, while you and the others all moved far away, chasing your dreams." Her eyes suddenly flashed with anger and resentment. "Does what I've done mean anything to you, Johnny? Where were you when we needed you all these years, especially after Papa died?"

I looked down at my hands. *Dear God. I never really thought about it. I had been too preoccupied with myself, with my own ambitions and adventures.*

Her eyes filled with tears, and she looked away. "You seem to forget that I, too, was happy as a child across the bay in Orphir. But then James went to Africa, and left little Helen behind for us to raise. William went to North America. You left for the Arctic. Papa died. Jessie and Hector moved to Canada West. Tom and Dick did the same thing. Mam had to leave the Hall of Clestrain. We hardly saw you after you left for Hudson Bay in 1833. You just sent money and the odd letter to Mam, as if that made your absence all right. If you really did care so much about those of us left behind in Orkney, surely you'd have made some kind of effort to come here and see us. Eventually, you did visit, but by that point I was tired . . ." John reached over and put his arm around Marion's shoulders as she wept.

"That idyllic life you apparently treasured so much is long over, Johnny," she said. "It is done."

Tara Gott.

"Marion is right," John added. "She has stood fast all these years, while everyone else trickled away and left your mother in her care. John, you should appreciate what your sister has done, and thank her for it! Not just you, but the whole lot of you Raes!"

I sighed. "Marion, I feel like a fool. I was selfish, absorbed in my own life, just as you said. It never occurred to me that you didn't have the time or opportunity to think of yourself. I just assumed that you were satisfied to take care of everything, raising your family, being close to Mam."

I wanted to reach out and hold her hand just then, but I was afraid she would snatch it away. "I do appreciate everything you have done — everything you do — but you couldn't have known that, because I never came home, never told you, hardly ever wrote to you! I took you for granted all these years. I can only hope you'll forgive me, because I am very, very sorry."

"The cold season here is so long, dark and damp," she sniffed. "The winds are relentless. It's hard on our family's health, our spirits. Our house in Stromness isn't big enough for all of us. We could move to something larger, but our decision to leave Orkney is about much more than the size of a home. The children — John and I as well — need room to grow, to expand our horizons, see our family in North America, learn something about the modern world beyond these islands." She looked at her husband. "There's a good hospital in Hamilton where John could put his skills to use, and the city has a growing population. We are all getting older, Johnny. John and I are well along in our forties now, and we don't have all the time in the world."

I thought about my remaining siblings and their families building new lives in Canada West. Settlements and cities in North America were growing, but the opposite was true in Orkney, where life had changed little during many centuries. I sighed. "As much as I find it difficult to accept the notion of our family leaving Orkney after only one generation — "

"Two, Johnny." Marion scowled. "We have nine children."

"Aye, you are right. There I go again, completely missing the obvious. Two generations." My eyes were burning; I rubbed at them, which only made it worse. "How could anyone fault you for wanting to make a new life in North America? How could I criticize you for that? You have earned it."

Marion rose, put her arms around my neck and kissed me on both cheeks. "Thanks, Johnny. I needed to hear that. I may sleep better to-night for it."

Later, John and I sat together in the library, drawing warmth from the fire. "Have you thought about what you will do while this terrible Franklin mess runs its course and eventually settles down?" he asked.

"Aye, I think about it all the time."

I looked at the Rae family portrait hanging on the wall. It had been painted in 1825, almost thirty years ago. I had a vague recollection of having to sit alone and unmoving on a stool for what seemed like an eternity, so the artist could capture the details of my child's face and body. Each of us in our turn had to endure that solitary sitting for the paint-ing — with all of us in it — to be completed. I smiled at the memory.

John's voice brought me back to the present. "Will you return to busi-ness as usual with the Company?"

"Sir George expects me to continue as chief factor," I replied, "but I can't see myself spending the rest of my life in the Arctic. It can be lonely over there, you know. I hate to admit it, but as I grow older, my tolerance for the outdoor life in such an unforgiving climate is dimin-ishing."

I looked at John's handsome, kind face, feeling envious of his life with a wife and children. I had always known that I wanted one day to have the same things as John and Tom, his wife Helen and their two fine boys, but the idea of settling down always seemed to be so far away in the future. Things were beginning to look different now.

"I'm thinking of submitting my notice to the Hudson's Bay Company as chief factor for the Mackenzie River District, John. Sir George may offer me a position closer to home, at least for a while. I do think I'm ready for a change, especially after this latest fiasco with the Admiralty. Before too long I want to have a family of my own, but definitely not in the Arctic."

He glanced up from the fire. "What about the immediate future?"

"So many ideas are tumbling about in my head. I may try to pay a visit to Tom and Dick in Hamilton next summer. The boys are still packing meats, you know, but they've also started buying ships, and they're even building them in the railway shipyard at the docks." I felt a wave of world-weariness at that moment.

Then, I thought again. Shipbuilding. Hamilton. Rae Brothers & Company. *Perhaps I could build my own ship there.*

John sighed. "There are rumours. Jessie writes that Dick disappears for days at a time. No one knows where he goes or what he does, and he offers no explanation when he returns. Tom told her that he arrives at the office unshaven, sullen and quiet. He refuses to answer questions about his absences. He lives alone these days, so nobody really knows about the nature of his double life."

"Alcohol? Gambling?"

"Quite possibly."

I pressed my thumbs into the corners of my eyes. "Tom's a good lad. So is Dick, but it sounds as though he's gone off course. You know I love my brothers, but it's no secret that I really looked up to William. He taught me how to sail. He was strong and adventurous, such a capable seaman. And funny as hell, too."

"Aye, Johnny, we will never know the full truth of what caused William to snap. I will say, though, that he was far from home, and I do not believe the Hudson's Bay Company supplied him with what he needed to properly run an outpost in such a foreign place. He spoke no Spanish . . ."

He settled more deeply into his chair. "From what I understand, the Company had for too many years shuffled the poor fellow here, there and everywhere throughout the Pacific Northwest. When he was sent south to Yerba Buena in the Columbia River district after marrying his employer's daughter, it all seemed to start out on a good footing. Apparently he worked hard to gain the trust of the people. It looked as though he had the world in his pocket. Eloisa gave him four fine children, the eldest named after you, Johnny . . ."

"Aye, and then William took a mistress."

"A very poor decision, indeed."

I rose from my chair and faced John, my back to the fire. My legs were stiff, and the warmth from the flames felt soothing.

"You know," he said, "William was an unreliable correspondent, at best. He made his own bed, so to speak, and not once did he indicate to any of us that his life was taking such a difficult turn. You read the letter his associates sent to your mother after his death. Everyone was taken by surprise."

I sat down again, and stared at the flames rising in the hearth. "Well, I will write a letter to Tom in the morning. You know, I miss the pip-squeak! Once my business with the Company is finished in London, I may spend some time in Hamilton, but I don't know if I would choose to settle there permanently. We'll see what the future holds. Maybe one day I'll purchase land in Orkney and live here with my own family."

"That's a splendid idea," he replied. "You can repopulate these islands with new generations of Raes!" We both chuckled at the thought. "You know, our move to Canada West will mark the end of this era, but for Marion, the children and me, it's the beginning of a new and happier one, I hope. God knows Marion deserves it. Of course, we'll remain here with your mother as long as necessary, and see to it that she is not alone." He paused.

"You said earlier that you don't wish to discuss the Franklin party controversy, or the people associated with it. I understand that, of course. You should get some rest . . ."

"I will, but I wouldn't mind sitting here in front of the fire for a while longer."

"D'you wish to be alone, Johnny?"

"No, I'm glad for your company." We sat in companionable silence. Later, I cleared my throat and turned to John.

"This is a difficult time for me, John, both personally and professionally, but mark my words — I'll be damned if I'll see the Esquimaux dragged through the mud like this without a fight. I'm not sure how, but I hope to figure out a way to straighten out the whole mess. Lady Franklin and her followers are on a mission to discredit me, the Esquimaux, and to place her poor husband on the highest possible pedestal as Britain's greatest explorer.

"By the way, John, do you ever read Charles Dickens' weekly journal *Household Words*?"

"I've heard of it. I think the newsagent along the road brings in a few copies each week. By then, they're out of date. I've enjoyed his novels, though. *David Copperfield*, *Oliver Twist*."

"Dickens calls himself the "conductor" of the news, as if he is leading some sort of writers' orchestra. How odd that is. Why doesn't he simply refer to himself as the editor or publisher? Pompous, arrogant fellow . . ."

John stared at me. "I gather you have some kind of argument with the man, Johnny."

"I saw him briefly in London. He has picked up on my news about the Franklin Expedition tragedy, with the encouragement of Lady Franklin and her husband's niece. I have a strong feeling that he's out for blood against the Esquimaux, and that he'll use his pen as a weapon against them."

John stretched out his legs towards the fire and crossed one foot over the other. "I suppose Dickens' writing does have some influence on public opinion." He frowned. "I'm a bit surprised to hear that he may attack your sources, though, since he purports to care deeply for all humankind, especially those less fortunate."

I nodded in agreement. "I fear that his charitable thoughts do not seem to extend beyond white-skinned, English-speaking Christians. He's a hypocrite, in my opinion. Soon we'll see if he decides to write about the Franklin story and, if so, what he will have to say about the Esquimaux."

"Johnny, have you given some thought to making a claim for the reward money offered by the Admiralty? Regardless of what anyone thinks of the testimony you gathered, you are certainly the man who has earned the reward. No one can take issue with that."

"I didn't earn it alone, you know. I had the help of a hunter who acted as a guide, an excellent interpreter and some others. To answer your question, aye, I did submit a written claim before I left London, and if the money is granted to me, I intend to see to it that those men receive the reward *they* so richly deserve as well."

John thought for a moment. "I'm curious about something. How would the Esquimaux put British currency to use in the regions of Hudson Bay and points west?"

"Well, the irony of the system is that they would be able to spend the money only at Hudson's Bay Company depots, to buy such goods as flour, blankets, tobacco, and so on, using currency supplied by the British government," I said. "There is nowhere else to spend it."

He tapped his fingers on the armrest of his chair. "By the way, isn't it true that Parliament is quite fed up with the Hudson's Bay Company's growing land acquisitions in North America?"

"Aye, the Company has been engaging in some ambitious expansionism in the North and West. As you can well imagine, this does not please Her Majesty at all. Tension has escalated between public and private enterprises, to the point where there is talk about a parliamentary inquiry into the Company's growing trade monopoly over there."

"How extraordinary!" he declared. "An imperialist government which has amassed great wealth as a result of aggressive expansionism around the world feeling threatened by a growing private enterprise, owned and operated abroad by its very own countrymen!"

"Aye, John," I said. "The nature of business is rife with strange twists and turns. That's one of the reasons why I would prefer to move away from Company dealings altogether, as soon as I can. It has all become too political for my liking.

"I have been thinking about something else," I added. "I don't know if it will ever amount to anything, but an idea seems to be taking shape in my mind. I'd like to ask your opinion, if I may."

"Of course."

"Will you keep what I am about to tell you to yourself, at least for now? I don't even want Marion to know. Then if nothing comes of it, no one will be the wiser for it."

"Agreed."

"I have been thinking about going back — "

Curious, he leaned forward in his chair. "To the Arctic? To search for more evidence? Surely not for the British Admiralty. With the Company?" He sat back. "Sorry, go on. I interrupted you."

"Well, the answer is yes, to look for British encampments in the area suggested by the Esquimaux and no, certainly not with the Royal Navy, even if they were to present an offer to me, which I highly doubt they would. Not necessarily with the Hudson's Bay Company either, John, because Sir George would surely direct me to attend to a number of other distracting matters along the way. No, if I were ever to go back, I would choose to be the one in charge of the entire enterprise, so the reward money would certainly be useful.

"While I was at sea on the way here, I sketched some ideas for constructing a sleek and modern ship, an eighty-ton cross between a brigantine and a schooner — yes, a schooner! — with a long-shafted screw propeller and the flexibility to manoeuvre through tight spaces."

He looked both surprised and amused by my outburst. "You are serious about this?"

"Well, it's only an idea right now, so it's too early to know if it will happen at all, but the more I toss the notion about, the more I wonder, why not? I could hire a small crew — perhaps six or seven skilled men — and sail the ship to the area, if weather conditions permit. We would carry the proper equipment for disembarking and working on the ice or on land when necessary."

He was leaning forward now, resting his elbows on his knees. I trusted John to honour my request for confidentiality, so I took a further step. "While we are on the subject of the Arctic, there is something else I will tell you, for your ears only. I am quite sure I found a section of the missing link in the Northwest Passage during last spring's expedition. I logged the coordinates, and I have a reasonable idea of how to get there by boat. As you know, I have travelled extensively in that region on snowshoes and on foot, but also by canoe, an inflatable Halkett boat, and even on a 22-foot clinker vessel with lug sails!"

"But you weren't aboard a full-sized ship!" he cried. "The history books clearly show that most vessels are either dashed to pieces or swallowed whole in the Arctic . . ."

We were both on our feet, now. "Aye, but think about this, John. Maybe they have been the wrong kinds of ships. Not lean or supple enough for moving around obstacles. Not piloted by sailors with the right kind of experience for the job. Remember the *Erebus* and *Terror*!

Both of them massive gunships, fitted to be floating palaces, but they were stout and clumsy, built for fighting battles at sea, not for hugging the shoreline or manoeuvring through pack ice. And you have seen with your own eyes how well I can handle a boat when the odds are against me."

"I'll give you a point or two on that one, Johnny. Clestrain Sound . . . Scapa Flow . . . what could be more challenging than that?" He chuckled at the thought, but then turned serious. "Well, mountains of ice, perhaps . . ."

"The channel I located last April was only lightly frozen, John. The pack ice was blocked by an enormous island to the north, so the ice in that channel was vastly different. Young. Possibly navigable in July."

He raised his knee, slapped it and laughed. "I have to give you credit for courage, for even thinking about such an ambitious undertaking. It would be quite an achievement, wouldn't it? If you were to succeed in solving the mystery of the passage, and if you located the Franklin Expedition encampments, then the knighthood you so richly deserve would surely be offered to you!"

"It's too late for that." I waved my hand dismissively, although I did care very much about being officially recognized for my achievements. Almost every man who had been actively involved in Arctic exploration — including my employer Sir George Simpson — had been knighted by the Queen. Even though I had charted over two thousand miles of Arctic coastline, I was certain the government would never admit a man who had "gone native" to such a hallowed brotherhood. I took pains to disguise the fact that the snub had a sting to it.

John poured us both another mug of strong tea from the kettle Bessie had left hanging by the fire. "All right, then. Let's suppose you do collect enough money to build this . . . this hybrid of a brigantine and schooner — "

"More schooner than brigantine," I interrupted.

"Schrigantine," he laughed.

"Brooner," I countered.

"Well, if this project moves ahead, have you thought about what name you might give to the vessel?"

"Aye, I have. But nothing I've come up with so far seems to be just right. I've thought of family names . . . you know, *Margaret Glen*, *Marion*. Then there are strong, unsinkable names such as *Intrepid*, *Dauntless*, *Arctic Fox* . . . do you have any suggestions?"

"Let's see . . . the first thing I think of when I hear the word Arctic is ice. Then snow, cold, polar bears, wind. *Wind Lass* comes to mind. How does that name sound to you?"

"Hmm . . . I quite like it, although you just said that ice is the first word that comes to your mind."

"Yes, and rather a lot of it." He rubbed his eyes. "Here's something," he said. "What d'you think of the name *Iceberg*?" He looked over at me, smiling, pleased with his idea.

Iceberg. Majestic white and aquamarine-coloured images floated before my eyes, and I thought of the strength and indestructibility associated with icebergs. "I like it very much, John. If my Arctic idea were to actually come to fruition, there could be no finer name than *Iceberg* for such a vessel."

We shook hands and retired to our respective bedrooms for the night. For the first time in a long while, I slept soundly.

→ *Stromness and Orphir, Orkney*
[NOVEMBER 1854]

I awoke long before daylight and lay in bed for a while, listening to Bessie humming to herself as she lit the fires and brought various kettles to a boil in The Haven's kitchen. For as long as I could remember, Bessie had been the cheerful anchor around which the Rae household revolved.

I poured water into the washing bowl on the nightstand, rinsed my face, donned my winter breeches and hunting coat, and snuck into Mam's room. She was lying on her back, still asleep, her form too small and her breathing too shallow for my liking. The nurse was dozing in a chair beside the bed. I adjusted Mam's blanket so it covered her tiny shoulders, and then slipped quietly down the stairs to the kitchen.

Bessie was stirring a steaming pot of oats over the fire, her broad hips keeping time with the rhythm of her arm movements.

"Good morning, Bessie," I whispered.

Startled, she turned around, her wooden spoon dripping splotches onto the floor. "Johnny! You frightened me! For heaven's sake, the sun hasn't even kissed the horizon yet! Where are you going in this cold? You'll catch your death . . ." I planted a kiss on her cheek, bent down and wiped up the sticky pools.

"Don't worry, Bess. I'll be back before you know it."

"Johnny, you and I both know what happens when you go on one of your wee walks," she scolded. "We probably won't see you until next week, for goodness' sake!"

I solemnly crossed my hands over my heart. "Bess, I will make you two promises. One, I'll be as warm as toast. Remember, our climate here in Orkney is like the tropics when compared to the Arctic! The second promise is that I'll be home before supper. Would you please bake some biscuits and a nice fruit pie today? I'll have my fowling piece and nets with me, so we'll have ourselves a good feast."

Her face relaxed. "Just like when you were a young lad."

As I was collecting my shotgun and bag by the door, she appeared at my side and pressed a cloth bundle into my hand. "Take this bread and cheese, Johnny. You'll need some victuals after you've walked for a while."

I laced my boots and stepped outside into a cold, cloying Orkney fog, settled a woollen cap onto my head, slung my bag over one shoulder and my gun over the other. I turned north and walked alongside the black waters of Hamnavoe, my stride on the Plainstones gathering speed and lengthening along the darkened route I knew by heart. When I reached the end of the bay, I turned east in the direction of Orphir parish, on the far side of Clestrain Sound. The mud did nothing to slow my pace; I drew in long, deep breaths of the damp earth and salty air, feeling better than I had in recent months.

Once I was out of earshot of the townsfolk, I lifted my head and sang out a song I had memorized when I was a boy combing the hills of Orphir with my Newfoundland dog, Leo:

At eve when glowed the setting sun
Above the western wave
A lofty barque, her full sail on
Full, beautiful and brave.
Robed in a gleam of golden smiles
She steers upon the Northern isles
She steers upon the Northern isles.

The low-hanging sky was beginning to lighten as I approached Orphir parish, with the outline of the Hall of Clestrain slowly taking shape in the distance.

I picked up my stride as I descended the hill past grazing cattle towards Orphir and the Hall. The building seemed to grow even larger as I approached, and there was no mistaking the familiar sounds and smells of my childhood: barking dogs, bleating sheep, shouts, the ever-present odours of manure and mud. My hearing was well adapted to identifying the most essential noises connected to safety and sustenance in the Arctic: the crunch of snow underfoot, the moans and cracks of the moving ice, the howling of wolves, the overhead approach of a skein of chattering geese, the thunder of migrating caribou herds. Whenever I returned home, though, my senses easily adjusted to the changes, perhaps because everything about Orkney was embedded in my soul.

I had paid a brief visit to the resident Mackay family at the Hall two years earlier. I took the wide stone steps two at a time and knocked on the door. The housemaid recognized me, took my coat, and showed me into the drawing room. I removed my gloves and cap, wiped my beard, smoothed my unruly hair into place with my fingers.

"John! How lovely to see you again!" Frances Mackay appeared in the doorway. She reached for my hand, her grip as firm and friendly as ever.

"Good day to you, Mrs. Mackay." I smiled back at her. "I just happened to be out for a walk in the neighbourhood . . ."

"Oh, don't we all know about your walking exploits, John! Do come and join us for breakfast. Mary is just now setting the table, and we would be ever so pleased to welcome another soul to take food with us."

"Perhaps my timing is a little bit presumptuous — "

She interrupted me. "Hush now, John! I will not take no for an answer!" Although I had never spoken the words to her, Frances seemed to understand how much I loved being in Orphir and coming to the Hall. "Your timing could not be better." She took my arm. "Come with me."

She led me to the dining room, a place which had once fairly rattled with the exuberant chattering of seven Rae children and various adults. Frances winked at me as she called for Mary, the kitchen maid. "Mary, where are you, dear? You will never guess who is here. We have a special visitor! Come, we shall need another place setting for Dr. Rae!"

A wisp of a young woman appeared at the doorway, shy and smiling. She lowered her gaze and folded into a curtsy, to which I responded with my deepest, most gentlemanly bow. "It is good to see you again, Mary," I said. Flustered, her cheeks pink, she whispered, "Thank you, Sir," and backed out of the room, tripping over the leg of a sideboard.

The breakfast meal of coddled eggs, sausages, hot biscuits and tea was delicious, a far cry from the flavourless, dry pemmican we tore at with our teeth when we were on the move in the Arctic. William Mackay arrived and made general enquiries about my latest expedition, and I was relieved when he did not mention the controversy surrounding my report to the Admiralty.

After the meal, William and I walked along the stone dyke line and down the hill to the beach at the edge of the water. The clouds hung low and the view across the sound to the isles of Graemsay and Hoy were obscured by mist, but I was profoundly pleased to be once again in Orkney's open spaces, free from the walls of London and the unexpected turn my life had taken.

I picked up one of thousands of tiny periwinkle shells left behind at low tide and blew into its miniature chambers, sending the high-pitched whistling sound deep into the fog. When we were children, we often amused ourselves by blowing into the shells in games of hide-and-go-seek, or made the noises from the beach, pretending to guide ships through the mist and darkness of Hoy Sound.

Esquimaux children were taught that whistling would disturb the spirit world, causing angered spirits to descend and rip off the offending children's heads. I assumed there was a good reason for instilling such fear in young people. The sound was sure to frighten away much-needed prey animals in the Arctic.

William put his hands in his pockets and faced me. "John, I hope you won't think me too forward in asking you this, but I'll get straight to the point. Do you believe Sir John Franklin's men consumed the flesh of their fallen?"

"Some of them did, William. Not all," I corrected him. "Some of the men were eaten, but we don't know how many. We have to be careful not to bundle the whole group together under one blanket."

"Aye, right you are. Some of the men."

"Do I believe it happened? In a word, yes. I have no reason to doubt the testimony of the Esquimaux." We regarded each other for a moment, as friends and as fellow northerners.

"That is good enough for me, John. I respect your opinion. I've heard that some of the younger lads who worked over in the Arctic like to knock back a few pints at the pub, and tell tall tales about the Esquimaux. They're just looking for attention to impress the ladies."

"The native peoples of the Arctic do not deserve to be disparaged by anyone," I replied. "Just as we are obliged to live by laws against lying and cheating, so are the Esquimaux around Hudson Bay. Their customs may be different, but they're human beings, too."

William shook his head. "I cannot argue with that. I did not intend to speak ill of the natives. To be honest, I was wondering more about the men of the British Navy."

"Extreme deprivation over a period of time does strange things to the mind, William."

"Aye, such a tragedy." He then turned to me with a half smile, as if he had just been struck by a far more pleasant thought. "John, on a more cheerful note, would you fancy taking one of the horses for the day? Rest your walking legs for a while? No doubt the man who is widely known as the 'Arctic Fox' can readily outrun a Galloway pony, but here's an offer for you. I've a fine, strong mare that needs a good stretch."

"William, I should be honoured to do the job of exercising your horse."

The diminutive, well-muscled mare measured just over thirteen hands high at the withers, but her breed was capable of carrying heavy loads over long distances. Her name was Thunder, and she appeared to have a most agreeable temperament. Her broad chest and back were light brown, her lush mane, tail and feathered legs black. After I secured my shotgun and bag to the saddle, I warmed her up on the road leading away from the farm, and then let her have her head for a good canter up the hill.

We wove our way around the Ring of Brodgar, and then circled the nearby Standing Stones of Stenness. I never failed to be astonished by the sheer height and numbers of those ancient and mysterious monolithic towers. The ring and the stones had supplied ample fodder to imaginative Orcadian storytellers over the centuries.

I shot two tundra geese, a mute swan and nabbed several tufted ducks, birds which had migrated across the North Atlantic from the Arctic regions to spend the winter season breeding in the Orkneys. When the first goose was wounded and fell out of formation, I thought of my own fall from grace in the eyes of the British establishment, and I felt pity for the poor creature. I tied it to my line, mindful of the gratitude the Esquimaux expressed to the animals and birds they killed. Later, I stood at the edge of a briny loch and dropped lines into the water, eventually bringing up a trio of good-sized Atlantic salmon.

Shortly after, I returned the horse to the Mackay's stables, gave two salmon to the cook, and politely refused the offer of a wagon ride home, preferring instead to return to Stromness on foot.

I stopped at The Haven for a moment and gave Bessie my catch. She reported that Mam was resting in her room; I told her that I would step out again and shortly return. There was one more thing I wished to do that day before the November darkness cast its shadow over the town and land.

I walked further along the Plainstones in the direction of Hoy Sound, and along the shoreline path to Warbeth Cemetery, where my father was buried. Here lay the man who had taught me the meaning of self-sufficiency. He had inspired me to be curious, brave and strong, and in that moment, I keenly felt his absence.

JOHN RAE ESQUIRE OF WYRE ISLE
DIED: 2 OCT. 1834 AGE 62

My father had been born in the Lanarkshire region of Scotland. When he was offered the position of overseeing the operation of the Hall of Clestrain and the lands surrounding it, he moved with my mother to Orkney. He had never really owned the Hall, but in my stubborn mind, it had always belonged to the Raes. Papa purchased land on Wyre Isle instead, as an asset for his personal estate. When I enquired about the wording on the gravestone, my mother had replied that it was his wish, because it was the only land he had ever owned in his life.

The grave site was badly overgrown and untended now that Mam could no longer manage such exertions and everyone else was preoccupied with other things. It saddened me to think that our mother would soon join Papa in the cemetery. I couldn't bear the thought of our only living parent leaving us, but seeing her trapped behind a mask of immobility was worse.

✦ *Stromness*

[DECEMBER 1854]

One evening after the children were settled, Marion, John and I lingered at the supper table, taking turns reading aloud from newspapers I had brought from London. The editorial section of the *Times* had published my responses to readers' accusations regarding the veracity of my information.

"It is my duty," I had written, "as well as my desire, to give every information on this distressing subject, not only to the relatives and friends of the lost men, but also the public at large." I was glad that the editors had published my letter. It is far wiser to openly discuss problems and misunderstandings than to turn away from uncomfortable conversations.

Marion and John were naturally curious to hear my theory about what may have overcome the men. "Tell us more about what you know, John."

"I can't verify what happened, but I will tell you of something that has bothered me. Apparently witnesses who saw the *Erebus* and *Terror* off the southern coast of Greenland in August of 1845 reported that the crews killed and salted a large number of waterfowl, which suggests to me that they had future consumption of the meat in mind. Perhaps the commander ordered the slaughter and salting as a contingency, in case the voyage took longer than anticipated and the supply of preserved and tinned victuals ran low. I have wondered if the greasy, rancid stores of birds would have been consumed only as a last resort, causing the men, who were in all likelihood experiencing symptoms of scurvy and other ailments, to suffer from serious bouts of intestinal disorders as well. In my letter to the *Times*," I explained, "I hoped to assuage the public's anger by appealing to its sense of pity." I read aloud from the paper.

"'. . . picture a party of gallant men reduced by want and perhaps disease, to great extremity, pushing their way to the mouth of a large river, such as Back's Great Fish, which they expected would permit them to travel southward in their boat.'"

Marion sighed. "Those poor men . . ."

"They would have had little to no strength left for such an undertaking." I read on: "'I wish I could have been with them . . . my greater experience of Arctic travelling and hunting might have been useful to those in such extremes and danger.'"

"Do my words sound immodest? I wanted the readers to understand that I truly did regret not being there to help prevent those premature deaths."

John shook his head. "Your grave concern about the men's suffering is clear in your letter. I wouldn't worry about how readers will interpret it."

The *Times* had also published a strange missive from a Mr. W. Parker Snow, in which he declared his certainty that not all hope was lost concerning the fate of the crews of the *Erebus* and *Terror*.

"His name is familiar. I heard that he had been to the Hudson Bay region once, as a civilian passenger aboard a search vessel."

Marion leaned forward, her chin resting on her hand. "Mr. Snow sounds optimistic. What did he write?" I picked up the paper and read his statement: "'I firmly believe the crews of the *Erebus* and *Terror* to be alive, among the Esquimaux, I have a strong idea where they may be found. I have always had the same idea and the various rumours obtained through the wild tribes on the coast of Continental America, all refer to corroborating the view I take.'"

I frowned. "Rumours . . ."

He concluded his letter by announcing that he had formulated "'a plan to submit to all calm thinking and humane minds. This I shall shortly lay before the public. Meanwhile, I once more urge the plea . . . with a hope that my voice may not altogether be in vain.'"

I slapped the paper onto the table. "Imagine that!" I shouted. "Such nonsense. Grieving people may find themselves clinging to false hope after reading this cluttered drivel. The poor fellow cannot even write a proper sentence, for God's sake!"

"But he went to the Arctic, you said, to search for the ships and men . . ."

"He is no one of importance, I can assure you both. His claim to fame — the attainment of which eludes him, by the way — is that he believes he possesses the gift of second sight, the ability to see things that are hidden from view or far away. I remember his name because he approached Lady Franklin three years ago, asking to join one of her search expeditions. He convinced her that he had experienced a vision of the missing ships, and that he knew precisely where they could be found. She hired him in 1851 as a civil officer aboard the *Prince Albert*, a ketch she had commissioned for the search, but the effort came to naught."

The romantic notion of second sight had become highly popular, and Marion was intrigued. "How extraordinary! Where did he believe the ships and men were positioned?"

"He claimed he saw them somewhere west of the Boothia Peninsula."

"Johnny, you reported — "

"It is a vast region, Marion. If Mr. Snow thinks he has knowledge of the locations in question, he could only have acquired it through incomplete maps. The *Prince Albert* never made it past the Boothia Peninsula anyway, because sea ice forced the captain to turn her back. I presume the writer is still basing his opinions on premonitions and visions. He is grasping at straws again, probably hoping to join another search."

"D'you think it's possible, though, that some of the men are living with the natives?"

"No one can know anything for certain, of course, but I expect I would have heard something about that during two months of interviews at Pelly and Repulse Bays."

John took her hand. "We will never know the full story nor understand what those poor men went through, my dear. Unfortunately, much of what happened must be left in the realm of imagination. It sounds as though our Mr. Snow is a charlatan. I wouldn't be surprised if more people like him begin crawling out of the woodwork, looking for ways to profit from the news."

"Aye, they are." I passed the newspaper to him. "If even one crew member is found alive, the Admiralty will have to make good on its offer of an additional £10,000 in reward money to those who bring him safely to England. There can be no doubt that many others will be seeking absurd ways to claim it."

I placed two issues of *Household Words* on the table. "I picked these up from the newsagent," I explained. "Charles Dickens has written a two-part essay called 'The Lost Arctic Voyagers.'" I began to read Part One, expecting the worst. He was generous enough in the opening paragraphs of his article, and I was relieved to see that he wrote that I had acted with integrity: ". . . we find no fault with Dr. Rae, and that we thoroughly acquit him of any trace of blame . . . faithful report to the Hudson's Bay Company . . . his report was made public by the Admiralty: not by him."

One of England's greatest living novelists was not afraid of informing his readers that the Royal Navy, which he publicly supported, had released scandalous news about its own men. That is the greater of the two stories, I thought.

I read an excerpt from the first essay to Marion and John: "'Of the propriety of his immediate return to England with the intelligence he had got together we are fully convinced. As a man of sense and humanity, he perceived that the first and greatest account to which it could be turned, was, the prevention of the useless hazard of valuable lives; and no one could better know in how much hazard all lives are placed that follow Franklin's track, than he who made eight visits to the Arctic shores. With these remarks we can release Dr. Rae from this inquiry, proud of him as an Englishman, and happy in his safe return home to well-earned rest.'"

"Well, Johnny," Marion smiled, "Mr. Dickens seems to have great admiration for you."

"He refers to me as an Englishman. I am a Scot, and he knows it."

She raised her eyebrows. "Aren't you being bit too sensitive? Perhaps his comment was just an oversight . . ."

"I have my doubts about that."

Mr. Dickens had printed decent words about me, but once the niceties were out of the way, his essay took a less congenial turn. Sure enough, he quickly and decisively moved beyond the flattery, swung around, and took aim at the Esquimaux. I continued reading: "' . . . no man can, with any show of reason, undertake to affirm that this sad remnant of Franklin's gallant band were not set upon and slain by the Esquimaux themselves.'" It seemed clear he was scattering seeds of hatred. The pen can indeed be mightier than the sword, and with his pen in hand, Dickens continued his assault on all natives, sparing no one.

Both Marion and John leaned forward, their eyes widening. "Listen to this," I said, as my eyes moved ahead on the page. "'We believe every savage to be in his heart covetous, treacherous and cruel . . .'"

An image of Dickens floated into my mind, his shoulders hunched over a writing table, his head close to the paper, his facial features drawn tight with determination. I continued reading: "'The word of a savage is not to be taken for it; firstly because he is a liar; secondly, because he is a boaster; thirdly, because he often talks figuratively; fourthly, because he is given to a superstitious notion that when he tells you he has his enemy in his stomach, you will logically give him credit for having his enemy's valour in his heart.'"

When it seemed that he had said more than enough, he moved in for the kill: "' . . . the noble conduct and example of such men, and of their own great leader himself, under similar endurances . . . outweighs by the weight of the whole universe the chatter of a gross handful of uncivilized people, with a domesticity of blood and blubber.'"

John shook his head. "Such nasty statements! Charles Dickens certainly doesn't mince his words, does he?"

I tossed the paper onto the table, as if it carried a disease. It was clear that, like most Britons, he had absolutely no knowledge or understanding of native morals and values. He, an intelligent man, could at the very least have made an effort to learn something about those people before he put pen to paper. His dramatic attack on the innocent Esquimaux was abhorrent.

"I have no doubt this vile portrait of the natives will sell many issues of *Household Words*," I said. "And that's exactly what he and his friend Jane Franklin want: to divert the public's attention away from the truth."

As we three read on, we came to the same conclusion. The central point in his essay — that the native testimony in my report was worth less than the paper it was written on — was weak, at best, because he had no information to draw upon in support of his vicious declarations. Instead, he wrote at length about other British sailors who had faced starvation but never stooped to the last recourse. Ad infinitum. He knew nothing of what really happened to the men of the *Erebus* and *Terror*, none of whom survived to tell any tales. And his ignorance was showing.

Marion was furious. "Are you thinking of writing a rebuttal, Johnny? Dickens is doing even more harm to the poor people who have lost their husbands, sons and brothers by suggesting they were murdered and eaten by savages!"

"I will challenge his accusations, although I can't imagine that my arguments will do much good. It seems as though Charles Dickens can do no wrong in the eyes of the reading public." We remained at the table for some time, lamenting the British establishment's ability to influence public thinking.

—

While the debate about what had really befallen John Franklin and his men raged on, there had been no communication from the authorities concerning the £10,000 reward money which was my due. The Admiralty had been in possession of my application for two months. In my opinion, the claim was clear but it was unnerving to know that the authorities were biding their time, waiting for Captain Richard Collinson's return, among other things. The HMS *Enterprise* must have surely reached port by now. I took my pen in hand in The Haven's library, with the fire warming me.

First Secretary
Lords Commissioners of the Admiralty
London

December 25, 1854

Sirs:

I take the liberty of bringing the subject before the notice of my
Lords Commissioners of the Admiralty, believing that their Lordships
have before this time become acquainted with the details of Captain
Collinson's despatch, and have been able to decide whether the tenor
of that document be such, as in any way to interfere with my claim to
the reward alluded to.

I have, &c.

John Rae
Stromness, Orkney

I wondered what other strategies Lady Franklin and Sophia Cracroft would be employing, in their relentless attempt to secure Sir John Franklin's Arctic legacy. It was a certainty that the ships' crews had fought for their lives, but it was completely irresponsible to blame bystanders for their demise.

Time was moving along at such a rapid pace. It seemed as though I had just arrived in Orkney; I was reluctant to leave Mam and the others so soon, but I knew that once December reached its end and January began, it was a certainty that my presence at Hudson Bay House in London would be expected.

PART IV

Life Changes

[1855–1858]

I arrived in the city on a dreary evening, and registered under the name William Hamilton at the Tavistock Hotel. In the morning, I made my way to Fenchurch Street to meet with Sir George Simpson at Hudson Bay House. As usual, he was in good spirits and eager to get on with the many tasks at hand.

"Well, my boy . . ." He leaned back in his chair, puffing on his pipe. "I'm quite sure we can find many things for you to do around here. As you know, our soaring profits have raised more than a few hackles in Whitehall over the years, and I've been advised by the board of governors to expect that a parliamentary inquiry will be called at some point. The thing of it is, you know — well, we are just so good at what we do! — private enterprises and governments have a tendency to lock horns when it comes down to who controls what, and so on. The British Empire is so vast; how could its leaders expect a company such as ours to stand still in North America, and let business opportunities pass us by?"

I nodded. "How right you are on that one, Sir. Perhaps I can make myself useful by gathering and documenting information about the Company's activities, so we will be well prepared for questions and challenges when they arise."

"Aye. That is precisely what I am thinking, John. If there is to be an inquiry, you will probably be called upon to testify on our behalf."

"Well then, if you will assign a desk to me, I'll get to work." I paused at the door. "By the way, Sir, who has been appointed in my place as chief factor for the Mackenzie River District?"

"James Anderson has stepped in. Are you personally acquainted with him? He seems to be a good man, reliable."

For a fleeting moment, I felt a twinge of jealousy at hearing that I had been so readily replaced. "James Anderson? Aye, I met him once. You are right, he's a decent fellow, and he is apparently capable of many things." I paused. "He did not strike me as an adventuresome type, though. More of an administrator, I suppose."

Sir George knew me well enough to understand why I was hesitant about supporting my replacement in the Arctic, but he was also adept at smoothing rough edges when he felt it was necessary. "He has a knack for numbers, John, and there is no denying that he lacks your skills as a traveller." He chuckled. "As I told you last year, no one can fill the snowshoes of the man known as the 'Arctic Fox' when it comes to getting around in the wilderness, my boy."

A short time after my conversation with Sir George, the British government awarded Captain Robert McClure of the HMS *Investigator* a knighthood and £10,000 for supposedly completing the Northwest Passage. To say that I was irked by that strange decision would be an understatement. McClure and his men had abandoned the *Investigator* in pack ice in the spring of 1853. In 1854, they were rescued after sledging and walking across a stretch of ice which was somehow presumed to be the missing link in the passage. At first, the Admiralty had court-martialled the captain for abandoning his ship, but later reversed its decision and lauded him for his exertions. McClure's report about his experience could not have possibly offered proof that he had discovered a *navigable* waterway, because he had no vessel with which to traverse the alleged link!

Richard Collinson finally returned from his five-year sojourn aboard the HMS *Enterprise*, but his much-anticipated discovery turned out to be barely noteworthy. During five long years of searching, he had found a small piece of wood bearing the broad arrow insignia of the Royal Navy. There was, of course, no proof that the object came from the *Erebus* or *Terror*, and in any case, it was a mere trifle in regards to further intelligence concerning the expedition's fate. The small amount of patience I'd held onto for delays was wearing thin; I had become fed up with those responsible for needlessly stretching out the reward process.

It was well known that the Admiralty was under great pressure from such outside influences as the widow of Sir John. I just couldn't imagine her letting go of a quest to see her husband crowned the king of all Arctic explorers. However, I kept my thoughts to myself as the list of claimants grew: Erasmus Ommanney, A.K. Isbister, Esq., Dr. Richard King, R. McCormick, Lieut. Bedford G.T. Pim, Captain William Penny, John Garland, Lieut. John Powles Cheyne . . . Exactly where had these men travelled, and why in the name of God were they all claiming that *they* had ascertained the fate of the doomed expedition? Infuriated, I took to writing more letters to the Secretary of the Admiralty.

"What 'further report' as far as regards the fate of Sir John Franklin and his party, their lordships expect to receive, I am at a loss to imagine," I wrote. There was no reply. The McClure and Collinson chapters in the story had been closed. Every Royal Navy vessel which had been involved in the Arctic searches had either succumbed to the pressures of sea ice and been abandoned by her crews, was back in port, or on duty elsewhere.

→ *Stromness*
[FEBRUARY 1855]

Before the annual spring exodus of winter birds and waterfowl from Orkney and the arrival of breeding birds from the north, Mam suffered a third stroke. This one was massive, merciful and final. According to John and Marion, she lost consciousness immediately and her exit was swift.

I was not there to kiss her on the forehead and say goodbye. The news reached me in London a week later, and by the time I arrived in Stromness, her body had been committed to the ground next to my father in Warbeth Cemetery, overlooking the great hills of Hoy. The minister held a brief second service at the graveside with just Marion, John and me in attendance. We bade Mam farewell on a clear and breezy day while sea birds soared, dived, circled and glided above us, their sharp cries at once loud and then carried away by the winds. We watched as a four-masted barque exited Hoy Sound with the running tide. Mam would have appreciated the sight of the great ship gaining speed, her multiple sails filling with fresh northeasterly winds as she left the Orkney Islands behind.

Marion placed a hand on my shoulder. "Spring is almost here, Johnny, and before long, the kirkyard will be greener. Our mam would have liked that. You know," she said, "her face looked decades younger just before she left us. It was like the face of a child."

"I will love you, Mam, always," I whispered. *Tara Gott.*

Soon after, the Hamilton family began making preparations to emigrate to North America. They invited Bessie to join them in their new home, but she declined their offer. She was getting on in years, and the change would have been too much for her. One evening as we sat together in The Haven's kitchen, she placed two cups of hot tea on the table. "These islands are my home, Johnny. They are all I have known in my sixty-four years of life, and I cannot imagine living anywhere else. My friends need looking after as they get older, and I've put away a tidy sum over the years, so I'll not be wanting for anything." She wiped at her eyes as they filled with tears. "I will miss you all terribly, though. The children . . ." I gave her my handkerchief.

"I understand, Bess. We will all miss you as well. Marion will see to it that they write letters to you." I sipped my tea. "I will be sure to visit Orkney when I can, and I hope you will invite me to your cottage for a visit."

Her face brightened. "Of course I will!"

"And who knows?" I added. "I may return here one day to raise a family of my own."

"Oh, wouldn't that be just fine, Johnny! I'll hope for it! No matter what happens, I will say a prayer for all of you every night as I have always done."

→ *London*

[APRIL–JULY 1855]

I was surprised when Sir George advised me that the Hudson's Bay Company had seconded James Anderson to the Admiralty to conduct a search of the area where I had reported the Esquimaux sightings of the missing men. I was further taken aback to learn that Anderson and his travelling partner James Stewart had been supplied with only two canoes made from the poorest of bark — such frail vessels — and a one-man inflatable Halkett boat for their arduous journey. What had Sir George been thinking when he agreed to let the men participate in such a poorly planned endeavour? Had he withheld the news from me in order to avoid the inevitable questions I would have asked him about it? If I had been consulted, I would have strongly advised against anyone being sent into the wilderness with inadequate equipment and resources.

The canoes were eventually destroyed by ice, the search was abandoned, and the men returned to Repulse Bay via Back's Great Fish River, lucky to be alive. They had found some metal fragments and a piece of wood floating in the water, engraved with the name *Stanley*. It was a small clue concerning the fate of the ships; Mr. Stanley had been listed as the surgeon aboard the *Erebus*.

→ *London*

[DECEMBER 25, 1855]

Precisely one year to the day after I had submitted my reminder to the authorities about my claim to the reward money, I wrote yet another letter to the Admiralty, inquiring again about the subject. My words were carefully chosen to disguise the fact that I was completely and utterly furious with the Lords Commissioners of the Arctic Council for the simple decision they continuously failed to make.

→ *London*

[1856]

The newspapers reported that the Admiralty continued to be under great pressure. Lady Franklin had not yet finished with them, far from it. She, her husband's niece and their leagues of supporters continued firing volleys at Admiralty House, the government and the newspapers.

They even went so far as to plead with such foreign dignitaries as the president of the United States and the governor of Van Diemen's Land in their ceaseless campaign to push for the money to finance more search expeditions.

The editors of the *Times* warned the naval authorities that it would be irresponsible to divert British money from more pressing matters at home and abroad. "We vehemently protest against the extension of any assistance from public funds, or from public establishments, to so preposterous a scheme as another expedition in search of Sir John Franklin's relics," they opined. "We are really so sick of the subject."

"Just give me the bloody reward money, you fools, and I will set the record straight myself!" I scribbled, after which I crumpled the paper and tossed it into a dustbin. In May, I sent the Admiralty still another letter. "It is now four weeks since the expiration date for the Lords Commissioners' decision concerning the reward. Don't keep me in suspense," I added.

In the early summer — after what had felt like an eternity of chasing after the reward — the Admiralty finally made a decision in my favour, and my battle for it was over. When I submitted my retirement notice to Sir George, he accepted it with great reluctance. "I wish the government had properly recognized you for your outstanding achievements, my boy. Such a bloody shame. As for the Company, I sincerely hope you'll consider taking on the odd project with us in the future. Leading expeditions, conducting research and so forth, when your schedule permits."

"I would be honoured to be at your service," I replied. And I meant what I said.

I directed the Hudson's Bay Company to divide the sum of £2,000 among Ouligback, Mistegan, and a handful of deserving men who had so ably assisted me during the fall of 1853 and that fateful summer of 1854. With the remaining £8,000 in hand, I bade farewell to Sir George, promising to visit him in his retirement in Lachine, near Montreal, and to remain in contact with the Hudson's Bay Company about future endeavours. I boarded a ship bound for New York, and then a train to Hamilton, Canada West, where Marion, John and their nine — now ten — children had settled close to Tom and Richard. It was time for a fresh start, and the idea of building the *Iceberg* was never very far from my thoughts.

✦ *Hamilton, Canada West*
[SEPTEMBER 1856]

"Tom! Over here!" I shouted as I disembarked from the train. My gangly, curly-headed younger brother was a fine sight for sore eyes. I lifted him off his feet in a bear hug, and we danced around one another in an imaginary boxing match, throwing false punches and ducking, just as we used to do as boys.

"Good to see you, big brother!" he laughed. The city air was hot, humid and thick with coal-fire smoke, much like the atmosphere in London at the same time of year. "We are in need of a good, strong wind right now, Johnny."

Tom was referring to more than just the weather. Rae Brothers & Company was moving forward with great speed. The company owned several ships now, and more were under construction at the Hamilton railway shipyard. He led me to the waterfront, where two brigantines and four schooners were anchored and ready to carry cargo, waiting for customers.

"How much have you got invested in this?" I asked.

"Fifty-five thousand dollars."

"That's a tidy sum."

"Dick and I finally managed to sell off the meat-packing equipment, and we took out a loan," he added. "Our first vessel is over there. We bought the *Princess Victoria* from a bankrupt builder. She's almost twenty years old, but she's a solid workhorse if ever I saw one."

"And the others?"

"All built in the last three years. Beauties, aren't they? I have a surprise for you. Look over there. We named that 200-ton schooner for you. The *John Rae* was finished in 1853."

"Bless you. I am flattered, but is she making money for you?"

His voice dropped. "She's getting there, slowly but surely."

"Perhaps I can contribute a modest sum to help."

"Thanks for the thought, Johnny. We can talk about that later."

"And how is Dick?"

"You'll see that he's much better and steadier on his feet now that he's employed as an immigration agent. In his free time, he's overseeing the building of another schooner, the *RH Rae*. He's been busy finding investors and raising the funds for the project."

Another one? This enterprise was growing into a full fleet. Would it be profitable?

The *RH Rae*. Richard Bempede Honeyman Johnstone Rae. I kept my thoughts about the extravagance of the boys' new venture to myself. Great Lakes shipbuilding was an emerging industry and full of promise, but constructing such a sizeable fleet in a short period of time was a risky undertaking, to say the least. It was my good fortune, however, that the facilities for constructing the *Iceberg* were right there and could be available for use. My brother and I stayed up and talked long into the night, about his wife, their two boys, about Hamilton, and Rae Brothers & Company. We also discussed the strange turn my own professional life had taken.

"Tell me about this mysterious vessel you're thinking of building, Johnny. You sounded quite excited in your letter."

"Well, while I was waiting for the decision about the reward money, I had time to give the idea a good deal of thought. Here it is, Tom. If I'm going to settle some unfinished business in the Arctic, I'll need to have a specially designed ship. The past two years have been gruelling. I've had enough of London and the British government's ineptitude. It's time to get on with other things."

"Go on."

"When I saw a brigantine under construction at the Aberdeen docks almost two years ago, a bell rang in my head. It's still ringing, reminding me of what I want to do. I don't know how to explain it exactly, but at that moment I knew I wanted to return to the Arctic one more time and be accountable for it to no one but myself. I've been working on plans, making sketches, looking at ships, and thinking about building an exceedingly strong schooner, partly based on the design of a brig. Sleek, light, easy to manoeuvre, and with a rake in the stem so she won't strike hard on the ice. I am also planning to build her with round sides, so she'll be able to tolerate being pushed upwards by pack ice without damage to her hull. And I want to fit her with the new, long-shafted screw propeller technology everyone's talking about. What do you think?" My excitement was rising to the surface; I couldn't stop myself from smiling as I spoke.

His eyes widened. "A schooner with some brig features," he repeated. "That's an interesting combination. So you're planning a return trip to the Arctic with your own vessel. Will you be searching for the remains of the Franklin Expedition?"

"I want to do more than that. My plan is to reconstruct what I believe to be the route of the *Erebus* and *Terror*, around the top of the Boothia Peninsula. Instead of bearing west from there and then south in Victoria Strait as I think Franklin and Crozier did, I will turn her south sooner, between the west coast of the Boothia Peninsula and the eastern coast of King William Island, where I believe the missing link to the Northwest Passage to be. I'll show you a map I've drawn — "

"Johnny, the British government has already rewarded Captain Mc-Clure for finding the route! He was paid £10,000 for his discovery, and he's now a 'Sir'!"

"I don't think he found the correct link. I plan to travel north anyway, and if my hypothesis proves to be correct, then I should be able to sail the ship between the southern shores of King William Island and the northern coastline of the continent. We can disembark and travel overland when needed — "

"— to locate the naval encampments and search for more evidence?"

"Aye, and bring back proof of cannibalism among the last survivors. Proof that the Esquimaux told the truth about all of it, about the marching men with their boat, the death camps, perhaps even information about at least one of the ships, although the chances of finding much material from the *Erebus* and *Terror* are slim at best."

"You may find pieces of them, though."

"Perhaps. I found part of a ship's stanchion off the coast of King William Island several years ago. At the time, I was quite sure it came from a Royal Navy vessel, so I gave it to the Admiralty. I didn't hear anything more about it. And there is something else I wish to do in the Arctic. I want to complete the Boothia Peninsula coastline survey I began in 1854. It nags at me that I didn't complete what I started. I've never liked leaving things half-finished."

He chuckled. "We all know that about you, Johnny."

"Aye, brother," I grinned. "I'll load up my ship with proof, and sail her back to England. I will send letters and reports in advance to the *Times*, the *Illustrated News*, the *Guardian*, the *Gazette*, the *Scotsman*, the British Admiralty, Lady Franklin, her unpleasant niece, and even to the 'Conductor' of *Household Words*, my friend Mr. Dickens."

I was breathing hard now. We both smiled. Tom knew me well; he was aware of how much it had stung when my report of 1854 had been criticized. "You've taken quite a beating at the hands of the London establishment, haven't you, Johnny? Perhaps the public will finally acknowledge the truth about your report. Lady Franklin and her companions may continue to be troublesome, but you'll be able to leave all that controversy behind you."

"I have already drawn up plans for this vessel, Tom. I can see how busy you are, but d'you think you could help me build a schooner here in Hamilton?"

A look of surprise swept across his face. "There's not much time to complete her. Winter will set in and . . .."

"I want to launch her next spring."

"What? Have you lost your senses? We can't possibly — "

"Just watch me. She will be ready to go if I have to hammer in every nail and turn every screw myself. Tom, others are probably well underway with their own plans to do the same thing! If this enterprise is going to be at all successful, there's not a moment to waste."

He sighed, knowing there was little point in arguing about it, and that I would fight hard to see the project through, come hell or high water. "God bless you. You never were one to wait patiently for things. You've got to understand that I have a business to run, and I can't devote all my time to this. By the way, have you chosen a name for her?"

"The name was John's idea. We tossed some ideas around when I was in Stromness, and we settled on *Iceberg*," I said. I watched his eyes for a reaction. He blinked, sat back and grinned.

"*Iceberg*," he repeated. "Aye, that's a fine name for such a vessel, considering where you plan to sail her. You'll be sure to encounter more than a few of those . . ."

"She'll have a crew of no more than nine men, including me, each of us properly experienced, trained in sailing, and equipped with survival skills. My plan extends beyond even that. If all goes well, the *Iceberg* could later be refitted as a commercial vessel and carry cargo around the Great Lakes. She could pay for herself and bring in some decent profits. Tom, with these tasks completed, I think I will be ready to settle down somewhere and start a family."

He laughed. "When are you ever going to settle down? You're forty-three years old! You've been restless since the day you were born!"

"Well, I've got to scratch this Arctic itch whilst I still feel it. Then, you'll see . . ."

It was pleasant to be grounded for a time, living with Tom and his family, seeing all the others for the occasional meal and at church on Sundays. Soon I fell into a state of undistracted obsession with my plans for the 80-ton vessel, sometimes waking in the night to write notes about her fittings, making sketches of her smooth lines all day, imagining her many angles and curves inside and out, thinking of her as a lover I was yearning to meet. With Tom's help, the materials were ordered, and construction of the *Iceberg* began the following week.

→ *Hamilton*

[FEBRUARY 1857]

Trying to finish her for a spring 1857 departure from Hamilton was indeed an ambitious undertaking. Tom was right about not having enough time to get her ready, although I was loath to admit it until I had no choice. After six months of frenzied work, often in poor weather conditions, it became clear that the chances of a spring launch were rapidly diminishing. As the days and weeks passed and she was nowhere near completion, my stomach became tied in what felt like a hundred knots.

On a cold and windy February afternoon, we watched as builders and fitters scrambled all over her like ants, trying to get her finished. "You have to face it, Johnny. She won't be ready in time. You — we all — did the best we could."

"I know. I appreciate all you've tried to do." I turned away. "With luck, we'll put her to work on the lakes as a merchant vessel sometime this summer. Let her start paying for herself." My feelings of reverence for the ship had been slipping away as if she'd let me down, which of course she hadn't. I suppose I expected her to rescue me as quickly as possible from the embarrassment of the past few years. I cursed myself for being so childish, for trying to believe in the impossible.

→ *Hamilton*
[APRIL 1857]

To make matters worse, the newspapers reported that Lady Franklin had raised enough funds to acquire a steam yacht named the *Fox*, and that she had retained Captain Francis Leopold McClintock to take command of the ship, which would set sail for the Arctic from Aberdeen in July.

"You'll get there next year, Johnny. You will, and it won't be too late for any of it. The *Fox* may run into no end of problems, especially leaving so late in the season. It could be years before they find anything, if they do at all." Tom was always the optimist in the Rae family.

→ *Hamilton*
[MAY 1857]

As it turned out, I wouldn't have been able to travel to the Arctic that spring after all, because I was called to London on a different matter. Just as Sir George Simpson had predicted, the British government ordered the establishment of a Parliamentary Select Committee in London, to investigate complaints about the Hudson's Bay Company's growing monopoly over commercial trade and land control in Rupert's Land, the northwest region of Canada. The Company had also been accused of failing to "civilize" the indigenous peoples. As its long-term governor, Sir George was expected to be a key witness in the Company's defence. My own history as a chief factor made it obligatory for me to testify at the hearings as well.

"Tom, I've got to return to London for a week or two." We were standing in the rail yard, watching men going about their tasks aboard the *Iceberg*. "It's a long way to go for such a short time, but I don't have a choice in the matter."

"Don't worry. I'll keep a close eye on things here." He moved a stone out of the way with the tip of his boot. "What will happen to the natives in North America, Johnny, if the British government eventually forces its own language, religion and way of life on them? It all seems to be so . . . against nature, for want of a better expression."

"Aye, brother, you just hit the nail on the head. I do not believe they will be able to cope with the changes. Indians and the Esquimaux are hunters. They don't settle in one place and stay there. They survive by constantly being on the move in search of food. They give thanks to the animals for feeding them, and if the animals aren't to be found, they believe they have not been kind enough to them. In their world, everything has a spirit. I cannot imagine them ever welcoming our God into their lives."

We were walking away from the rail yard now, breathing in the fresh green scent of spring, thinking about the conflict between the Hudson's Bay Company and the Crown. The two opposing enterprises were espousing completely different views about how to maximize the commercial potential of colonizing the outer regions of North America.

"The directors of the Company are in favour of expansionism," I said, "but there is general agreement that the natives' way of life should be left alone. The indigenous people are used to trading with us; they understand how it works, and our methods are successful for them as well. There is no need for the natives to alter their way of life and sense of identity." I stopped and turned to face Tom. "That's the part I don't understand. The British colonial powers plan to bring in thousands of settlers to Rupert's Land, and convert the natives to being exactly like them."

"D'you mean teaching them English and making them into farmers?"

"Aye!" I cried. "Forcing them to adopt English names, forbidding them to speak in their native tongue, dressing them up like English men, women and children!"

Tom shook his head. "If we were ordered to change who we are and how we choose to live, I know we would fight them every step of the way," he declared.

⇾ *London*
[JUNE 1857]

When I arrived at the Fenchurch Street offices of the Hudson's Bay Company after a week at sea, Sir George was waiting for me. He clapped me on the back as we shook hands. "Good to be in London again, and to see you, my boy." As usual, he got straight to the point. "The powers that be in government are accusing the Company of having a stranglehold on the northwest of the continent. Our enterprise is moving along quite nicely, but we must try to disabuse them of the notion that our plan is to take control of everything."

He offered me a chair. On the wall behind him was a map of Rupert's Land, with a circle around each Hudson's Bay Company trading post and depot. There could be no doubt that the Company was expanding its business and territory.

"Apparently, our pious friend Sir John Richardson is deeply disappointed that the natives aren't the least bit interested in being converted to Christianity, as if we have failed the people," he grunted. I thought of Richardson's fervent belief during our travels that the natives' starving souls could be "saved" if they would only surrender to the teachings of the church. For a fleeting moment, I missed being in John Richardson's company, but so much had changed since our time together. He had not only turned his back on me when I needed his support, but now he was accusing the Hudson's Bay Company of doing a great disservice to the people of Rupert's Land and beyond.

"Well, Sir, I stand firm with you in my belief that assimilating the native peoples of North America into a British colonial way of life would be a great mistake," I said.

He tapped his fingers on the desk. "If you see me getting hot under the collar when I'm testifying on the Company's behalf, John, give me a nudge to remind me that losing my temper will only do more harm than good. You know how much I dislike politics in general — and politicians in particular."

"I'll do my best, Sir."

During the inquiry, we expressed our concerns to the committee, explaining why it would not have made sense to change the natives' way of life by persuading them that their lot would improve with a transition to agriculture and resettlement under foreign rule. We predicted that the forced implementation of such systems would do far more harm than good to British relations with the Indians and Esquimaux, and we emphasized the negative impact that cultural assimilation would have on business overall. We even went so far as to query why no natives had been consulted concerning the matter and its potential outcome. The committee's explanation was simple: the people were apparently too undeveloped to know what was best for them.

I explained why the Hudson's Bay Company's system of working with the natives had been successful. I pointed out that we gave them fair treatment, acknowledged their humanity, and we employed a sensible system of reciprocity in all of our dealings with them. I testified that our methods of doing business in the Arctic had beneficial effects for all concerned parties.

A member of the committee asked, "What say you about the allegation that Company employees gave alcohol to the natives?"

"The practice of distributing spirits to them was discontinued long ago," I replied. "It was a mistake ever to allow it to happen. As we all know, a small amount of alcohol may be useful for medicinal purposes, but anything beyond that clouds the mind and interferes with making sound decisions."

The inquiry was still underway when notice was served that Upper Canada's colonial legislature had passed into law the "Gradual Civilization Act," meaning that the process of assimilation would begin regardless of any debates or inquiries in London. Sir George was confident that the Company would weather changes in the political landscape. My heart was heavy with concern for the future of the native peoples and their way of life, but I had no power to influence the changes to come. With my participation in the inquiry completed, I departed for North America.

➔ *Hamilton*
[AUGUST 1857]

The finished *Iceberg*, resting on a crib in the railway·yard, was indeed a sight for sore eyes. I was disappointed to have been away during the later stages of her construction, but eager to move forward with planning an Arctic expedition in the early spring of 1858. When we climbed aboard the vessel, I hugged my brothers. "Tom, Dick, you have done far more than a fine job with her. Congratulations and thank you. You have served the *Iceberg* well. Now, the celebration begins."

We had not told anyone outside the family about my Arctic plan for the ship. All others knew was that I had decided to put her to work as a Great Lakes cargo vessel. If we did make it to the frozen north and the expedition succeeded, her mission would soon enough capture the attention of the public.

On August 9, 1857, we launched the *Iceberg* to great cheers and applause from an admiring audience on the pier. She was a splendid sight to behold, with her slender, polished frame holding three masts, each sprouting an array of new canvas sails. We were a crew of four, including Tom, Dick and our brother-in-law John, and I soon forgot about my disappointment in the delays and interruptions as I piloted her around Hamilton Bay and beyond.

She was a lovely creation: everything I had dreamed of and more. Smooth, steady and fast, she responded to the lightest touch of the wheel, coming about again and again, without a moment's hesitation. There were no adequate words to describe the pride I felt in being at the helm of such a fine ship. When we fired up the steam engine, the propeller shaft spun effortlessly, affording us additional power for times when the winds dropped, for outrunning storms and for slipping around ice blockages when we reached the Polar Sea. As we sailed around Lake Ontario on that beautiful summer day, I fell hopelessly in love with the *Iceberg*.

→ *Lake Ontario, between Welland and Kingston*
[AUGUST 17, 1857]

As had befallen the *Erebus* and *Terror*, fate has the power to interfere with plans in a most cruel and punishing manner. Less than a week after we launched the *Iceberg*, I hired her out to carry a load of coal from Cleveland to Kingston. Battered by monstrous waves in a fierce storm, she never made it across Lake Ontario. Broken, she bucked, snapped, groaned and rolled over, before sucking all hands down to the lake bottom with her. My lovely creation was suddenly gone and I felt shattered. I had sunk more than £2,000 of the reward money into building her. My Arctic plan had suddenly disappeared, taking the money down with it. Shortly after the ship was lost, I sank into a state of profound melancholy.

→ *Hamilton*
[OCTOBER 1857–FEBRUARY 1858]

Family members gathered around me in Hamilton during that bleak and bitter time, offering me nourishment and soothing words, but I was inconsolable. I withdrew into a dark, cold place and stayed there, lying in bed all day, walking the neighbourhood streets after sunset. Sometimes during my nocturnal wanderings, I experienced hallucinations. My grief at the loss of the *Iceberg* and the death of my Arctic dream caused me to lose my grip on reality. Caught in a dreamlike state, I imagined that I was reaching out from the bank of a roiling river, trying to grasp the arm of a man who was being dashed about like a rag doll on the rocks in the rapids, spun into swirling eddies, disappearing, reappearing and gone from sight again. I repeatedly grabbed his wet, limp hand and held on with all of my strength, to no avail. Seven years after the tragedy of losing Albert One-Eye in the rapids of the Coppermine River, I was hallucinating that terrible event over and over again. I was too ill to tell the difference between my memory and imagination.

Nakka, Albert . . . *Nakka!*

Nakka. Nakka! I'm sorry. I'm sorry!

The illness caused my grieving mind to envision watery images of my Esquimaux friends standing on an enormous iceberg, smiling and waving to me as they drifted away from me. I was heartbroken to be leaving them. But somehow I knew they would be all right, although I was sailing towards my own certain death. *Tavvavusi! Goodbye!* I sobbed as they faded from sight.

In yet another terrifying vision, I believed I was driving a team of dogs through a blinding blizzard, desperately trying to avoid running them into danger. Everywhere there were crevasses, cliffs, open water. The dogs were going to tumble or drown, and I was going to perish along with them.

Qimmiq ikajuq! Ahu! Dogs, stop! Help!

I deserve this! I shouted in the dream.

At one point, Tom informed me that I had been outside, walking in my sleep. Startled neighbours had come timidly out of their homes and watched me as I called out commands, wild-eyed, dressed in deerskin and wielding an imaginary whip above a team of invisible sled dogs. He said they were afraid to approach me when I was like that. During those sleepwalking episodes, I seemed to become someone else, not the quiet doctor who lived with his brother and family. At first, I did not believe him, because I had no memory of what I had done.

I was prescribed a course of medicine to calm me, stop the nightmares and put an end to the sleepwalking. The tonic helped smooth some of the edges, but my days and nights were filled with darkness. I had no desire to eat, to write letters, to listen to music or engage in any kind of human interaction. I lost myself and became a thin, pale shadow, not caring whether I lived or died.

→ *Hamilton*

[MARCH 1858]

One morning, Tom entered the kitchen as I sat half-dressed at the table, staring at the vapours rising from a steaming mug of tea. His wife and children had gone to the market; the solemn silence of the home was measured only by the ticking of a grandmother clock in the hallway.

"Johnny, listen to me." He spoke through gritted teeth, his voice strained. I didn't want to look at him, let alone hear his voice. I covered my ears with my hands.

"It's been seven months," he shouted. "The good Lord knows you've been through hell and back during these past few years, but I have to tell you something, and you must listen to me. It's well past time for you to start living again. Your mood is contagious. Helen and the boys are afraid to laugh, to disturb you in your fitful and melancholy state. We are all terrified you'll walk in your sleep again and frighten our family, the neighbours, and everyone else out there. And I'm sorry to say this, but I can hardly leave the house quickly enough in the mornings, just to get away from you, my brother who used to be so bright and full of spirit."

A flash of irritation came over me. "Are you saying you want me to leave, Tom? Is that what you are telling me? Of course, I will do just that, right this minute," I snapped. I jumped up from the chair and shoved it aside.

He took a deep breath and sighed. "Sit down now, Johnny. Sit and listen to me. Something has got to change. You must pull yourself out from under this dark cloud and get on with life. Can you imagine Papa and Mam looking down on you these past months, shaking their heads in disbelief? John, we Raes do not quit. Everyone experiences setbacks, failures, disappointments. Look at me! Richard and I have trouble enough on our hands with trying to keep our ships in use. It's not easy. Dick has worked hard to find his way back from his own despair, and I am proud of him. You can't just give up on life when things go wrong."

"William quit."

"That is surely the point, John! William quit, and we all — especially you — suffered horribly because of it. When life dealt him a hard hand, he chose the easy way out, because he didn't have the courage to face his losses and get on with things. You are the bravest man I know, so why are *you* giving up? For God's sake, brother! Are you going to roll over and surrender to bad luck the way William did? I, for one, would never forgive you if you did. I promise you that."

My eyes began to fill. I turned my head away so Tom wouldn't see the tears. I tried to say something, anything, but words failed me.

"Johnny, you are my best friend in the world. You have always been there for me, and I'd do anything for you. You were my hero, my older brother, the famous surgeon, scientist, hunter, the explorer who walked, sailed and sledged more than ten thousand miles in the Arctic, a courageous man who never gave up on anything he set out to do! We've lost enough in this family already, wouldn't you agree?"

His tone softened. "It seems as though you've gone somewhere and you're not coming back. Whenever you went away, I always believed you'd come back because you were stubborn, strong and brave. Now, I don't know . . . and it frightens me." Tom wiped at his own eyes.

"Damnit, Tom!" I brought my fist down hard on the table. It sounded like the report of a gun, and then, just as suddenly, the ticking of the clock was once again the only thing breaking the silence. We did not look at one another after my outburst of temper. Eventually, Tom turned around and straightened his back.

"I want you to come and look at something with me. Have the bath you so desperately need, shave, get dressed in clean clothes and meet me at the front door in thirty minutes."

"What on God's earth are you chattering on about? Have you lost your senses?"

"No. I may be many things, John, but crazy I am not."

Forty-five minutes later and much against my wishes, we were standing at a nearby corner, in front of a handsome stone house with a flagstone chimney. Large leaded-glass windows looked out onto views of a leafy garden. It was not a large home, but it projected the same kind of elegance as a stately mansion.

"It's for sale, Johnny, and I swear it's got your name on it."

"What in God's name are you talking about? I've never owned a house. Why would I start now when everything has just fallen apart? Everything's temporary, Tom. Everything. A snow house melts into the ground. A stone house crumbles with age. A ship sinks in a storm."

He stood fast, his expression firm, resolute. "Is there any harm in looking? You've got the time . . ."

"All right, I'll look at it, but that's all. Would that make you happy? I'm not in the frame of mind to make any commitments, you know. As I just said, nothing lasts anyway."

"Aye, but let's just have a poke around. There's nothing to be lost by looking."

———

One month later, I purchased that stone house at the corner of Bay and Nelson Streets. It was attractive enough, and Tom had put forward a compelling argument. He was right. The Raes should never quit, and it was time for me to concentrate on getting well enough to rebuild my life. I set up a small medical clinic in one of the ground-floor rooms. It took time, but eventually I grew stronger, recovered some of my former vitality and became known once again as the quiet, cheerful doctor. Neighbours slowly began to visit me for their ailments.

I re-entered the world of news and invention by subscribing to the *London Times* and *Hamilton Spectator*, along with assorted scientific and medical journals from overseas. I picked up my pen again and wrote articles for such prestigious periodicals as *Nature* and the Royal Geographical Society newsletter. I delivered lectures about my experiences with the Esquimaux to assorted interest groups. I took some pleasure in being a founding member of the Hamilton Association for the Advancement of Literature, Science and the Arts, for which I served as vice-president and then president.

I learned that there had been no communication from Captain McClintock, who had sailed for the Arctic aboard Lady Franklin's steam yacht the *Fox* in July 1857. Was something wrong? Had the vessel become beset in ice? Had they found anything related to the Franklin Expedition? I was curious but tried not to dwell on the recent past, knowing that those kinds of thoughts could resurrect the terrible darkness within me.

One day, a letter from London arrived in the post. I was surprised to see that it was from Gerald McIntosh, the King's College professor who had so kindly taken me under his wing at the Royal Society on the day the dreadful news of my Arctic discoveries was released to the public. His handwriting was much like the man himself, large and generous. He wrote that he had acquired my Hamilton address from Sir George Simpson. He advised me that he was planning to retire from teaching soon, that he had often wondered how I was getting along, and he hoped the arrival of his letter would find me well and cheerfully occupied in Canada West.

He mentioned that he and his wife had seen the play *The Frozen Deep* at the Royal Gallery of Illustration in Regent Street. It was authored by a man named Wilkie Collins, but heavily edited by his friend Charles Dickens, for the purpose of extolling the virtues of men in the Royal Navy. In the letter, he gave me his assurance that despite silly rumours, the character of a scheming Scottish servant had nothing to do with me. I was grateful for Gerald's kind thoughts and words, but I was still recovering from my illness and didn't wish to think about Charles Dickens or Wilkie Collins, or his play at that time. I finished reading the letter and tucked it away.

→ *United States*

[JULY 1858]

An invitation to accompany Sir George Simpson and fellow Scot, Edward "Bear" Ellice, on an expedition through the northern United States turned out to be an excellent tonic for what had ailed me. A man of great intelligence, political power and enterprise, "Bear" and I journeyed well together, departing from Toronto by rail and travelling to Minnesota, where we joined Sir George on a riverboat and travelled down the Mississippi River. The 4,500-mile journey took my mind far away from the intrusion of any melancholy thoughts and kept my spirits aloft.

– PART V –

Love, Courtship
& Marriage

[1858–1860]

→ *Toronto*

[OCTOBER 1858]

Upon my return to Hamilton, I was pleased to receive another invitation, this time to deliver a lecture to students of Natural Sciences at the University of Toronto. The requested topic was a personal favourite, and one I knew well: Patterns of Migratory Birds in the Arctic Region. I sorted through my overflowing boxes of papers and notebooks, most of which I had not touched for years. The process of preparing for the lecture by reviewing my meticulous notes and maps was quite satisfying. I looked forward to sharing my knowledge — and a generous portion of anecdotal material about my own observations and experiences in the frozen north — with a youthful and energetic audience.

After the lecture was over and I had answered many questions — most of which concerned my Arctic adventures, not birds — I was escorted to the spacious apartments of the Dean of Natural Sciences. Dr. Kitson was a genial and methodical man with silver hair, an easy smile and striking blue eyes; I liked him right away. After we finished a fine meal of roasted duck, fried potatoes and blood pudding, my host and I relaxed together in front of the fire, exchanging notes about ornithological matters and generally enjoying each other's company.

I was in no hurry to leave Toronto on Saturday morning so I decided to spend the day walking, exploring the city's lively neighbourhoods, and taking a lengthy stroll alongside the rocky shores of Lake Ontario. I felt better than I had in some time. When Dr. Kitson extended an invitation to me to stay another night, I readily accepted his kind offer.

On Sunday, I attended services at St. James Cathedral, a short walk from the university. It was an impressive structure, distinctly Gothic in design, with soaring ceilings, splendid buttresses and exquisitely stained glass windows. The day was bright and mild. Warm breezes drifting across the lake from the south brought unseasonably warm temperatures, which Hamiltonians often referred to as an "Indian Summer," the reason for which I never quite understood. My closest guess was that the expression had something to do with a longer harvest period, as well as more fish and game to catch for hungry families facing a long, harsh winter.

On that warm October morning at St. James Cathedral, the voices of the choir and congregation joined together in song as members of the clergy slowly processed up the centre aisle towards the sanctuary. When I turned with the others to watch the procession, I was struck by the profile of a slender, petite young woman across the aisle and one row behind mine. She was dressed in green, which suited her colouring very well. An unruly strand of curly red hair had broken free of its ties under her stylish hat, which appeared to be slightly off-centre, and I smiled at the thought of the whole affair — hat and hair — tumbling from atop her head with even the slightest movement. There was something exceptional about her posture, her bearing, the way the corner of her mouth appeared to be slightly upturned, as if she was on the verge of smiling.

I didn't know why, but I experienced the wishful and ridiculous sensation that she was intentionally revealing half of herself to me. Of course, this was not the case, because she had not yet — and perhaps never would — notice me. She turned and raised her face to sing, and in that moment, my heart missed a beat. Her green eyes caught me quite off guard; I think I jumped slightly when I saw them. I was relieved to see that she did not notice me looking at her, because I sensed that I momentarily lost control of the neutral expression on my own face, such was my feeling of surprise at seeing such an extraordinary young woman.

There could be no doubt that she was considerably younger than my forty-five years. I knew that my reaction to seeing her was inappropriate at best, yet despite her youth I found it nearly impossible to turn my eyes away from her and face the front of the cathedral once the procession had moved past our rows of pews.

It did not escape my notice that she was flanked by a straight-backed, red-haired father figure and a dark-haired, diminutive mother. I failed miserably in a promise to myself that I would not attempt to look at her again. At first, she didn't notice me casting furtive glances in her direction, but she must have been intuitive, because before long she seemed to sense, well, *something*. I could tell by the sudden squaring of her shoulders, a subtle turn of the cheek. To my chagrin, her glowering father seemed to catch on as well, from his position beside her on the aisle. He attempted to block her from view, which annoyed me greatly.

After the service, many members of the congregation gathered in the church hall to drink tea and socialize after the service. Although I knew no one, I joined the group, hoping to meet the beguiling young lady who had caught my fancy. I looked about for her in vain, declined the proffered tea, and slipped out the side entrance. I strode around to the front of the church where carriages were lining up to collect parishioners and take them home. Suddenly, I spotted her from behind, waiting for a carriage with her parents, two other young ladies and an adolescent boy. I approached the family group from the side, appearing to search for my own carriage, which did not exist.

They all turned as one and looked at me, expressionless. I pretended not to notice them and then, apparently absentmindedly, tipped my hat and said, "Good morning! Excellent service, what a fine day it is!" — all a bit too cheerfully, I realized afterwards. The young woman blinked in the bright sunlight, and my heart took several turns to the point where I thought she would be able to hear it thumping in my chest. I took half a step back. My face felt hot. It was not in my character to be quite so forward with strangers. I drew a deep breath and took the plunge.

"Please excuse me," I said to the father and mother, as if I had taken no notice of the children. "I thought I spotted my carriage."

The father was burly, his demeanour formal; his expression was anything but friendly. He nodded and looked away. I felt an utter fool standing there, hoping to strike up some kind of conversation. At that point, anything at all would have sufficed.

"I wonder if we have met previously, Sir." I lowered my hat to chest level, in a gesture of deference. "May I introduce myself?" I did not dare wait for an answer, because the chances were quite high that none would be forthcoming.

"I am Dr. John Rae of Hamilton. Did you attend my lecture at the university here in Toronto on Friday evening? There was a gentleman who — "

"No, I did not. You have mistaken me for someone else." The father of the young lady did not identify himself as he turned away.

"Oh, I beg your pardon." I pushed on, hoping that introducing myself as a lecturer at the university would warm him up a little. "You bear a strong resemblance to a member of the audience." I glanced over at the young woman, because now she was looking at me. Her eyes were exquisite, the colour of green sea glass. She did not look away; to my surprise and delight, she appeared to be suppressing a smile. If that awkward exchange was amusing her, there was hope for me.

"Good day to you." I replaced my hat, bowed and moved away, pretending to look elsewhere for my carriage. I took my time turning around again to look for her; when I finally did, the family was gone. I returned to the church hall, introduced myself to the minister and initiated a friendly chat, again using the ploy that I was quite convinced I had seen the man with the red hair at my Friday lecture, but did not catch his name . . . that he had attended today's service with his wife, three daughters, and son.

"Oh, you must be speaking of Major Thompson, Doctor."

The minister, a most congenial gentleman, revealed through casual conversation all I needed to know, and much more. Catherine "Kate" Thompson — only nineteen years of age! — was the youngest daughter of Major George Ash Thompson and his wife, Emma. The family had recently emigrated to Canada West from County Londonderry, Ireland. The major was now retired and the family had settled in Hamilton. I was ecstatic to learn that Kate Thompson, the lovely young woman with the unforgettable eyes was, in fact, my neighbour.

I was so elated that I picked up my bag and walked all the way home to Hamilton along the shores of Lake Ontario, a journey of more than six hours, with my feet barely touching the ground.

→ *Hamilton*

[OCTOBER 1858]

By good fortune and feigned coincidence, I bumped into Kate Thompson a week later at Sunday services in Hamilton. Although I greeted her as if we had just met again by chance, she had been squarely in my sights since worshippers began arriving at Christ's Church Cathedral thirty minutes earlier. Her parents were standing on the other side of the vestibule, chatting with parishioners. Kate was nearer to the entrance with her sisters; my heart skipped a beat when her green eyes glanced in my direction. I tipped my hat and bowed. "Good day."

The charming corners of her mouth turned upwards ever so subtly when she saw me. I nodded at the other two young women, hoping I did not appear too awkward. I felt like a silly schoolboy in her presence.

She held out her hand in greeting. Her grasp was pleasantly firm. "Good day to you, Sir." This was the first time I had heard her voice, although I had been trying to imagine the sound of it for a week. It was strong and clear, with a lovely Irish lilt.

I took an awkward step towards initiating a conversation between us, aware that she could turn her back on me at any moment. "What a coincidence!" I said, too enthusiastically. "John Rae," I introduced myself. "I believe I spoke with your father outside of St. James Cathedral in Toronto last Sunday."

"Yes, indeed," she replied. "Doctor Rae, is it?"

"Yes, Miss . . ."

"I am Kate Thompson," she offered without a trace of shyness. "And these are my sisters, Emily and Sarah. My brother William is over there."

"I am honoured to meet you." I tipped my hat again in their direction, but my eyes seemed to be irretrievably locked onto Kate's. One of the girls placed a gloved hand to her mouth, and suppressed a giggle.

"My family lives here in Hamilton," she said.

"Aye, as do mine. Do you attend services here every week?"

"Usually," she replied. "We were visiting with our cousins in Toronto when you spoke to my father on Sunday." She blinked, just as she did in Toronto, and my heart took yet another turn. How could such an ordinary act as the blink of an eyelid elicit such a strong reaction in a man's heart? Time seemed to move more slowly for me when I watched her eyes.

Our light conversation was barely underway when Kate's father interrupted. He was clearly not amused by his daughter speaking to this older man. The major took Kate firmly by the arm; I thought I saw her flinch slightly at his grip. Wordless and staring straight ahead, Major Thompson led his family into the church. I dared not sit anywhere within sight of them and annoy him further. I took a seat at the rear and exited just before the service had ended, wondering if Kate would look for me a few minutes later as the family proceeded along the aisle. I did not stay for the post-service gathering nor did I linger outside, because I did not want to jeopardize my chances of meeting her again by making myself too visible to her father.

My thoughts remained scattered because the image of Kate was repeatedly surfacing in my mind. Later that day, I attempted to focus on Tom's words as we sat in front of the fire in my home at Bay Street, discussing Rae Brothers & Company business. Tom had good reason to be worried about the stability of the company because more money was flowing out of the venture than into it. I had invested a modest sum from my reward purse after I arrived from London, but I experienced a further loss of money with the drowning of the *Iceberg*. I was reluctant to invest more in Rae Brothers because I was not convinced of the viability of a sizeable shipbuilding enterprise on the Great Lakes.

Tom held his hand to his forehead. "The numbers do not look promising, Johnny. You knew it three years ago, didn't you? I can't believe I was naïve enough to think we could keep all seven of them moving most of the time around the Great Lakes, up the St. Lawrence River, across the Atlantic and back." Tom rubbed his forehead hard, as if he could banish thoughts of potential bankruptcy.

"How many vessels do you have on the market right now?"

"Four, including the *John Rae*. This is a terrible time to be selling ships. Winter will soon be upon us, and the market is already saturated with vessels for sale. The bank is sending letters . . ."

"Let's ask Dick to join us today," I offered. "We three can surely put our heads together and figure out some way of lightening the load at the shipyard. Maybe we can look into selling ships in other markets — the United States and even further south to the Caribbean, perhaps — "

Without warning, my personal thoughts intruded again, and I couldn't hold back. Impulsively, I interrupted myself.

"Tom. How do you know when you are really in love?"

"What?" Tom moved his hand away from his forehead and shook his head.

"I am quite serious. Well, I think I might be. I don't know really. You see, I think I'm in love, but I hardly know the girl. I just can't get her out of my mind." I took a sip of tea and looked out the window, embarrassed by my eagerness.

Tom reached out and clapped me on the shoulder. "Well, I'll be damned, brother! It's about bloody time! You've been in love with yourself for too long! Maybe now you'll stop spending so much time in front of the mirror," he teased.

"Well, I — "

"Ah! Don't bother. Tell me about her. I need to hear some good news today."

I told Tom of the moment when I first laid eyes on Kate's profile in church, how exquisite her face had looked from the side, her nose straight and pert, how the corner of her mouth turned up ever so slightly as if it were just on the verge of breaking into a smile, how everything about her seemed to be so small and beautiful, except for a generous bosom —

"Johnny, you fell in love with *what*? Come on, don't be ridiculous! You can lust after lovely breasts, but you can't fall in love with them. You have to look at the whole person, and — "

"Stop it!" I shouted, laughing. "I met her, Tom! I spoke to her! I met her officer father. An unpleasant-looking Irishman, at that . . ."

"All right. All right. Calm down, now. Where does she live?"

"Here in Hamilton."

"What's her name?"

"Catherine — Kate — Thompson. Her father is Major George Ash Thompson, originally from County Londonderry in Ireland. He was a career military man with the British army."

"Aye. I know of him. Red hair? Rather stiff? A dour sort of fellow?"

"Must be him. I tried to strike up a conversation, but he wanted nothing to do with me."

"I heard he is unwell, ruined by the drink. A veteran of too many

British wars. Unfortunate." He brightened. "And what about Kate? How many times have you seen her?"

"Twice. Once at church services in Toronto and again this morning, here at Christ's Church Cathedral."

"Well, it's quite simple then, isn't it? Continue going to Sunday services, and you'll know soon enough if you're in love. Perhaps you'll eventually learn if she fancies *you*."

"She strikes me as someone who is confident about herself, not afraid to speak her mind. And she's friendly. At least, I don't think she hates me. Not yet, anyway." I couldn't hide my stupid smile, so I looked out the window again.

"Tom, will you, Helen and the children accompany me to services next Sunday? I'll ask Marion if she'll bring her family as well."

"So you want the lot of us to be your personal entourage?" he laughed. "D'you think we'd give you an air of respectability in Major Thompson's eyes? We'll see. I can't promise you that we'd all be on our best behaviour, though. There are quite a few of us, you know — and don't forget, we're Orcadians — a bit of a wild bunch, sometimes!"

I cleared my throat. "The situation might be sensitive for another reason, Tom. There is a wee problem you should be aware of. It's about Kate. Well, it's not a problem with *her*, but there's one significant difference between us."

"What's that?"

"I think she is quite a bit younger than I."

"How young?"

"Perhaps half my age."

Tom raised his eyebrows and shook his head again. "Aye, my foolish older brother, I agree with you. You may well have a problem, especially with her father. You never were one to keep things simple, were you?"

Our brother Dick joined us soon after. We three spent the rest of the day discussing the excess number of their ships in port, and how to prevent Rae Brothers & Company from slipping into receivership. Every so often, Tom would catch my eye and wink at me, a small enough act, but one which I found exceedingly annoying.

→ *Hamilton*
[1858–1859]

Under the dark cloud of her ailing and disapproving father, I gingerly began to strike up a friendship with Kate. There I was, well into middle age, thinking of little else than attending Sunday services at Christ's Church Cathedral, with the hope of seeing that lovely young woman who made me feel weak in the knees. As a spiritual man, I had always enjoyed the ritual of engaging in communal worship. As a besotted man, I felt light-headed just knowing that Kate was in the same building. I trimmed my beard and moustaches to a more fashionable length, hoping to make myself appear more youthful. Various members of my family were present on most Sundays. I was glad for their company, and it was reassuring to think that Kate and her parents might at least see that I was not an uncivilized man.

To my chagrin, Kate's stern and worried father continued to herd his wife and children away from me, but his efforts were destined to backfire. Kate began to take regular notice of me, and Major Thompson's actions only served to add fuel to our mutual attraction. We became quite adept at communicating through glances, winks, the subtle lifting of eyebrows, half smiles and gestures, to a point where we developed our own secret but rather efficient language.

In December, I arranged with a nephew for the first of a series of letters to be secretly delivered to Kate after Sunday services, to which she promptly responded with lengthy replies. I devoured every letter she wrote to me; her words became increasingly friendly and engaging as we came to know each other through that age-old method of communication. At the end of January we made arrangements for a secret assignation, away from the church and her father's prying eyes.

When we first met alone in a snow-covered gazebo at the Royal Botanical Gardens, my hand was trembling when Kate reached out to grasp it in greeting. Embarrassed, I loosened my grip and her gloved fingers slipped away.

"If I am to be honest about it, I'm a bit nervous, Miss Thompson," I sputtered. "Well, quite nervous, actually." I had never been very articulate when conversing with pretty ladies, but this was downright humiliating.

"I shouldn't be surprised that you are uncomfortable, Dr. Rae," she replied. "My father has gone out of his way to cause you great discomfort, which is an embarrassment for me as well. Despite his unpleasant behaviour, though, I see no reason why you and I cannot be friends."

Her clear voice had that beguiling Irish lilt. Its musicality both thrilled me and soothed my nerves at the same time.

"Well then," I replied, "if we are indeed to be friends, please call me John."

Her face lit up, her green eyes dancing. "Good. John it is. And you, John, may call me Kate."

Our secret meetings — along with daily letter-writing — took on their own rhythm as the seasons changed. By the time of spring's early arrival in 1859, hiding our growing love for one another had become too challenging for us. Something had to change, so I decided that it was my obligation, as Kate's suitor, to initiate face-to-face contact with Major George Ash Thompson and declare my love for his daughter.

"Kate, my dear, we can't go on like this. We are both adults, yet we are pretending we hardly know each other. I want to meet your father soon."

She pulled away from me, aghast. "Oh John, my father is the most rigid man I have ever known! As much as I am growing to know and care for you, he apparently considers you to be uncivilized, unsuitable and far, far too old for me." She blushed. "I'm sorry. I should not have said that. He has read about you in the newspapers."

I held up my hands. "Kate, I am guilty on all counts, except for the unsuitable part. I am also a gentleman, even though he does not consider me to be one. It's time for me to tell him about my feelings for you."

Kate placed her hand on my arm. "He is not well."

"I am aware of that, my dear. I have noticed the yellow cast in his eyes."

"He is an angry man. He may be unkind to you."

"No more so than he has been thus far. What else am I to do? I have fallen in love with you. If you think you feel the same way about me, we should not be hiding it as if we're committing some crime. We've been seeing each other for months now. Tell me, are we harming others by wanting to be with each other? I have never approved of deception, Kate. I don't want to do this anymore."

She tilted her head and stared at me, her green eyes wide. "Do you really love me, John? You just said you've fallen in love with me."

"I'm afraid I'm a fallen man, Kate," I laughed, "and I suspect that my condition is incurable."

"Good Lord!" she cried. "Oh, now that you've said it, I guess I can say it as well. I love you." She threw her arms around my neck and kissed me. "I love you, too. There, I said it again! I love you!"

"Let me arrange to see your father now, so we can come out of hiding. Hold on. Do you need some time to think about it first?"

She paused, looked away for a moment and laughed. "I'll be sure to hide all his weapons somewhere before you knock at the door."

"Sensible idea, you lovely creature."

One of the many things that drew me to Kate like a magnet to metal was the fact that she was indeed an exquisite creature with a beautiful heart, and not simply a lovely creation. Kate was the real cure for the sense of rejection and loneliness which had ailed me since my return from the Arctic.

Her mother Emma responded favourably to my note requesting an interview with her husband. I was surprised that she approved of her daughter having a romance with an aging explorer who had been embroiled in public controversy. Perhaps she was able to see something of value in me, beyond my mixed reputation. More likely, she knew her daughter well enough to realize that opposing Kate's wishes could result in an estrangement — which would be heart-rending for any mother. In Mrs. Thompson's reply, she promised that she would urge the major to have the courtesy to meet with me and listen to what I wished to say. Of course, she knew what the subject of the meeting would be.

I could just imagine his response when she approached him: "I already *know* what he is going to say, Emma! What in the devil's name is the point?" He finally agreed to a brief meeting in his house — his territory — at an hour which suited him best.

—

He awaited me in the spacious, high-ceilinged parlour of the Thompson home, just three city blocks from my own house. His back was turned to me when Mrs. Thompson showed me into the room, and I was instantly reminded of Sir James Graham displaying the same sort of distaste for me at Admiralty House some five years earlier. When Kate's father finally turned around to face me, I offered him my hand, which he brusquely declined. He was clearly in no mood for pleasantries. The first words he uttered confirmed that he considered any discussion with me to be a battlefield, and since the battle was taking place on his home ground, he wasted no time in firing the first shot.

"*Leave her alone!*" he thundered. I was not surprised to notice that he had fortified himself for our meeting with some form of spirits. I was also no stranger to the politics of intimidation, and I knew there could be only one response: never back down.

"I understand that this is difficult for you, Sir, and I must tell you that I sincerely appreciate your agreement to meet with me this evening." He scowled and shook his head, because he refused to believe that he had agreed; he had only given in to stop his wife from badgering him about it.

His hostile expression had little effect on my enthusiasm. "I can assure you of my absolute sincerity when I tell you that I have grown very fond of your daughter. Kate, for her part, has indicated to me that she shares my feelings — "

"What do *you* know of feelings? You are every bit as hard-hearted as those man-eating Esquimaux whose company you favour! I've heard eyewitness accounts of you wandering the streets of Hamilton at night, a madman clad in animal skins, hallucinating and shouting incoherently at nothing. Go back to Orkney or the Arctic where you belong! Why did you come chasing after Kate that day in Toronto when you knew nothing about her, nothing of us! Leave my daughter and my family alone!"

I had been expecting something unpleasant, but his attack against my life among the Esquimaux and my personal values caused me to see red. I felt my face flushing with the heat of anger, but I drew a deep breath; this was not the time to lose my self-control. I was also quite sure that Kate, her mother, sisters and brother were listening on the other side of the parlour doors, because I heard a stifled gasp after he shouted at me. I held my temper.

"You might feel differently if you know more about my history and character, Major — "

His dark eyes were ablaze with anger. "*You* are the wild man who accuses Royal Navy men — the salt of the earth — of consuming each other's flesh, for God's sake! You set out to single-handedly destroy the impeccable reputation of Her Majesty's finest . . . how dare you?"

Even though I had expected that particular volley to be fired, it stung me deeply, coming from the father of the woman I loved. I stood firmly in place and never took my eyes off him.

"Oh yes! I know enough about you," he continued. "Rumour has it that you sleep with Esquimaux men's wives, that you take their women and your bastard children into your ridiculous snow castles! You are a filthy old man, and I'll not stand for you having any contact with my nineteen-year-old daughter who, by the way, is young enough to be your own child, God forbid!"

"That is enough!" I roared. The force of my shout surprised the unsteady major, causing him to grab hold of the back of a chair to prevent himself from losing his balance and falling. He stood fast, swaying with rage and indignation. I held my ground, unbending in the face of his hostility, ready to duck if he tried to throw a punch. "I shall say one final thing to you before I take my leave, Major. Your daughter is an adult now, old enough to make her own decisions. If she chooses to spend time with me, then it is God's will — and Kate's — and it will be one battle you cannot win. Good night."

The major seemed to be struck silent, still holding onto the back of the chair as I reached for the door. I heard the sounds of scurrying in the hallway, as the eavesdroppers scattered. A servant awaited me with my coat and hat. I slipped quietly out the front door and vanished into the night. There was nothing more to be said.

Monday

Dearest Kate,

I heard sounds in the hallway at your home this evening, prompting me to think that you most likely overheard the brief conversation (if one can call it that) between your father and me. Your father has made assumptions about me that are, quite simply, not true.

I do not hold him to blame. I understand why he draws certain conclusions from chatter about my unconventional life in the Arctic. I also sympathize with his wish to protect his beloved daughter from a suitor who is more than twice her age.

I ask you to trust me when I say that I never have, and never will, lead a "double life."

I have no personal connections to women or children in Scotland, London, the Arctic, or here in Hamilton. I have no doubt that those who know me will attest to this fact if your father wishes to interrogate others and further investigate my background.

As for the other subject, I will not waver in my belief that the Esquimaux testimony was accurate. I will stand by the report I submitted to the British government until I have drawn my last breath.

As I told you, I have fallen in love with you. There is no hurry for making decisions about the future. In time, I hope that the dust will settle.

Meanwhile, I carry you dear to my heart, lovely Kate.

John

Her reply was swift and to the point. I was greatly relieved to read that her father's temper had not caused her to bend. If anything, she sounded more resolute, but patient nonetheless, and I admired her for those qualities. Patience had never been one of my strong points.

Monday

Dearest John,

You know that I, too, have fallen in love with you.

Even though my father is unwilling to see you as the honest and kind man you are, I feel I have come to know you well. My mother has begged him to learn more about you, and I can see that his refusals are growing weaker. I worry about his health, but he is the only one who can take measures for improving it.

I carry you dear to my heart as well, John. I do not want to be parted from you, ever. Know this, my love, and as you say, all will be clear in the fullness of time.

Your Katie

We continued to meet one another as the months went by, while Major Thompson's health worsened. By early August, he was no longer able to attend Sunday services, which was a blessing in one way, because I was spared from being on the receiving end of his angry stares. On the other hand, it was unfortunate that he was losing his battle with his health, which was a source of great anguish for his family.

→ *Fort Garry, Manitoba*
[SEPTEMBER 1859]

The letter from Kate arrived hours before an elaborate hunting party, including Sir George Simpson, James Carnegie the Earl of Southesk, Lord Milton and a gentleman named Dr. Cheadle, was about to embark on a lengthy expedition in the regions around the Red River, under my leadership. The last of the preparations had been attended to when a clerk handed the envelope to me. I recognized the handwriting immediately.

August 26, 1859

My Dearest John:

I hope this letter finds you well.

My father claims to have discovered proof that you have several "country wives," native women who give you comfort and with whom you have children, in the regions around Hudson Bay. My mother, sisters and I have begged him to speak to those who really know you, but as a result of acquiring this so-called information, he has forbidden me from ever again seeing you or communicating with you. He has laid down an order that if I do not sever ties with you immediately, I will be turned out of the family home, removed from his will and shunned — for life — by all of our relatives.

My heart is broken, John. When I finally fall to sleep at night, I soon awaken with a start as if something terrible has just happened. The sight of food repels me, and just when I think I cannot possibly shed even one more tear, the flood begins again. You have promised me that you have no country wives, and I have believed you. I try hard to hold onto my faith in your words —

Papa is resolute in his decision and, alas, I am well and truly lost, thinking of running away from here but to where, I do not know. Whatever happens, remember that I want to believe there is no truth in his accusations.

Your Kate

I stuffed the letter into the pocket of my coat and looked around. Fort Garry was a beehive of activity; our hunting party was being as- sembled with horses, carts, provisions and munitions. Sir George ap- proached me, leaning heavily on a cane for support. He was no longer in condition to engage in physical exertions, but his enthusiasm was as boundless as ever.

"Well, my boy," he trumpeted, "this should be a fine day for our de- parture, with a cool breeze to keep some of the flying insects away from us. I shall be quite comfortable riding in a cart, cushioned by Company blankets. Wouldn't want to miss this adventure for the world, you know!"

I pulled the crumpled letter from my pocket and shook it, taking care not to let him see the feminine handwriting. "Sir George, I'm afraid that an emergency has arisen at home . . ."

The excitement drained from his expression. "Has someone taken ill?"

"Yes, you could say that, and this matter is very serious indeed. I deeply regret that I have to take my leave from this journey at once — "

"You are leaving us?" He looked incredulous. I had never done such a thing before.

"Yes, Sir, I'm afraid I must. Our travelling party is well organized, and the supplies are more than adequate. As you know, we have hired the very best guides, interpreters and hunters. I shall have a word with them, and then I will express my regrets to our British travelling companions."

He shook his head. "This is quite out of character for you, John. I suppose there's no point in trying to change your mind."

"No, Sir. I am sorry, but the situation is urgent, and my presence is required immediately. I wish you the very best on this journey."

I felt badly for causing disappointment in the others, but their lives would continue as usual, and mine was on the verge of another collapse. I could not afford to let that happen. St. Paul was several days' journey south from Fort Garry with a pair of horses, and from there, I could return to Hamilton by train.

I could not find it in my heart to forgive Major Thompson for his vigorous attempts to ruin his youngest daughter's happiness, but neither did I wish him ill health. I was saddened to learn upon my arrival that he had passed away just two days earlier, and the Thompson home was in a state of mourning. His body, dressed in full military uniform with his sword in its scabbard at his side, was on view in the parlour. Kate held on tightly to my hand and together we approached the open casket. He looked younger in death than he had in life; the deep lines on his face had all but disappeared. He had been, after all, a man who had survived many battles, the second to last one being the protection of his loved ones. He had lost his final fight against the demon alcohol, which was a tragic end indeed.

"I pray that you will find comfort and peace with God, Major Thompson," I whispered. Throughout the funeral service and burial at Christ's Church Cemetery, Kate and I seldom left each other's side. When the formalities were over, her mother suggested that I return with the family to the Thompson home for some coffee, a generous invitation which I did not refuse.

Later, I noticed that the others, including Kate, had excused themselves from the parlour, leaving me alone with Mrs. Thompson. Kate's mother wasted no time. She brushed at her skirts with her hands, fixed me with her green eyes, and came straight to the point.

"Dr. Rae, you love our daughter very much, don't you?"

I felt my cheeks growing warm. "Aye, Mrs. Thompson, I do. With all my heart. I — "

"Why?"

"I beg your pardon?"

Tears came to her eyes. "I'm sorry for being so forward. Quite clumsy of me, really. It's just that with George's passing, I believe we can speak freely now. I am tired of pretending not to notice how challenging Kate's friendship with you has been. These have been such difficult times for all of us. I do not think you would have dropped what you were doing and returned to Hamilton from so far away, if you didn't love her."

I leaned forward in my chair. "You are right, Mrs. Thompson, and I don't blame you at all for asking me why I love your daughter." She sighed, as if she felt some relief. The forbidden topic was open for discussion now, and I could feel my own muscles relax.

"She is a beautiful woman, I'll grant you that," I said, and she nodded in agreement. "But my feelings for Kate run much deeper than what is so obvious to the eye. There is something unique about her spirit, her sense of confidence, her friendly nature and intelligence." I placed my hand over my heart. "She touches me right here, as if our souls have known one another for a long time. To be honest, I am at quite a loss to explain it . . ."

She wiped at her eyes. "I think I understand, Dr. Rae. I believe George once felt the same way about me. He wasn't well, you know . . ."

She looked directly into my eyes. "George wrote to your friends from York Factory, James and Letitia Hargrave, to inquire about your northern activities. I never saw their reply, so I will ask you directly. *Did* you ever have country wives, Dr. Rae? More to the point, would you tell me if you did?"

I cleared my throat. "I have no doubt that James and Letitia would have vouched for my good character. As you know, I lived and worked in the Arctic for more than twenty years. It would be dishonest of me to tell you I was celibate throughout that period. But never, ever did I take a so-called country wife, and that is God's truth."

"Is it possible that you fathered children in the Arctic?"

"I am sure I did not. If such a thing had happened, I would certainly have known. In the world of the Esquimaux, secrets do not exist. Information travels with great speed and accuracy."

"You are so much older than my Kate . . ."

I shook my head. "I know. It is a fact which I have no power to change, although I wish I were twenty years younger, believe me!"

We both smiled. "I promise you, Mrs. Thompson, that if Kate will agree to take me as her husband, and if you grant us permission to marry, I will honour her, cherish her, be faithful to her and take care of her for the rest of my life."

"Please, call me Emma."

"Only if you will agree to call me John."

We were both on our feet now. Emma took my arm. "Let's see what Kate has to say about all of this, shall we?"

At that moment, Kate threw open the doors to the parlour. It was clear from her smile that she had been eavesdropping again.

"My dear Kate, the walls in this house certainly *do* have ears, don't they!" I cried.

➔ *Hamilton*

[OCTOBER 1859]

Shortly after Major Thompson's death, it was reported that Captain Francis Leopold McClintock — who had left England aboard Lady Franklin's *Fox* in the summer of 1857 — had safely returned to London. The steam yacht had been twice beset in Arctic pack ice, and the captain was praised for his fortitude and persistence, because he had apparently wasted no time in putting his previous overland Arctic experience to good use. He wisely employed a skilled Esquimaux interpreter during his travels and gathered more information from the natives concerning the fate of the Franklin Expedition. Captain McClintock had lost three of his men on the two-year journey, but he and his crew did not return empty-handed. They arrived with more Franklin Expedition relics he had acquired from the Esquimaux, along with a Royal Navy sledge and whaling boat containing the skeletal remains of two of Franklin's men.

A Royal Navy document retrieved by one of McClintock's men from a stone cairn at Victory Point — on the northwest coast of King William Island — proved to be of great value in piecing together the mystery of the party's disappearance. In May 1847, Lieutenant Graham Gore of the *Erebus* had noted on the standard-form document that although the two ships were beset in ice, there was no great cause for concern. He had added, "Sir John Franklin commanding the expedition. All well." But the men's situation must have dramatically deteriorated after the note was cached in the cairn.

By the following year, all was clearly not well. On April 25, 1848, the document had apparently been retrieved from the cairn and annotated in the margins by a member of the crew: "Sir John Franklin died on the 11th June 1847; and the total loss by deaths in the expedition to this date has been 9 officers and 15 men." What on earth had caused so many deaths — including the commander — in two years? It was unfortunate that the author of the note provided no information about what had killed the men. Perhaps the reasons for such a great number of deaths in a short period of time had been as much of a mystery to the men of the *Erebus* and *Terror* as it was to others when the record was found and published.

If that melancholy news were not disturbing enough, the next line quoted in the *Times* was bone-chilling in light of what had been previously revealed to me by the Esquimaux I had interviewed. According to the annotated document, the *Erebus* and *Terror* had later been "deserted" by the crews. *Terror* captain Francis Moira Rawdon Crozier had then begun leading one hundred and five "souls" south, in search of rescue: "— and start (on) to-morrow, 26th, for Back's Fish River." I pressed my palm to my brow and sighed. "Back's Fish River," I said aloud, recalling the Esquimaux' stories about seeing marching Kabloonans in 1854.

Those poor Royal Navy men had indeed been trying to get to the mouth of Back's Great Fish River in 1850, just as In-nook had told us, with Francis Crozier in command. I recalled my difficult meeting with Sir James Graham at Admiralty House. He asked me if I had any ideas concerning the identity of the officer found under the overturned boat at the place where many men died, and I had replied that I did not. In the absence of a body, it was pointless to engage in conjecture about who may have been the last of the British men to fall. Identities were of no consequence anyway, because at the end of a torturous attempt to reach safety, all of them had suffered unspeakable hardship and perished.

Sir John Franklin, commander of the expedition, had died in June 1847, when John Richardson and I were in the Arctic searching for the ships and men. At least he had been spared the agony of that terrible death march. How I wished Sir John Richardson and I — or anyone at all — had managed to save them. Waves of melancholy washed over me, and I was once again reminded of the darkness in my heart.

Her Majesty awarded Captain McClintock £3,000 and a knighthood. I was sorely disappointed when a short time later, he suddenly declared himself to have been the first person to ascertain the fate of the Franklin Expedition. To my horror, Sir John Richardson publicly agreed with him, as if my findings had never happened. What in God's name caused the Admiralty to forget the truth, which was my own discovery in 1854, and for which they had awarded me £10,000?

When I read that McClintock's absurd announcement went unchallenged, I was even more infuriated. It was disappointingly clear that a member of the Royal Navy stood much taller than anyone else in the eyes of the Crown. There was nothing to be done about politics in London, however, and by then my eyes were looking ahead to life as a married man who would one day — soon, I hoped — be the proud father of a good number of little Raes.

→ *Toronto*

[JANUARY 25, 1860]

A tremendous snowstorm was well underway when I slipped a gold wedding ring onto the slender finger of Catherine Jane Alicia Thompson at St. James Cathedral. The cavernous church was icy cold, but our mutual joy warmed the group of family members who gathered there to witness our marriage ceremony. Just over two years had passed since Kate and I first spotted each other — in that very building — on a sunny October morning.

After the reception, we lay in each other's arms in a grand suite at the Rossin House Hotel on King Street, watching the snowflakes swirling outside the hotel window. We laughed about how my life had now changed from sleeping in self-constructed snow houses, with howling winds and –50° temperatures outside.

"You know," I mused, "I liked living in the Arctic wilderness. There were periods of utter silence, broken by the sounds of ice cracking, the calls of migrating geese, the howling of wolves, barking foxes, thundering hooves of migrating caribou many miles in the distance. The Esquimaux say they can hear hissing and crackling sounds made by the aurora borealis."

"Really? Is it possible that northern lights can be heard?"

"I've listened for it, Katie, but I've never heard it myself. Quite extraordinary, when you think about it. I wonder if they have a heightened sensitivity to sound, because their survival has always depended on it."

Kate stroked my beard with the back of her hand. "Tell me about walking on snowshoes, dear. They resemble paddles more than shoes to my eyes, but you have travelled hundreds of miles on them. What did it feel like to walk on top of the snow, Mr. Arctic Fox?"

"You can sprint when the load is light and the snow is soft enough, but you have to be careful about where you place the shoes with each step. If the surface is crusty, it's easy to lose your balance, and the strands of fine leather mesh can snap occasionally. I made my own snowshoes under the guidance of the natives. Come to think of it, Kate, we are both skilled at sewing. You produce award-winning needlework, and I have been known to work well with leather and beads!"

She half sat up, her sea-glass eyes twinkling. "But how on earth can a person walk on paddles?"

I laughed. "You've seen my snowshoes. The tips of them are turned up, for traction. You set off at a steady pace by pushing off with your toes, and lifting up the front of your feet. The rest just seems to follow along. Someday, you can try it for yourself. We'll have a race against one another!"

"Oh, I think I would be terrible at doing that! You'd just leave me lying at the starting line, on freezing clouds of snow!" Her face turned serious. "Tell me, though: what was it about walking on snow and ice for thousands of miles in the far north that you loved so much? At least, enough that you waited until now to settle down?"

I looked up at the ceiling and thought for a moment. "I am not sure I can describe it, really."

"Try anyway."

"Well, I think a long day's march on snowshoes is about the finest exercise a man can take, Katie. For me, the feeling of moving forward at a fast pace is exhilarating."

She giggled. "Does it make you feel strong?"

"Yes, and healthy, alive. The further I walk or travel on snowshoes, the more rhythmic it becomes, and I can cover long distances before any sort of fatigue sets in. My body seems to recall a set of instructions when I'm moving like that, and I lose my sense of time."

"What do you think about?"

"To be honest, I don't think about much at all. The past doesn't exist when I'm walking on the snow, nor does the future, come to think of it. The moment is on my mind, along with how to navigate the next bend, where rocky obstacles may be hiding under layers of snow, the position of the sledge I'm dragging behind me, all those sorts of immediate things. I am more alert when I'm on the move; my senses are heightened to what's around me. When I'm not travelling alone, my habit is to think about the others travelling with me, listening to the sounds of their breathing, checking on them, so I know where they are and the condition they're in."

"And when the weather's especially harsh?"

"D'you mean when it's blowing a gale and the ice is driving needles into your eyes?"

"Yes. What kinds of thoughts are you having then?"

"Placing one foot in front of the other, and keeping my head down as much as I can without falling on my face."

"Do you think you draw pleasure from physical hardship, John?"

"Aye, I suppose I do, love. Stretching beyond my limits of endurance is like a drug for me, as strange as it may sound."

She kissed me then, and suddenly, I was thinking about nothing else at all.

⇢ *London*

[APRIL 1860]

"John dear, our European honeymoon has seemed like a most wonderful dream." Kate was gazing out the window of our hotel room in Kensington, watching the continuous parade of horses, carriages and pedestrians flowing by.

"You know, I never felt settled in Hamilton," she said. "When my parents told me we'd be moving to Canada West after Papa's retirement, I was miserable. This side of the Atlantic is where I feel at home. Everything over there seems so new and boring, so lacking in character and history . . ."

"Well, North America is still undergoing major settlement, Katie. But I agree with you. Although I like having family nearby in Hamilton, there's an absence of antiquity in the buildings and on the streets. I wonder if we should consider settling over here. I don't know about living in London . . ." I kissed her. "How about Orkney?" I held my breath and waited for her response. She pulled away, surprised.

"Orkney?" she cried. "John dear, from everything you've told me about the Orkneys, I can only picture a place that's wild and remote! I think of the wind blowing everything sideways, and you say there are hardly any trees. I know you had a happy childhood there, but it sounds so bleak. It's one thing to visit for a holiday in fine weather, but I just can't imagine myself adapting to that sort of life . . ."

I realized that I had taken the discussion a step too far. My sister Marion's words from six years earlier floated up from my memory and pricked my conscience. "I suppose my longing to return to Orkney sounds selfish."

"Orkney may be lovely during the summer months, but I can't imagine living there when the gales of winter set in." Her expression brightened. "London's so lively and colourful with all the carriages, the shops, the theatres. We've only just returned from our honeymoon, darling. There's no rush to make decisions just yet, is there? Let's take some time to think about all the possibilities."

PART VI

Enterprises &
Family Life

[1860–1880]

A few weeks later, a familiar face greeted me when I entered one of the reading rooms at the Royal Society in Somerset House. Gerald McIntosh heaved his generous body out of a leather wing chair and waved me over.

"Good Lord, if it isn't my old friend, John Rae!"

As we shook hands, I apologized for not replying to his letter. "Gerald, these past few years have been busy, indeed. I've been travelling and assisting my brothers with their business in Canada West. I hope you'll forgive me."

"Of course I forgive you, John! Come, have a seat. It's good to see you. My heavens, you look well. Your retirement from the Hudson's Bay Company must be agreeing with you."

He held up his pipe for emphasis, but I could see that now it was empty of tobacco, most likely on doctor's orders. "I still participate in the odd expedition for them," I replied, "and for other organizations. I lead the occasional hunting party in North America as well, which I enjoy."

"Good, good! Work keeps us honest, I always say. Now, let's catch up for a few minutes. I'm sure you are aware that Lady Franklin and her supporters are still tirelessly pushing to convince the authorities that Sir John officially discovered the missing link in the Northwest Passage . . ."

I sighed. "Gerald, Captain McClintock's report of last year — and the testimony of the Esquimaux — clearly indicated that the *Erebus* and *Terror* sailed south on Victoria Strait, to the west of a potential passage — "

"Hold on, John. It is now quite certain that the ships were trapped by pack ice and never did manage to achieve the goal, but tell me, do you think they may have passed an entrance to the link before they reached Victoria Strait?"

"Aye, I suspect they did, but the entrance may have been filled with ice at the time. The conditions can change dramatically from one year to the next. My own exploration of the area between the Boothia Peninsula and King William Island revealed the distinct possibility of there being such a route, which may at times be free of ice for part of the short summer season. I charted the co-ordinates on a map."

He looked astonished. "Have you told anyone of this?"

"I informed the first lord of the Admiralty in 1854, but he and the official cartographers expressed no interest in discussing my findings. The co-ordinates I submitted were excluded from being recognized on the Admiralty's maps." I waved a dismissive hand, because I was loath to resurrect the topic. The series of events following my return from York Factory could not be altered. In addition, I did not wish to discuss my disastrous *Iceberg* project with anyone but those who were closest to me.

"John, I hope you will forgive an aging mathematician and amateur historian for being so forward, but there is something about the discovery of the passage that confuses me."

"Feel free to ask me questions, Gerald, but be warned that I may not have the answers you are looking for."

He rubbed his hands together. "Do you know that five years ago, the government paid £10,000 to Captain Robert McClure and awarded him a knighthood for discovering the missing link in the Northwest Passage?"

"Aye, I am aware of it."

"Well, I've always felt the story of his discovery was confusing, because he had left his ship behind. It is my understanding that the link was meant to be navigable by boat. Is that correct?"

"That was the objective all along. The Admiralty made it absolutely clear that the passage was meant to be navigated by a sea-going vessel. When I charted its possible location in 1854, I did not have a boat in which to sail it. It is ironic that a year later, Captain McClure was rewarded for *walking — not sailing —* across a proposed link, the existence of which has yet to be proved."

"What a bloody shame, John." He leaned forward again. "Since a link has yet to be navigated by a vessel, would you consider trying to sail the route, just for the satisfaction of being the first to complete the passage by boat?"

My heart skipped a beat before I answered his question. "No, Gerald. I have other interests now. A few months ago, I married a lovely lady I met in Toronto. We would like to start a family, either here in London or perhaps in Orkney. I am too busy to consider such a time-consuming undertaking."

"You've married! Well, isn't that good news!" He reached over and shook my hand with gusto. "Who is the lucky lady, may I ask?"

I didn't want to bring up the name of Kate's father, in case rumours about his hatred for me had somehow reached London. "Her name is Catherine — Kate."

"Congratulations to you both, John. The love of a good woman is the highest form of praise a man can ever hope for in his life."

I changed the subject. "How are you faring, Gerald?"

"Oh, I am now retired and tired. Bored. Fat and disgruntled with my physician for nagging at me, I suppose. Other than that, I have no complaints. The society rooms are too crowded now." He waved a hand to indicate that most of the reading room chairs were full. "There are discussions about moving to a larger building, possibly sharing space with other scientific institutions. I rather like it here, but the decision lies in the hands of the board of governors. I had a seat on the board for a time, but removed myself because of petty differences among the members." He sighed. "The meetings were tiresome and rather unproductive, I'm afraid.

"You know," he added, "it still bothers me that you have been so undervalued in the minds of the British establishment, although I suppose you don't hold a great number of them dear to your heart anyway. In my opinion, your achievements have been nothing short of remarkable, John."

"I appreciate your kind words, Gerald. I am sure I will never quite understand how the clumsy government machine operates, particularly concerning its vast overseas interests. So secretive and unreachable, and many important decisions are made behind closed doors with little input from the citizenry."

"Aye, I agree. We elect our leaders to make decisions in the best interests of the nation, but we seem to have no control over their actions."

The fact that the failed Franklin Expedition was now being hailed as the finest British achievement in Arctic history irked me to no end, despite my efforts to ignore it. "There is talk of Sir John Franklin being immortalized as the discoverer of the Northwest Passage," I said.

"Aye, it's all quite a mess, isn't it?"

Gerald cleared his throat and briefly studied the pipe he was holding, as if he regretted not being able to fill it with tobacco and light it. He placed it on the table beside him and rubbed his hands together. "John, I think Great Britain is in dire need of a symbol of a successful British enterprise right now — a heroic figure whose memory will outshine all others in the history of Arctic exploration." He leaned forward.

"In my personal opinion, that hero should be *you*, not John Franklin. Knowing what I do about your history in the Arctic, I believe you have accomplished far more than anyone else over there." He sat back. "There you have it, my friend." Both flattered and embarrassed, I felt heat rising in my cheeks.

He shook his head. "Disasters such as the loss of the Franklin ships and men, our failure to reach the Orient by means of a northern route, and our terrible defeat in the Crimean War are placing a great strain on the people of Great Britain.

"I do wonder if Britain can claim to have any heroes these days, John. I believe that because of his widow's carefully crafted public campaign — and despite his many failures — Sir John Franklin will be posthumously recognized as Britain's Arctic hero. Indeed, what qualities must such a figure possess in order to reach such an exalted status in the eyes of his countrymen? Well, for one thing, I believe he should be dead. Secondly, he must have perished under horrific circumstances whilst performing notable service to his Queen and country. As such, his name will always be associated with sacrifice and martyrdom. History will never forget him."

"Aye, you've made some good points, Gerald. I suppose one could also add the fact that in this case, there is a despondent widow who has sacrificed her own resources — not to mention the purses of many sympathizers who have been drawn to her plight — in a desperate effort to find him."

He nodded. "Lady Franklin has now suffered the further blow of knowing that her husband's body will likely remain in the wastelands of the frozen north." He wiped his brow with a handkerchief. "The myth is usually greater than the man himself, isn't it?"

"True enough. I suspect that the memory of Sir John Franklin will forever be associated with the Northwest Passage, Gerald, whether or not he ever came close to it. Wasn't it Sir Francis Beaufort who recently declared '. . . let the name of the discoverer of the Northwest Passage be forever linked to that of Sir John Franklin'?"

My companion relaxed his posture and mopped his forehead again with a handkerchief. There was really nothing more to say about the matter. We chatted on for a while longer, and then I went on my way. *Tara Gott.*

◆ *Kensington, London*
[MAY 1860]

Kate returned from an afternoon walk with her mother and sister. "The tulips at Hyde Park are exquisite! It all looks like a splendid drawing on a postcard. People are strolling with baby carriages and dogs, children are playing on the grass . . . and the Serpentine is lovely, with ducks splashing around and chasing after each other. The songbirds are in fine form — it's all such a feast for the eyes and ears! I am so glad that Mama and Emily are here with us." I appreciated their visit as well, partly because the time had come for me to get back to work, and also because Kate enjoyed their company so much.

I had been approached by the governor of a newly formed private enterprise called the Atlantic Telegraph Company, and invited to participate in conducting the land portion of a telegraph cable survey between Britain and North America. The company's offer of a generous contract certainly caught my attention. The notion of travelling in the northern wilderness across Scotland, the Shetland Islands, the Faeroes and Iceland appealed to me, as did the thought of driving a team of dogs across southern Greenland. Now that Kate's favourite companions were nearby, I hoped she would encourage me to participate in something new and challenging.

"John, the project sounds well suited for your experience and skills, but you would be travelling so much of the time. I don't like to think about that part of it, because I'd miss you terribly. When would you go? For how long?"

"If I accept the offer, we will leave in mid-July and return in late September. I don't want to be separated from you for so long either, but it would be difficult to turn down the chance to participate in such an ambitious technological enterprise. It is quite an opportunity, Katie . . . and the thought of travelling in the northern wilderness again . . ."

"Sometimes I wonder if you love the wilderness more than you love me!" she laughed.

"Katie . . . how could you . . ."

She took my hands. "I'm teasing you, dear. You know, some wives worry about their husbands taking up with other women, gambling, leading double lives. I never think about it, because I know that being in a cold and wild sort of place with all the elements raging around you is *your* other passion. Of course you should go on the expedition! But try not to leave me and our family-to-be for too long at a time." She put her hand on my heart, and I covered it with my own.

"I'm grateful to you, dearest Kate. You have my solemn promise that I will never be away for too long."

⇢ *Southampton, England*
[JULY 19, 1860]

The royal party's yacht, HMY *Fairy*, steamed alongside the *Fox* at half past ten, and the lavishly attired Queen, Prince Albert, several of their children and a sizable entourage were escorted aboard. Captain Allen

Young — a well-known veteran of previous searches for the missing Franklin party — and I, along with the other members of our survey expedition, bowed in greeting as we were introduced to them. The Prince Consort paused to admire our Royal Geographical Society medals for our Arctic accomplishments, forcing me to consider the irony of the situation.

Just three years earlier, I had felt as though I was in some sort of race against Lady Franklin when she purchased the *Fox* and engaged Captain McClintock to search for the *Erebus* and *Terror*, while Rae Brothers & Company scrambled to finish building the *Iceberg* in Hamilton. I had been desperate to beat the *Fox* to the area where the Esquimaux had seen the Kabloonans, but fate intervened and I lost the race.

Here I stood — aboard the *Fox*, of all vessels — exchanging mundane pleasantries with the head of the British Empire and her family about a telegraph expedition. They gave no indication of recognizing my name, nor did I expect anything other than their attitude of regal detachment when we spoke. It was a relief when they disembarked and we set about our various tasks for getting the ship underway.

→ *The North Atlantic*
[JULY–SEPTEMBER 1860]

I missed Kate as we travelled from island to island aboard the *Fox*, alighting to explore the land on foot, horseback and later with dog teams, in search of suitable locations for the placement of telegraph lines, but she was right. It was stimulating to be braving rough conditions once again. The journey required a good deal of stamina and, despite feeling the odd twinge from aging knees, the exertions caused new energy to flow through my body and mind.

→ *London*
[OCTOBER 1860]

I was saddened to learn that while I was away, Sir George Simpson, the former Governor-in-Chief of the Hudson's Bay Company, my mentor, employer and friend since I first arrived on the shore of Hudson Bay in

1832, had died at his home in Lachine, near the Lower Canada city of Montreal. I had planned to take Kate with me on my next journey to North America, so she could meet the man who had seen potential and something of his own character in an eager and adventurous young doctor. I certainly hadn't expected that my summer employment twenty-seven years earlier as ship's surgeon aboard the *Prince of Wales* would turn into a long and adventurous career with the Company in the Arctic.

Sir George and I had experienced our differences over the years, but for the most part I regarded him as a father figure and a man upon whom I could depend. It was unsettling to think that I would never see him or hear his boisterous laugh again, nor could I attend his funeral, because I had been at sea aboard the *Fox* when he died.

↦ *London*

[NOVEMBER 1860]

It was disheartening to learn a month after our return from the survey expedition that the newly formed Atlantic Telegraph Company had failed to secure the contract for building the cable system across the Atlantic. The company was soon disbanded. *Yet another disappointment to add to the list*, I thought. Why had my connection to northern enterprises been so fraught with losses ever since I submitted my report to the Admiralty in 1854? Even though I had not failed professionally on this latest endeavour, I personally felt as though my reputation was doomed to be forever tarnished by poor outcomes.

↦ *Kensington, London*

[JANUARY 1861]

"Darling! Come here at once!" Kate was standing in the hallway of our home, her head lowered, hands on her stomach. I dropped my book, leapt from my chair and ran to her. "What's the matter, Katie? What's wrong?"

She took my hands and held them to her belly. "Do you feel that?" I shook my head. She raised her head and broke into a wide smile. "I felt something move in there. I did feel something move, I swear it!" She threw her arms around me. "I felt our child. I know I did! Oh, John . . ."

I was smiling now. "Tell me about it, Katie. What did you feel?"

"I . . . I don't know. I can't describe it exactly, but at that very instant, I just knew what it was! It's the life inside me, John! Oh my goodness . . ." She looked up at me. "Do you know what a woman feels when she has been carrying a child for three months? Your patients must have told you . . ."

"Aye, my love, but mothers-to-be feel movement at different times. Generally speaking — "

She was bursting with excitement. "What, John?"

"Well, women sometimes describe it as a sort of fluttering feeling . . ."

"Yes, that's it! That is exactly what I felt. At first I thought it was butterflies, how your stomach feels when you're nervous, but then I realized it was something more . . ."

"I can assure you that there will be many more of those to come and, as the date of the child's birth comes near, the movements will keep you awake at night!"

"Oh, I shouldn't mind that at all!"

We stood in the hallway, holding each other for a long while. After we extinguished the bedside lamp that night, we talked about how we would raise our child: with books and games, outings in the park, playmates and most importantly of all, with love.

→ *Kensington, London*

[JULY 1861]

To our horror, the child's heart stopped beating just prior to its birth. In our initial state of shock and mutual grief, we could barely meet each other's eyes. I held Kate while she wept, whispering into her hair, trying to be strong and stop the tears from rolling down my own cheeks. Poor, poor Kate. Nature could be so cruel. The love of my life had been robbed of the new life growing inside her. How could God have allowed such tragedy to befall her, to hurt us so badly?

The child was a son we would never know. I thought back to the time when I was four years old, and my baby brother was lost soon after his birth at the Hall of Clestrain. I shivered as I recalled catching a glimpse of my mother's grief-stricken face. Now, I was holding my wife as she sobbed. If it was a boy, we had decided to name him Thomas Glen Thompson Rae; we chose the name Emma Glen Thompson Rae for a girl. I had dreamed of taking young Tom or Emma for long walks in the park, to church, to Orkney and beyond. The thought of teaching Tom how to fish, shoot and sail, just as my father and older brothers had taught me, was never far from my mind while Kate was with child. Telling him stories about my adventures in the Arctic. Helping Emma with her schoolwork, letting her play with my violin, patching our children up when they skinned a knee.

Kate clad our lost son Tom in a silk bonnet and beautiful white gown she had sewn for his christening. We laid his tiny body in a velvet-lined, polished mahogany box and buried him in the yard of the church where we attended Sunday services. With this agonizing task completed, we held each other and vowed to try again.

→ *Kensington, London*

[FEBRUARY 1864]

On a chilly Tuesday afternoon, I opened the door to our home, hung up my hat and coat, and rushed into the kitchen, where Kate was supervising the preparation of the evening meal.

"Good heavens!" she cried. "Something has got you all in a fluster. Is everything all right, dear?"

I could hardly contain my enthusiasm. "Yes, of course. All is well, but I do have something exciting to discuss with you."

She gestured for me to meet her in the parlour, where she joined me with two cups of tea. "Well, you've certainly got my attention. Your face looks flushed. Your news must be very interesting."

"Aye, it is! As you know, I was called to a conference at the offices of the Hudson's Bay Company today. It turned out that the purpose of the meeting was to discuss a new expedition requiring someone with my surveying skills and wilderness experience!"

Kate raised her eyebrows. "Another long journey?"

"Aye, but listen to this: the Company is joining a newly formed private venture called the American Western Telegraph Company to explore the viability of setting up an intercontinental telegraph line through Siberia, the Bering Strait, Alaska . . ." Kate's hand flew to her mouth. "*Siberia?* Alaska? So far away this time!" she cried.

"Oh no, don't worry, Kate. I wouldn't consider being involved in all of it. My part of the journey would comprise a portion of the survey in Rupert's Land." I pulled a map from my pocket, and drew a finger across it from Fort Garry — the Hudson's Bay Company trading post positioned at the confluence of the Red and Assiniboine Rivers — to the mouth of the Fraser River in western British Columbia. "I've been asked to conduct a survey from the fort, to identify and chart the locations of suitable trees to be fitted as poles for carrying the telegraph wires to the Pacific Coast. And *if* the new company wins the contract, we might consider making a modest investment . . ."

A shadow of concern crossed Kate's lovely face. "When would you go, and for how long?"

"This spring. And, my dearest Katie, I hope you'll agree to travel with me as far as Fort Garry. We can make a wonderful holiday out of it — sail to New York together, visit with family and friends in Hamilton . . ."

Kate jumped up, surprised. "Oh, John. D'you mean it? Oh my goodness! I don't know what to say!" Now, *her* face was flushed with excitement. Throughout the remainder of the evening, she peppered me with questions until I begged her to let me get some sleep and resume the conversation in the morning.

→ *North America*

[1864]

Kate and I set sail for New York from Liverpool on a fair spring morning, arriving in New York a week later. The journey aboard the RMS

Persia delighted both of us to no end. We strolled along the decks arm in arm, dined extravagantly, and I thought that I had never seen her look so vibrant and well. We travelled by train to Hamilton and then to St. Paul, Minnesota, and took a steamboat north on the Mississippi River until we were transferred to horses and carts. At this point, the comfortable aspects of our expedition abruptly ended, and the conditions became almost unbearable.

When I was in the area years earlier, I had marvelled at the lush landscape and abundant lakes, naïvely assuming that the region would be in the same green late-spring condition this time. The final leg of our journey north was grim, however, due to the worst drought conditions I had ever witnessed. Prairie fires had destroyed tree and plant life; lakes had dried to nothing. There were times when the clouds of smoke, dust and insects were so thick that I was unable to see the horse I was driving. I could hear it coughing, though — a dreadful sound I will never forget.

The atmosphere slowly changed from brown and foul to green and fair, as we pushed our way north along the Red River Valley and arrived at our destination in late June. "Katie, if I had known what the conditions were going to be like . . . I should have checked ahead of time. I wish it had been like this all along — "

"Hush, dear. What an adventure this is. I'm thrilled to be here with you. Never for one moment did I think we wouldn't make it through the rough patches, safe and sound."

The following six weeks kept me occupied with preparations for the survey expedition. Kate enjoyed the companionship of several other women who were staying at Fort Garry, and we usually dined with employees of the company and their families. The topic of native dissatisfaction with the growing influx of white settlers was frequently brought up in discussions, and I was reminded of how native people were expected to adapt and change at the behest of British interlopers. I couldn't imagine the Esquimaux being forced into the same trap, because no white man in his right mind would try to settle in the frozen north.

Preparations were completed by mid-August, at which point Kate and I bade each other a fond farewell. She was escorted north and east to Hudson Bay for her journey home to England by ship, while our party of eight men travelled west alongside rivers with horses, carts and wagons. We moved at a painstakingly slow pace, because of my mandate to stop often and evaluate various species of trees for their durability and longevity as telegraph poles. Treacherous conditions sometimes forced us to leave our horses behind and continue the expedition on foot — my preferred method of conveyance on rough terrain — although the heavy load of equipment and supplies made the task particularly arduous when we pushed further west and were forced to traverse Rocky Mountain passes.

After we crossed the continental divide at Yellowhead Pass in British Columbia, I purchased two dugout canoes, declined the offer of a guide and, along with three of my men, undertook a most challenging and stimulating journey of two hundred and seventy miles down the Fraser River to Fort Alexandria, averaging seventy miles each day. So many bends, twists and turns to be navigated!

We left the canoes behind and, with my portion of the survey finished, I journeyed on to the newly incorporated city of Victoria, where I received a most welcoming reception from the local government. From there, I travelled south by ship to the Isthmus of Panama and boarded a train to the shores of the Atlantic Ocean. During the sea journey from Panama to England, I was mostly occupied in my cabin, preparing maps and a report on the survey. It was gratifying to write that, given the quantity and quality of suitable trees between Fort Garry and the West Coast, the proposed telegraph system would be 100% viable.

The latest venture had done me a world of good, but I was glad to return to my Kate and our London home. Perhaps this time, I thought, a post-Arctic enterprise in which I had been an active participant would be successful. Much to my disappointment, however, this was — yet again — not the case.

As it turned out, our extensive survey expedition had been for naught. Before my arrival in England, the Western Union Telegraph Company announced from its New York headquarters that it had won a contract from the American government for building a much larger telegraph system in the northern United States and beyond. The Hudson's Bay Company withdrew from the competition, and the American Western Telegraph Company was disbanded. *I had been involved in another failed enterprise.*

Kate insisted that I had not failed professionally — that I never had at any time — and despite my feelings of melancholy about what I perceived to be failures, she was right. She also reminded me that I had not come away from the experience empty-handed. Our holiday had been splendid, and the survey portion had afforded me the opportunity of taking a very close look at the pristine northwest regions of Rupert's Land. I made a strong effort to distance myself from the string of unfortunate outcomes associated with my involvement in private enterprises, but the deep feeling of having failed would not abate.

→ *Kensington, London*
[1865]

After the loss of our first child, Kate suffered two further miscarriages. Our confidence in having a family began to waver, and our spirits were very low. "Kate, my love," I whispered. "We should consider investing in a home instead of filling the pockets of a landlord. What do you think of the idea? If it is your wish, I will purchase a fine house here in London for us."

She moved away, smiling. "Oh John dear! You would?" Then her lovely face darkened, as she understood my reference to living in London as being *her* wish. The phrase had come out unexpectedly from my lips. What I meant to say was "if it is *our* wish."

"John, you've never really left Orkney in your heart, have you? Be honest with me. Tell me exactly what you are thinking." I held her more tightly and sighed. "I cannot deny how I feel about the Orkneys, but I also understand your fondness for London. Maybe we can figure out a middle ground."

"Well," she replied, "as much as I would love to buy a house here, we could wait for a little while. I am willing to spend some time with you in Orkney when the weather is fair. The sea air might do us both a world of good. What do you think of that?"

My heart missed a beat. "Katie, you are always full of surprises! I never thought you would consider spending time up there. Perhaps we could rent a splendid cottage in Orkney next summer, and you can see if that sort of life suits you at all. I promise you, my love, if you are unhappy, we will return to London and make our permanent home here."

"A summer holiday," she said, her expression brightening. "Well, I can think of no reason why we shouldn't spend the summer months in the north, dear. Maybe Mama and Emily would be able to join us. You, above all people, deserve a respite from the city, and I think I could use a change, as well." Tears filled her eyes. "If it's God's will, perhaps we will conceive a healthy child in your homeland."

She placed her hands on my chest. "I'll keep an open mind about Orkney, John. You can show your favourite things to me, share your knowledge of the flora and fauna, teach me how to fish, take me walking with you in Orphir and lead me to the Hall of Clestrain. I'll give it a good try. Just promise me one thing: we'll return to London if I don't feel I can adapt to life beyond a fair weather holiday on the islands. Cross your heart twice, now. Not once, but twice; once for you and once for me."

I crossed my heart once and then twice, relieved that this woman of the city was willing to give my beloved islands a chance for a few months. I kissed her forehead in gratitude. "Katie, I make you this promise here and now, and I will stand by it."

Later, after her soft breathing deepened and took on the rhythm of sleep, I lay awake and fretted about what my young wife was about to do. It would not be easy for Kate to cope with a transition to those windswept isles in the northern sea. On the other hand, if she had an opportunity to experience the kindness and warmth of the Orcadian people — a congenial blend of Viking settlers and their gentle Scottish descendants — maybe she would develop an attachment to the place. And if we were to find ourselves expecting another child, perhaps she would consider raising it in those natural surroundings for a few months of each year. I made a vow to find a comfortable residence close to the city of Kirkwall with a view over the waters of Scapa Flow, just a short carriage ride from the town and St. Magnus Cathedral, which was celebrated for its active social community.

→ *Berstane House, St. Ola, Orkney*
[JULY 1866]

"Katie, the wind is picking up nicely, so I'll be off for a sail while you go to your meeting." It was a cool, bright day with brisk winds out of the northwest. The conditions were fine for sailing, so I gathered up my jacket, cap and gloves.

"Wait a few minutes, dear," she called from upstairs. I stood in the hallway, leafing through the latest issue of the *Scotsman*. Kate came down the stairs wearing woollen gloves, a warm jacket over her dress, and tying the strings of a bonnet.

"I'd like to come with you," she declared.

"I beg your pardon? Katie, you've never been sailing, my love!"

"Don't I know it," she laughed, "and that's why I plan to come with you this afternoon. Don't look so shocked, John. You always talk about how stimulating it is out there. We've been living in Orkney for a while, now — don't you think it's about time for me to share in one of your more daring recreational pursuits?" She giggled.

"But you'll miss your meeting at the cathedral — "

"That's quite all right, dear. There will be other meetings. I'll give them my regrets on the way to the harbour. I want to try something that you love to do, and see how well I fare at it. Maybe I will like sailing, and we can enjoy it together sometimes."

I didn't dare to voice my doubts about her ability to withstand the cold breeze, not to mention the frantic scrambling of a sailor to keep the boat steadily moving no matter how often the winds changed direction.

"Well, what a nice surprise, my love." I kissed her cheek and offered her my arm. "Shall we go?"

I kept an 18-foot yole — very much like the one we Rae children used to sail when we were growing up on the shores of Clestrain Sound

— at the docks in the bay of Kirkwall. I had named her KATE in honour of the adventurous woman I had been fortunate enough to marry. I crossed my fingers and hoped she would find some pleasure in the experience. I raised only the jib and mizzen sail, and we pushed off for an easy glide into the freshening breeze. The motion was smooth and sedate, which seemed agreeable to my wife. I vowed to maintain a slow speed for her sake, but then she surprised me even more.

"Let's see if we can go a little faster," she said. "Will you put up the big sail?"

"Are you certain about that, Kate? Conditions can suddenly change and become quite challenging — "

"Of course I am!" Her reply was somewhat brusque, but endearing all the same.

"Only if you'll let me teach you a few things first — for safety's sake, Kate."

As we gently sailed back and forth across the bay, I showed her what her responsibilities as first mate would be, reminding her that I was the captain and therefore in charge of the vessel, just as my brother William had been all those years ago. An excellent pupil, she listened intently and executed each practice manoeuvre as instructed. After a while, she requested that we seek more demanding conditions, so I hoisted the mainsail and we set off on a course away from the shore. She shrieked with delight as the sails caught the extra wind, the boat leaned to starboard and we sped farther out into the firth.

As we moved along, another yole approached us with a group of youths, who shouted that they would be to the shore of the isle of Shapinsay, an Orkney island off the eastern coast of Main Isle — before we were halfway there. I explained to Kate that they were inviting us to race against them, but that we were under no obligation to accept their challenge. "Let's go!" she cried.

I shouted back, "Shall we beat them to it?"

She didn't hesitate, not even for one second. "Oh yes, please!"

I positioned the sails, with Kate in charge of holding the jib firmly in place so we could pick up full speed. The boys were well ahead, but I could see that they were heading for a cross-current, which we could avoid by altering our course. We maintained our good speed, while they faltered. We wasted no time, took maximum advantage of the wind, and soon enough we were passing them. We arrived at the southwest shore first — with Balfour Castle in view beyond it — and the boys well behind us. Conceding defeat, they all doffed their caps in our direction, before sailing back across the firth to the bay.

"Oh John, that was the finest race!" Kate declared. I told her that memories of my childhood adventures trying to outrun the tricky winds around Hoy and Clestrain Sounds had helped me give these youngsters a lesson, but I couldn't possibly have managed so well without such a capable first mate. From that point on we had no more sedate sails, and I was reminded that my lovely wife was game for almost anything.

→ *Berstane House, St. Ola, Orkney*
[FEBRUARY 1867]

Seven months later, when the days were short and the winds were fierce and cold again, I leaned over Kate to extinguish the lamp on her bedside table. The book she had been reading was face-down on her chest, but her eyes were open, her expression melancholy.

I rested my hand on her shoulder. "What's wrong, my love?" She set the book aside and rolled over to face me.

"I don't think I can be happy living in Orkney forever, John. We came to Kirkwall for a summer holiday, and I was the one who suggested we stay longer, but now we've been here for almost two years. Please don't misunderstand me. There is much here to like — the glorious views of the water, sailing with you, the hills, the church and the generous people, their music — but I just can't do it forever. I'm so sorry," she whispered. "I tried, I really did try, darling."

I suppose the only thing that surprised me about her declaration was that she had waited so long to make it. My heart sank, but a promise was a promise. "Yes, you did, my love. You tried your hardest."

"I've been afraid to tell you because I can't bear the idea of disappointing you. I know how much these islands mean to you." She took hold of my hand, and I squeezed it to hide my disappointment.

"You know," I said, "I thought your moments of melancholy were because we haven't yet had a child." I took her other hand. "I wish you hadn't kept your unhappiness about Orkney a secret, Katie. Two years is a long time to be miserable about where you live."

"Of course I am wishing for a child, always. I don't know, I guess I wanted to believe there's some magic in the air and water here, that staying longer would be the best thing for us, and we would have a family by now. I hoped I would come to love this way of life, but it just didn't happen. It's a wonderful place to visit for a summer holiday, you know." She looked at me, worried.

"It's all right, Kate. Orkney isn't going anywhere, and I can always return for a visit. Would you come with me sometimes, when the weather's fine?" She threw her arms around me and buried her face in my chest.

"Oh yes, I'd do that in a heartbeat."

Later, when she was asleep, I got up and stood at the bedroom window. Even though it was dark, I watched skeins of sea-foam being scooped up by the wind and thrown across the black surface of the sea, troubled by the thought that if children were to be in our lives, we would raise them in the crowded, noisy city, and not in Orkney. On the other hand, our family could spend holiday time on the islands. Perhaps a return to London would bring us what we both wanted the most.

➤ *4 Addison Gardens*
Kensington, London
[JUNE 1867]

The sale of the house in Hamilton and my medical work in Kirkwall had provided us with enough savings to purchase a modest house on a leafy street in West London. Our move marked a new chapter in our lives, another beginning in the city I both admired and disliked in equal measure. While Emma, Emily and Kate set about making our house a comfortable home, I reacquainted myself with members of the scientific community, and I was gratified to receive a warm reception from my peers. Topics such as the Franklin tragedy and cannibalism were carefully ignored in our discussions, much to my relief.

↳ *London*

[SEPTEMBER 1868]

My brother Tom and I had exchanged letters frequently, but then he stopped writing to me. I was already worried about the financial stability of Rae Brothers & Company in Hamilton, and now the railway system was rapidly expanding as settlements grew in North America. The movement of goods and people was safer by rail, with a much farther reach than by boat. My brothers had invested in building too many vessels, and on May 16, 1865, Rae Brothers & Company had been forced to declare bankruptcy. Tom had poured his heart and soul into the shipping enterprise, and Dick had made a good effort as well.

After I learned of the news, I sent a number of letters to both of my brothers, more often in an attempt to lift their spirits, just as Tom had lifted mine when I was suffering after the loss of the *Iceberg*. Despite my efforts to reach out, however, Tom survived less than three years after the company closed its doors.

September 12, 1868

My Dear John and Kate:

With great sorrow, I must inform you that our dear Tom passed away yesterday from a heart attack. It happened while he was sitting in his favourite chair in the parlour, reading a book. He fell unconscious straightaway, and the doctor assures me that any suffering he experienced was brief. Thank goodness for that. He was only fifty-one years old, and too young to die of an older man's disease. He had not been eating well or taking exercise for some time, despite my efforts to encourage him to look after himself.

Marion and John are here, looking after us while the arrangements are made. The boys and I send you our love and best wishes.

Helen

At first, I could not believe that Tom was gone. Every loss leaves a fingerprint on a person's heart, and I was no exception. Kate and I made arrangements to visit what remained of my family in Hamilton. It was good to spend time with Marion, John, Dick and the others, but with Tom gone, there was a great emptiness in my heart.

→ *4 Addison Gardens*
Kensington, London
[NOVEMBER 1869]

Despite our mutual passion and fervent desire to have a family, Kate and I remained childless, which became a source of continuing sorrow for us. After Kate had suffered another late-term miscarriage, our physician was resolute in his advice that we not try again. Her health had been compromised by the multiple traumas, and the doctor expressed his concern that she might not survive another pregnancy.

We were utterly devastated, but in another way I was relieved to hear the finality in the doctor's tone of voice. Despite my own medical background, I had been powerless to prevent the cruel losses of our unborn children and the risks to Kate's health. Each successive conception had brought with it hope but also a terrible fear of having to endure yet another heartbreak. As much as I wanted to have children with Kate, her life meant more to me than my own. I simply could not bear the thought of losing her.

After the doctor left the house and in the quiet of our bedroom, I held her while she cried — her thin, exhausted body wracked with sobs, her beautiful heart broken.

"Is this truly the end, John?" I tightened my arms around her, trying to slow her shudders.

"No, no, my lovely Catherine Jane Alicia Rae . . . this is not the end." I felt clumsy, searching for words to soothe her. "Perhaps this brings us to another beginning." Startled, she looked up at me, frowning.

"What can you possibly mean by that? The doctor just told us it's over, John. It's over . . ."

I buried my face in her neck and sighed. "I didn't intend for my remark to sound that way. What I meant to say is that we now face a new passage in our life together, another beginning. I am forcing myself to look at this change with some optimism. As long as we have each other, I still believe that we are truly blessed." I cleared my throat to hide my own grief. She had been wounded enough by so many losses.

"Kate, we must try to accept that however painful this is for us, perhaps it is God's will. I have asked the Almighty Father over and over again for an answer. Does He have a different plan for us?" I turned my face away so she would not see that my bravado was slipping away, that my own chin was trembling.

"Let us find ways of bringing joy into our lives, every minute of every day," I added.

"John, I don't have the strength right now to move beyond my sorrow . . ."

"I know, my love. There is no hurry, you know. Finding our way through this grief will be a long journey, but we will make it *together*, one step at a time. Our sadness will always be with us, but perhaps if we hold on tightly to our faith in God, we'll be able to find hope and joy in other things."

"Hope for what?" she cried. "All I wanted was children. Was that too much to ask?" She was sobbing again.

"No, it is never too much to ask. Never. If I could exchange everything I have for a child, I would, my dear Katie, but if trying again carries even a tiny chance of losing you, we cannot take the risk. Let's make a promise right here and now," I whispered. "I vow to you, Catherine Rae, that I will find a thousand — well, at least a hundred — ways to make you feel even a small measure of happiness every day for the rest of our time together on this earth." I placed our hands over my heart so she could feel it beating, and looked deeply into her watery, sea-glass eyes.

"I promise you this, my love."

Kate was still weeping, struggling to hold on to my gaze. "Please say a prayer with me, Katie. Let's say it together, even if we don't much feel like it right now."

> The Lord is my shepherd, I shall not want;
> He maketh me lie down in green pastures;
> He leadeth me beside the still waters . . .

In a halting voice, she joined me in reciting Psalm 23, not once but four times, each repetition for a lost child. That simple act gave us comfort, and in spite of our inexplicable losses it helped us to grow even closer to each other, to rise above the pain as best we could and get on with the job of living.

→ *London*
[FEBRUARY 1870]

As time went on, Kate slowly picked up the threads of her busy life. The daily routine of household care and management seemed to give her a sense of purpose and comfort, and she eventually resumed her habit of taking long walks in the parks. Her mother and sister remained with us, and they encouraged her to join them in performing charity work and other activities, while I escorted them all to the theatre — we enjoyed it tremendously — as often as I could. I continued to be hired for surveying projects, speaking engagements and consultations, which kept my mind alert and active. I walked to and from every meeting, sometimes accompanied by Kate along the way.

→ *London*
[JUNE 1870]

> We humbly beseech thee O Father that we may be honest and true in all our dealings, and gentle and merciful to the faults of others, remembering how much gentleness and mercy we stand in need of ourselves; That we may earnestly try to live with true faith, honour and love, and in charity and goodwill with all our fellow creatures . . .

I winced as I read aloud part of a prayer written by Charles Dickens. Kate listened, her sewing in her hands. "Katie, doesn't it strike you as odd that a man who publicly expressed his disgust with the innocent Esquimaux, actually penned a prayer beseeching *all* men to live 'in charity and goodwill with *all* of our fellow creatures'?"

The prayer was published in the newspapers following Dickens' death from a stroke at the age of fifty-eight. What a prolific and admired author he had been! He had preached compassion in his writings, but it pained me deeply to recall that in *Household Words* his claim to respect and love others had excluded people whose skin was of a darker hue, whose customs and spiritual beliefs were different from those of the white man.

On the one hand, Dickens drew attention to the plight of poor children in vermin-infested orphanages. This effort was noble, indeed. He also expressed great pity for the poor heroic men of the Royal Navy, who were caught in an epic struggle for survival in a hostile land. How right he was!

In my view, however, Dickens' unforgivable error occurred when he repeatedly asserted that people with dark skin and unfamiliar customs were sub-human. On this subject, his writing was downright irresponsible. Naturally, his reputation as a champion for the afflicted remained intact, just as he wished. I wondered if he had ever experienced second thoughts about his attacks on the Esquimaux and regretted them. I told Kate that although I felt a twinge of guilt about it, I did not feel saddened by the news of his death.

⇢ *London*
[JULY 1875]

During the summer of 1875 and shortly after Lady Franklin's death, Kate and I paid a visit to the dimly lit chapel of St. John the Evangelist in Westminster Abbey to view the marble bust she had commissioned in honour of her late husband, Sir John. When we entered the chapel, we looked to our left and were greeted by an extraordinarily handsome and flattering rendition of Sir John Franklin's countenance. A carving of a ship trapped in ice formed the base, and there was an inscription composed by the poet laureate of England:

NOT HERE: THE WHITE NORTH
HAS THY BONES; AND THOU,
HEROIC SAILOR-SOUL, ART PASSING
ON THINE HAPPIER VOYAGE
NOW TOWARD NO EARTHLY POLE.
— ALFRED, LORD TENNYSON, 1875

Kate stood back to look at Franklin's face. "His expression appears to be so strong and self-assured, doesn't it, John?"

"Aye, my love." I recalled my conversation with Gerald McIntosh: "The history books will see to it that he is remembered as a hero." In many ways, Sir John had been heroic, a veteran of fierce battles at sea and on land, including the treacherous push to open the Great White North on behalf of the British Empire. His failures would be written out of history; I supposed they didn't really need to be recorded there anyway.

I had won many battles against the elements, but I was certain that British historians would have little interest in my accomplishments. Their collective memory of me would centre on one thing: my distressing report on the terrible fate of the last survivors of the Franklin Expedition.

Kate understood the nature of my thoughts in the chapel that day. She placed her arm around my waist and leaned into me.

"You, John Rae, are a hero, and don't you ever forget that."

→ *Burlington House, Piccadilly Wing*
Piccadilly, London
[JUNE 3, 1880]

Nullius in Verba — Take Nobody's Word for It. This was the motto of the esteemed Royal Society. In my view, it was a bittersweet expression, considering the numbers of Londoners who did not take my word for it when I returned from the Arctic in 1854 with the tragic news about Sir John Franklin and his party.

I had been a member of the Royal Society for more than thirty years. On that bright day in June, I was summoned to Burlington House on Piccadilly to affix my signature to a document confirming that I had now been elected a Fellow of the storied institution. It had been almost twenty-six years since I took shelter from the press under the wing of Gerald McIntosh in a Royal Society reading room at Somerset House. The society had moved to the other building in 1867, but the memory of that distressing October day was as fresh to me as if it had taken place just yesterday.

Kate and Emily stood at my side as I signed the document. "Mama would have loved this so," Emily whispered. Kate put an arm around her sister's waist, and held her close. I found myself wishing that Gerald could also be with us. I had last seen my feisty old friend in November of 1866. He had been suffering from a nasty cold, and he complained that his physician was making far too much of a fuss about the whole thing. I reminded him of the importance of following his doctor's orders, but he assured me that he would be perfectly fine. I was saddened to learn that he succumbed to pneumonia just two weeks later. I missed him. No doubt he would have been delighted and amused to see his fugitive friend honoured like this.

My wife was even lovelier now, dressed in a plum-coloured damask gown with a delicate white lace collar. She touched the silver locket I had given to her on our tenth wedding anniversary, ten years earlier. Inside the locket were the inscribed words:

MY DEAREST LOVE, KATE
FOREVER IN MY HEART AND SOUL
JOHN

"I think my father would have been very proud of you on this day, dear."

"It's a nice thought, Katie." I did not mention my true feeling that I cared not a whit about what her father would have thought.

PART VII

Messenger from the North

[1881–1886]

→ *Kensington, London*
  [JUNE 1881]

As was my custom during my daily walk, I stopped at the Kensington
Post Office and retrieved some letters, along with a package which had
been forwarded to me from York Factory by the Hudson's Bay Company. I settled on a bench in a nearby park and sifted through the various
senders' addresses: Kirkwall, London, Edinburgh, London and Hamilton. The package from the Arctic intrigued me; it looked, felt and
smelled like dried deerskin, and it was bound in leather ties. The address read: To Doctor John Rae, Hudson's Bay Company, Great Britain.

I cut through the leather strips with my pocket knife. As the wrapping gave way, I was surprised to discover four intriguing objects: a
length of dried caribou hide, white feathers which were probably from
a snow goose, a string of blue beads, and a round, flat stone. How delightful, I thought, as I turned the stone over in my hand and observed
letters carved into it in English: REPULSE BAY.

I unfolded the caribou skin. On one side, the hair was a soft, reddish
brown. On the other, there was a message, again in English. The faded
letters appeared to have been carefully drawn using the blood of an
animal:

Dear Doctor Rae

I send this to you in spring time on HBC ship, to give to you.
I do not know where you live. My mother died. Her name was
Atuqtuaq. You saved her life long ago. I wish to meet you.

Yours truly
Irniq
Repulse Bay

How curious, I thought. An errant goose feather fluttered like a leaf to the ground. I bent down, picked it up, returned it to the package along with the other contents, and walked to a nearby library. I found an empty desk in a corner, reopened the parcel and looked at the signature again: IRNIQ.

Who was Irniq? I wracked my brain, trying to think of the hundreds of Esquimaux I had treated as a doctor and explorer during my twenty-three-year residency in the Arctic region. There had been many of them, from the very young to the very old. I could not recall their faces, let alone their names, although the name Atuqtuaq sounded vaguely familiar.

I examined the threaded beads. A slender string of dried ligament connected them, with a carefully tied knot at each end. I had seen those intricate types of knots before, and recalled tying them over and over again with clumsy results until I eventually got them right.

I lifted the stone and the beads to my nose and smelled them. Their wild, faintly fishy scent had survived the sea journey from the Arctic. Suddenly, I longed to be in Repulse Bay again, to meet and laugh with my old acquaintances, to share food, watch them dance, listen to their drums, their songs and stories, even if I didn't know what most of them meant. I looked up at the library's ceiling, clasped my hands behind my head, stretched my legs out in front of me. After some thought, I decided to make an inquiry before telling anyone about the package.

The next morning, I requested a meeting with the president of the Royal Geographical Society. I had known Richard Johnstone for many years.

"Well, John, it is nice to see you. I catch sight of you at meetings and events, but it has been a while since we last engaged in a real conversation."

"It is good to see you as well, Dick. How are Mary and the children?"

He frowned. "Ah, as well as can be expected I suppose, given that all four girls — the twins included — are currently in the process of becoming young *women*. Their temperaments seem to change by the minute. Lord knows what we will be facing during the next several years! My long-suffering wife will be the one to bear the brunt of it, I expect."

His expression softened. "Tell me, how is your lovely Kate? Mary assures me that her exquisite needlework is the talk of the town. It is inspiring to know that she donates it to charities, along with her prize money."

"She is well, Richard. We do enjoy our life in London. Kate encourages me to set off to the Orkneys when I feel the need to stretch my legs in the wilderness, but she also likes to join me there for the occasional holiday when the weather is warm. There is much for us to see and do here in the city, and I'm glad for my associations with members of the scientific community."

"I understand, John. You were raised in a unique northern space. You can take the child out of its birthplace, but you cannot take the birthplace out of the child. Now, to what honour do I owe this visit from you?"

I cleared my throat. "Well, as you know, I often have some small project of interest in the works."

"Small?" He laughed. "Do you refer to engaging in expeditions all over the North Atlantic and North America as minor activities?"

"Aye, your point is well taken, but you will likely agree that this one is just a trifle in comparison. I am curious to explore some Esquimaux names, with a view to understanding their origins and meanings. For example, an Esquimaux child may receive a name after having a notable experience or displaying a particular talent for something. A young man who has had an encounter with — perhaps even killed — a polar bear, may from then on be known as *Nanuq*, polar bear."

Richard listened with interest. "As you know," I continued, "Arctic explorers often assign English names to their Esquimaux aides. In my case, I named a most trusted guide and friend 'Thomas' after my younger brother, Thomas Rae. In hindsight, I wish I had taken the time to learn the man's true Esquimaux name."

He leaned back in his chair and stretched his arms across the desk. "How may I be of assistance to you, John?"

"Do some of your documents and correspondences contain Esquimaux names along with their meanings? It is a bit of a shot in the dark, but you never know . . ."

"Would you like to have access to our Polar Region archives?"

"Yes, indeed I would, if it's no trouble."

He waved a hand towards the door. "Good, then. I'll get the key and let you in." Before long, I found what I was looking for.

Atuqtuaq. Meaning "singer." Irniq. Meaning "son."

The humiliating aftermath of my return to London with scandalous news about cannibalism had caused me to bury many fond memories of my time spent with the Esquimaux, but now with the arrival of the package, I felt as though I were there again. I placed the other objects in my bag and walked home with the stone in my pocket, turning it over in my fingers, feeling its smoothness, the narrow lines of the carving. Eventually, I picked up my pen and composed a reply to Irniq. I did not know if I would actually send it to him, but after giving the idea some thought, I realized just how much I missed the companionship of people I had once known and been fond of. I felt comforted by the idea of having even a small connection with one or more of them as I journeyed through old age, because it was a certainty that I would never return to the Arctic.

June 18, 1881

To Irniq,

I am pleased to receive your package from Repulse Bay. Thank you for sending these gifts to me. I am sorry to hear that your mother, Atuqtuaq, is dead, but glad to know that I once saved her life. I will say a prayer for her.

I am married and live in London, England. I am very happy here with my wife. Her name is Kate. Every year I travel to Orkney, north of the Scottish mainland, where I was born. When I am there, I hunt and fish. I am too old now to travel to the Arctic.

Do you know William Ouligback Junior? Do you know Thomas Mistegan? If you wish to write to me, this is our mailing address: 4 Addison Gardens, London.

I wish you and all of your relatives well.

Sincerely,
John Rae, M.D., LLD.
London, Great Britain

"Kate, I need your opinion about something."

She was sitting by the fire, her hands casting tiny stitches onto a length of cloth. "What is it, dear?"

"Yesterday, I received a package from York Factory. It was sent by an Esquimaux. It was quite a surprise, since I've not been in contact with any of those people for so long."

She put the needlework down. "How does this person know where you live?"

"He doesn't, but he seemed to be able to write enough English, or have some help with it, to write to me in care of the Hudson's Bay Company."

"What was in the package?"

I showed her the deerskin wrapping, the stone, feather, length of hide and beads. She wrinkled her nose when she smelled the dried skin. She looked at the stone. "Repulse Bay," she repeated. "My mother died," she read. "I cannot possibly pronounce her name correctly."

"I'm not sure how to say it, either. I was never any good at their language, even though I made several weak attempts to learn it."

She looked at me, her eyes soft. "You saved this woman's life. Do you remember anything at all about it?"

"I'm afraid I don't. I treated so many men, women and children during my time there. I stopped by the society and looked up the meaning of her name: singer. The Esquimaux people often sing and dance in a ritualistic manner. It sounds and looks as though they are communicating with spirits. I think I told you about the extraordinary art of throat-singing . . ."

She nodded. "Yes, you tried to explain the sounds that come from deep within the throat — not a growl, but more like a strong vibration, as if it is a stringed instrument."

"That's it, or at least the closest I can come to describing the sound. Perhaps Irniq's mother was a throat-singer, a storyteller. I could never understand the messages expressed in throat-singing, but when an interpreter was nearby, he would occasionally translate some of the meanings to me: Seal hunter drowned off ice floe. Son of . . . father of . . . sister of . . . forever committed to the stars and meteors, to the dancing lights of the aurora borealis, to the moon and the sun and the sea."

"And the name of the person who sent you the package?"

"Irniq. It means 'son.'"

Kate resumed sewing. "Well, he has taken great trouble to find you. Do you think you should reply to him?"

"Yes, I do. Would you have a look at this letter I have written, and tell me what you think of it?" I stood beside her chair as she read. She smiled up at me. "It's a good reply, darling. You have expressed your wish to learn more about him, and I must say that I am growing quite curious, too!" I leaned over and kissed the top of her head.

"Good. I'll send it off in the morning."

→ *Kensington, London*

[OCTOBER 1881]

Irniq's reply arrived in the fall, and he wrote of his connection to the Ouligbacks.

To John,

Thank you for your letter. William Ouligback is my cousin. His father is dead for a long time. I wish to meet with you in Orkney and show you my appreciation for saving my mother's life. Maybe next year.

Irniq

"I suppose he's thinking about travelling to Orkney on a Hudson's Bay Company ship, Katie. Perhaps I could suggest that we meet for a short time next summer, and arrange for his passage. What do you think? If I invite him to join me and he decides to come, would you come with me?"

"We'll see about that, dear. Emily has been talking about going to Canada for a holiday to visit some old friends from her years in Hamilton. She has asked me to go with her. I don't know if I will join her, but I do think you should go and see Irniq. It will do your heart good to meet with him."

"Although I try not to think about it, sometimes I miss the friends and travelling companions I had over there. Does that surprise you?"

"Not in the least. You've spent a good part of your life living and working in the Arctic. It seems quite natural that you would miss the people from time to time."

→ *Stromness*
[JULY 1883]

I knew straightaway which man was Irniq when he disembarked from the *Prince of Wales II* at the port of Stromness. He was diminutive in stature, stocky of frame, and his face was round, with a pleasant expression. His thick, black hair fell close to his shoulders. He wore a reddish-brown deerskin jacket with trousers and moccasins to match. A deerskin bag was slung across his back.

We stared awkwardly at one another for a moment, and then touched hands in greeting. I welcomed my visitor with the Esquimaux Inuktitut language greeting: "*Tunnasugit.*"

"*Naqurmiik,*" he replied. "*Thank you.*"

I had almost forgotten the characteristically wide smile of the Esquimaux. There was sincerity in this young man's greeting.

"You are a tall man, just as they told me," he said.

"Well, I was even taller when I was younger, of course." We both laughed.

"You were a legend among my people. It is still true."

The twenty-five-day journey from York Factory to Scotland had been difficult for Irniq. He was accustomed to sealing and fishing in the choppy waters of the Polar Sea, but he said the massive North Atlantic swells had brought him to his knees with nausea and dizziness. I complimented him for his courage in travelling aboard the massive barque for such a long voyage.

We took a ferry to the northern isle of Westray and walked to a croft I had rented near the Bay of Skaill on the west coast. Irniq was intrigued by the sight of grazing sheep dotting the islands; he had never seen that kind of animal before. He was further amused by the sound of them calling to one another.

He followed me around the rocks and over stones, the topography of this place so far from his home. I noticed that he was sure-footed and had a good stride. Westray, "Queen o' the Isles," and her smaller sibling — named, oddly enough, Papa Westray — were two of my favourite islands, their ancient red sandstone cliffs at once desolate and beautiful, with rocky beaches created by the rhythms of the sea. There was mostly silence between us as we walked several miles to the croft, because I was uncertain about how to open a casual conversation with my visitor, and no doubt he felt the same way about me.

A faint outline of the stone croft appeared in the distance, and then grew more distinct as we neared the place where we would sleep, eat and spend time together. The thatched roof had been repaired many times over, but the owner reassured me that the structure was sound. The building's small size offered little space for any kind of privacy, but with a good peat fire in the hearth of a stone fireplace, we could keep it warm enough for the cool Orcadian nights. The island was unable to support tree life, so there were no buffers against the punishing winds. In some ways it reminded me of the Arctic, only warmer.

"Here you are, Irniq." I gestured towards a wooden plank with a goose-down mattress and pillow in a corner of the croft. He set down his bag and sat beside it, showing signs of fatigue for the first time.

"Thank you, Doctor."

I roasted a plump goose over the fire, and we consumed our fare with biscuits and gravy in near silence. After our meal, I handed him a mug of hot tea. As he sipped the tea, his eyelids began to grow heavy.

"And now to sleep, young man," I said.

"Thank you for the food, Doctor Rae. It was good. Good night."

"Good night, Irniq. Oh, one more thing . . ."

"Yes, Doctor?"

"You do not need to call me doctor. My name is John."

"*Unaukkut*, John." *Good night.*

"*Unaukkut*, Irniq."

He rolled over then, facing the stone wall, taking the blankets with him for warmth. The cabin smelled of roasted meat. For a little while, I watched the growing expansion and contraction of my companion's solid frame under the blankets as sleep overtook him. I reclined by the fire trying to read a book, but it was no use; my mind was full of questions about him, his community, his mother, his life. After a while my own eyes grew heavy, so I extinguished the reading lamp and lay awake for a while on my own mattress, exploring my memories of the Arctic. Eventually I fell into a light sleep.

When I later opened my eyes, I was reluctant to disturb Irniq but he awoke soon enough with the light, as was his custom. I set about preparing boiled oats and tea. He lifted his head, rubbed his eyes, and propped himself up on one elbow, looking puzzled, as if he wasn't sure where he was.

"*Ulaakut*, Irniq. Good morning. Did you rest well?"

He shook the sleep from his head. "*Ulaakut*. Yes, I think so."

After breakfast, I picked up two shotguns leaning against the wall beside the entrance to the cabin. I checked the safety latches, and handed Irniq a leather pouch containing ammunition. I pulled fishing nets from a hook on the wall, along with pouches containing clippers, fish hooks and leather threads. To this, I added two woven baskets for our catch, along with packets of bread and cheese. The day was cool, fine and not too gusty, excellent for walking, shooting and catching a few fish.

I was counting on that day's excursion to reveal some of Irniq's character and a more clear understanding of his decision to travel all the way from Repulse Bay to the Orkneys. The day's activities began with a walk to the shore, arriving at Noup Head on the northwest headland. The white-splattered sandstone cliffs stood tall — their nooks home to the nests of thousands of seabirds — and abundant with fresh eggs during the breeding season. There had been a time when I thought nothing of dangling over the summit of a cliff and bagging a bird or two with a long-handled net. Those days were over for me, but I was curious to see what Irniq could do in the same situation. The constant cries of circling seabirds drowned out any attempts at conversation.

I made a few gestures with the net, and Irniq understood what to do. He divested himself of most of his kit and, with net in hand, he stretched out flat on his stomach and hung over the edge of the cliff. For a man whose survival depended on a limitless supply of patience while hunting for seals and other such prey, I was not surprised to see him remain motionless for a long while.

Slowly, almost imperceptibly, Irniq reached out with the net and trapped an unsuspecting guillemot as it hovered nearby, trying to defend its nest. He held the bird with one strong hand, twisted its neck with the other, then carefully collected two eggs from the nest, placing them in the net with the bird. The triumphant young Esquimaux inched his body back from the edge without cracking an egg and showed me his catch. I was pleased beyond measure to observe the young man's skill, fearlessness, confidence and patience. He reminded me of myself at the same age.

With the bird and eggs wrapped in cloth and stowed inside Irniq's basket, we walked to the loch of Burness, in which an abundance of fine trout could be found. He required no guidance from me in setting his fishing lines. Before long, two good-sized sea trout were snagged on the hooks. He deftly removed the hooks and pressed the struggling fish together on a rock. I reached for my hunting knife, but he boldly placed his free hand on my arm, indicating that he wanted to finish off and fillet the fish. I was pleased to stay out of the process and watch.

He felt for a leather sheath fastened to his belt and withdrew something which caused me to gasp. It was the very knife I had seen in the hand of my interpreter William Ouligback Junior during our journey across the Boothia Peninsula in the spring of 1854. I had given it to his father in 1849 to express my appreciation for his guidance and help as a translator.

"Where did you acquire the knife?"

"Mar-ko, as you called him, asked me to show it to you. To prove that he knows and respects me. That he respects you. He told me the story of when you gave it to his father before he died."

For a moment, I couldn't think of anything to say. I stared at the knife and watched as he quickly dispatched the fish, using the knife with great precision. He gutted them both in a matter of seconds, tossed the entrails into the loch, rinsed off the fish and wrapped them in a cloth I had packed in his pouch, cleaned his knife and returned it to its sheath.

Irniq broke the silence. "Mar-ko," he said again. "William Ouligback

Junior. He journeyed with you on the Boothia Peninsula. He was with
you when you found part of the link that joins with the Northwest Passage. He was there when you turned back so your two young men
would not die. He helped you bring the relics of the Franklin Expedition to Repulse Bay. He was the interpreter for your interviews with our
people about the British sailors and their ships. He told us how the men
starved and tried to stay alive by eating the flesh of their dead. William
Ouligback Junior is the cousin of my mother, Atuqtuaq."

There was quiet between us, while I digested all he had just said.
"Irniq, you wrote that I saved your mother's life . . ."

"If you had not saved her, I would never have been born."

"Tell me more."

"She told me that you were a miracle man of Kabloonan medicine,
and that you made people get better when they were sick. She said you
saved many lives when you lived among our people, and that sometimes
you walked great, long distances to heal people when they were too sick
to be brought to you. She said you were a famous hunter, that you shared
your food with us, and that you always showed respect to our people
and the animals." He smiled. "She said you were terrible at speaking
our language!"

We both laughed. "Aye, I can't deny that, young man."

His face grew solemn. "She told me that you saved her life when she
lost my sister, before I was born. That is why I wanted to meet you and
say thank you, man to man."

"What happened, Irniq?"

"She gave birth to a girl while her family was following migrating
caribou across the tundra. The child was no longer alive when it was
born. My mother began to lose much blood. Her life was flowing out of
her body. The shaman came. He chanted over her body for a long time,
casting healing spells on her, but her life was still draining away. She
hardly remembered it all because she was so weak, but my uncles said
messages were sent to you. You left your travelling party and walked for
a long time to reach their snow hut. You brought Kabloonan medicine
with you. You knew what to do to save her. You brought her back to her
family when she was leaving them." Tears welled up in his eyes.

I had treated hundreds of young women — in Scotland, England, the Arctic — who came close to perishing during or after childbirth. Their faces were blurred in my memory. As a physician, my obligation was to keep my mind focused on the tasks of evaluating and fixing problems during life-threatening situations, however impersonal that may have appeared to some observers. I could not allow natural sympathy to get in the way of clinical decision-making. For that reason and because many of my patients did not survive, I intentionally removed their faces from my memory.

"My mother was famous for her singing, especially for her gifts as a throat-singer. She was a famous Inuk storyteller. She was a messenger for the spirit world, too. When she sang, everyone stopped what they were doing and listened to her." Irniq's lips began to tremble and I instinctively reached for his arm.

"How did she die, Irniq?"

"When I was changing from a boy into a man, she became very sick. Her skin was burning like fire and she spoke in many tongues."

"*Ogguarpunga*." I am sorry.

"Now, she lives among the stars, where the hunting is always good and no one starves or gets sick. I visit her almost every night, and I ask her to tell me stories. When I am asleep, she tells me everything about our ancestors and the lives of our people."

How tragic it was for a boy to lose his mother, I thought. How unfair. It happened all the time, especially in places where harsh conditions often dictated the difference between life and death.

"Who took care of you after she died?"

"I became a man when her spirit moved to the stars. My uncles and brothers took me everywhere with them, hunting, sealing, fishing."

"Where was your father?"

Irniq vigorously rubbed his hands together in the water to remove the blood stains. "My father's name was Amaquaq. He drowned off the ice when he was sealing, just after I was born." He slowly wiped his hands dry with a cloth.

"How did you learn to speak such good English?"

"My cousin gave me lessons every day. He took me with him when he went hunting. I was with him when he translated for English speakers on fishing and hunting journeys south to the big rivers. He spoke to me in English, so I could have an honourable trade, like him." He smiled, as if he was recalling something. "Some of the Hudson's Bay Company men are still teaching me to read and write in their language, but it is difficult!"

I thought of how hard it would be for a hunter and guide like Irniq, who had little access to the Esquimaux' own burgeoning writing system, to grasp the meanings of Roman symbols on paper. "And now are you a professional guide for English and American explorers?"

"Yes, Sir. They hire me because of my hunting and tracking skills, and because I speak English." He paused. "My people told me you also saved William Ouligback Senior's life."

I remembered that event well. We were near the North Pole River in 1847, searching for the missing Franklin party. The weather conditions were terrible. "Aye, the poor man fell on his dagger and suffered a severe injury to his arm. He refused to let me treat it at first . . ."

He nodded. "They told me that when the shaman came, Ouligback believed that salves, chanting and healing rituals would heal the wound, but despite the shaman's good work, it refused to get better because an angry spirit got in the way. The shaman tried to banish the spirit, but it was too strong."

"That's right. Mr. Ouligback's arm was unfortunately infected, which put his life and work at risk. At the very least, he could have lost his arm. He was a brave man. He finally gave me permission to tend to the wound."

"Your medicine makes miracles. My mother and many others told me this."

"Well, it's not really my medicine, you know. I learned it from teachers in my native land, Scotland. But shamans make important contributions to healing as well, Irniq. They can cross the kinds of boundaries I can never hope to breach. I'm afraid I have no power to work with the spirit world, although I'd like to think that God, the spirit guide of my homeland, sometimes listens to my prayers." One of the many things I admired about the Esquimaux was their relationship with nature and the spirit world.

Irniq looked at his hands. "Why did you never return to Repulse Bay or the Arctic, John?"

"This may surprise you, but I once made a plan to return to the Arctic."

"Why didn't you come?"

"There was an accident. The ship which was constructed for the journey sank in a storm. The crew perished, and my heart was broken. Later I met my wife Kate, and my life went in another direction."

He rubbed at his eyes. "Do you have children?"

"No, we do not. Do you?"

"Yes, two boys. Anu is five years old. He was born when there was fresh snow on the ground. Taktuq is three. He was born when there was a great fog, during the migration of the caribou. When we have a girl, we will name her Atuqtuaq, after my mother."

He looked thoughtful, as if he were trying to decide whether or not to ask a more personal question. "It's all right," I said, sensing what was on his mind.

"Did you ever wish to have children?"

I cleared my throat. "Yes, we did."

→ *4 Addison Gardens*
Kensington, London
[AUGUST 1883]

I stroked the nape of Kate's neck as we lay in each other's arms. "Tell me about your visit, John dear," she said.

"Irniq told me that long ago I saved his mother's life when she had just lost a newly born child. I do not recall the event, because there were far too many just like it." Kate shivered, distressed for the women who had suffered that way, and I knew that her own losses were never far from her mind. I held her more tightly.

"He wanted to meet the man who made it possible for him to be born, and to thank me in person. He said he loved and respected his mother very much, that she visits him at night when he is asleep, that she tells him stories."

Kate's eyes widened. "Oh my goodness. He dreams of her as if she is really there, but then he awakens . . ."

"Aye, Katie. He awakens, but he never feels that his mother is far away."

She smiled, and it struck me that hearing this gave her a sense of relief about her own losses. "They are not unlike us then?" she asked.

"That's right, with one interesting difference. They believe that their deceased are always busy visiting one another in what they call *qilak*, the heavens, above the rocks, the ice and snow. The people take great pleasure in watching them shoot across the dark skies in the form of meteors, to spend time with each other. They believe that the spirits dance in the aurora borealis. It's quite a beautiful way to look at death, don't you think?"

"It sounds lovely, actually. We pray to God and Jesus Christ in heaven, and we believe the souls of our departed ones live with *them*." She giggled. "I think the idea of travelling as a shooting star is far more exciting."

I held her tightly. "So do I."

"Does Irniq have children?"

"Yes, two boys."

After Kate had drifted off to sleep, I lay awake, thinking about Irniq and his reasons for wanting to find me after all these years. I understood why he would have been curious about the man who had saved his mother's life, and it seemed as though he had learned much about me from his people. There was no question that I liked the young man; I had grown increasingly comfortable with him as our time together on the Westrays went on. I could even imagine inviting him to join me for another fishing and hunting holiday in the Orkneys.

The idea both pleased and worried me. Did I wish to spend more time with Irniq because of my grief about not having a son of my own, and was he somehow brought to me for that reason? Although I had faith in God, I was not given to believing in such unproved notions as destiny, yet here was a young Esquimaux who had travelled all the way from the Arctic to meet me and thank me for saving his mother's life. He was also a relative of my travelling companions. As I lay beside my sleeping wife, I thought about what life in the Arctic had meant to me. I didn't want to let go of it completely, even though I was too old to travel there.

→ Westray and Papa Westray, the Orkneys
[JULY 1886]

When Irniq and I next corresponded, we agreed to meet again in the Orkneys the following summer, a plan which gave me much satisfaction. We met in Stromness and took the ferry to Westray, then sailed a borrowed yole over to Papa, its small sister isle. We landed the sailboat on a sandy beach. As we unloaded our things, Irniq handed me a small deerskin package.

"This is for you, John. To show you my appreciation for meeting with you again." I unwrapped the animal hide and withdrew a smooth, stone carving of a seal.

He was smiling. "I made it for you."

"It is exquisite, Irniq. I am most grateful."

On that visit, I taught him how to sail. We fished, caught birds and shot hares for sustenance, and we built a small cairn with rocks to mark our island holiday. We competed against one another with my rifle at target practice. Irniq had the advantage of being many years my junior; his aim was consistently steady and true. I — a man who had at one time earned a trophy for marksmanship — had to accept that I was losing my magic touch.

Words flowed more fluently between us during that visit. I asked Irniq to tell me some news from the Arctic.

"My cousin Tukkuttok had a baby girl and named her Uqi."

"What does the baby's name mean?"

"It means 'survivor.'"

I smiled. "That is a good name."

One evening, when our bellies were full and our bodies tired from the exertions of the day, I asked Irniq to tell me what his people thought of the Kabloonans who came to explore the frozen north. "White men think differently than your people do," I said.

He grimaced. "Yes they do. Our people and Kabloonans do not speak the same language, so both sides make many mistakes because we do not understand each other. I can tell you what has been passed along to us by our relatives and ancestors, what we tell our children, and what they will tell to their children. Are you certain you want to know the full truth of what our people think of the Kabloonans?"

"Yes, I am curious. Whatever you say may be difficult to hear, but your honesty will not personally offend me."

He hesitated, as if deciding how to choose the right words. "My people do not understand why Kabloonans want to kill everything. They do not care when an animal suffers, or if they take more than they need. We are bothered and unhappy that they never give thanks to the animals for providing them with food and warm clothes. They think they own the land, the animals, our bodies and minds, but *we* don't even own these things and places. We borrow something, and then we give it back."

I could not deny the truth of his statement. "Go on. I am listening carefully to your words."

"As you know, our people believe that hunting should be gentle, that the hunted should trust us enough to accept our snares, our arrows and harpoons, our gratitude. Hunting should be quiet, so the animals are not shocked by the cracking sounds of many guns and the horrible, stinking smoke that fills the air. Kabloonans wonder why the animals stop coming to them, why they almost starve because the animals stay away. We try to explain the reasons to them, but they do not listen to us. They shove food into their mouths and hardly chew on it, or taste its goodness."

"My God — "

"Should I stop now?"

"No. Tell me all of it."

"You know that we take what we need, and cache the rest for our return journeys and for others who are hungry. Your travelling parties did the same thing, John. That way, everyone has a chance of surviving when conditions are bad. Why do other Kabloonan explorers throw so much away? We do not understand this at all."

I shook my head. "Perhaps because those white men have too much, they don't want — or know how — to stop doing those things. You know, I'm not quite sure myself. Greed is a disease of the mind. I don't know of any medicine that can cure it."

"Another thing that makes us unhappy is when they force themselves on our women, our mothers and daughters, our sisters. If they treated us well and then asked to be close to our women, maybe the ones they desire would make their own decisions and reward them. My people tell me you never did that, John."

"No, I did not. It's barbaric."

"Bar . . . ?"

"Barbaric. The word means everything you just said. Cruel treatment of others, the animals, of people's belongings. Taking more than you need, not sharing what you have." John Franklin's earlier expeditions in search of the Northwest Passage came to mind. There had been rumours about his men's crude behaviour towards the Cree, Ojibwa, Yellowknife and Esquimaux guides who accompanied them.

"Are stories of Kabloonan expeditions from long ago still told by the native people, Irniq?"

"The stories are still told to warn our children about the evil ways of some Kabloonans. We heard of treachery, murder and cannibalism. Our people were taught to stay away from English explorers like John Franklin and George Back, because the first man was too weak to control his men, and the second one treated our people like slaves."

There was no point in pretending that the behaviour of explorers towards native people had been exemplary over the years, because there had been plenty of talk about their antics. "Aye, I heard about a disastrous Royal Navy journey up the Coppermine River long before I first came to Hudson Bay. The leader was Lieutenant John Franklin, and his travelling party was under orders to explore the Arctic shoreline."

Irniq frowned. "Do you know John Richardson?"

I nodded. "He was a doctor from Scotland."

"My uncles spoke of him. They said that he shot a voyageur through the head."

"I have heard about that. Apparently, the man Richardson executed had done something terrible, and he deserved to be shot."

"What did he do?"

"It was said that when hunting conditions were poor and the men in the British party were starving, the voyageur killed at least one man, ate his flesh and offered it to the others. Some of Franklin's men consumed the meat, and then realized that it was from the remains of a human. Apparently this man was dangerous. Dr. Richardson shot him through the head with his pistol, when he was found next to a white man's body with a gun in his hand.

"There are many rules in the Royal Navy, Irniq. For example, a man must never leave his fellow sailors unless he is ordered to do so by an officer. If he does and he is caught, he is punished for abandoning his duties."

"Did the natives travelling with the Kabloonans live under those same rules?"

"Yes, it was expected of them."

"The Kabloonans who left the big ships and died . . ." he began.

"Their sad situation was different, Irniq. The men of the *Erebus* and *Terror* were dreadfully ill when they were marching on the ice, so I imagine that after a while, they were no longer thinking about rules. Each person likely died from natural causes, not from murder. The survivors probably consumed the dead men's flesh because there was simply no alternative."

I talked about the many Kabloonans who must have felt trapped like penned animals aboard the ships, and how frightening it would have been to listen — month after month — to the sounds of pack ice squeezing the hulls, grinding past iron sheaths and against wooden boards, alternately lifting the vessels and their terrified occupants up, pushing them forward, then suddenly releasing them, only to grip and drop them again.

He slowly shook his head. "John, can you give me advice?"

"Of course, I will certainly try."

"What should my people do when we are guides and hunters for the Kabloonans, and they do not listen to us or treat us with respect?"

I let out a long sigh, troubled but not shocked by the knowledge that white explorers still treated the natives poorly. "Refuse to assist them, Irniq."

"Just like that?"

"Yes, just like that. If your people do not help them, they will not survive, and they know it."

It was important for me to know those unpleasant truths as the Esquimaux understood them. I knew that white men had done harm to native peoples while they pressed on to open up the north for passage and trade, but the things I heard from the young man were personal and raw.

When our time together came to an end, we waited at the docks in Stromness for the arrival of the *Prince Rupert*, which would take Irniq across the Atlantic to York Factory. I could see that he was feeling melancholy about saying goodbye, and this time I felt it too. We had grown much closer since his arrival two weeks earlier. He turned to me as we stood side by side looking out at Hamnavoe Bay.

"Our time together has been a good experience for me," he said.

"And mine with you," I replied.

"The only thing I want from you, John, is to never forget us, your Esquimaux friends. My wish is that you will always think of our people and the land, the birds, the fish and animals, our ice and snow."

"You have my word on that, young man," I replied. "In fact, I have an idea. If you can withstand another ocean crossing, come and meet me here at the same time next year. We will walk, sail and fish together, and I promise you that I'll beat you at target practice!"

His reply was swift. "I would like to return, but I must warn you that if we are to meet again, it is *I* who will beat *you* at shooting!"

I told Kate all about the surprisingly close friendship which had arisen between Irniq and me. She listened with interest as I described how their people suffered at the hands of the white people, and how they survived living in such a harsh environment by sharing everything they had with each other. She was particularly moved to hear about Irniq's gratitude for everything he had, and about his deep love for his family. I told her that I wished to meet Irniq in the Orkneys every year. I could afford to pay for the rental of a simple croft, and as a retired chief factor for the Hudson's Bay Company, I was able to pay for his Atlantic journey at a greatly reduced price.

"Kate, he doesn't make much as an interpreter and guide . . ."

She hugged me. "Don't worry about the cost, dear. Your time with him does your heart good, and the good Lord knows you deserve it."

Before each of these summer visits, I made a point of inviting Kate to join us. She consistently declined, but I always left for our holiday with an item she had sewed for him: a cap for the windy Orcadian weather, a neck warmer, a bookmark. Whenever I kissed her goodbye, she reminded me to give Irniq her very best wishes.

Irniq had never known his father, and I have no children. I have grown to feel as though that fine young man has become the son I have longed for. How blessed I am that he has made the effort to find me.

EPILOGUE

On Saturday July 22nd, 1893, just as the mid-summer sun was setting, my beloved husband of thirty-three years passed away. "He had been suffering from bouts of influenza for over three months, but his death came as a shock because his eyes had recently been brighter, his expression more cheerful, his strength slowly returning.

My sister Emily and I made arrangements for a private funeral service to be held at St. John the Baptist Church in Addison Gardens on the following Friday. We decorated his coffin with wreaths, crosses, anchors, shields, bouquets and a colourful basket of fresh flowers. I carried a simple wreath of the heather John so loved.

We had issued no invitations for the service, so we were taken by surprise when we arrived at the church and were greeted by a gathering of John's friends and companions from the Royal Society and Royal Geographical Society, who stood waiting near the entrance to pay their respects. After the service, Emily and I accompanied John's coffin to Euston Station, where we departed by train for the north of Scotland.

We arrived at Kirkwall with our sad cargo aboard the steamer vessel *St. Magnus*, to the sound of church bells from St. Magnus Cathedral on the hill above the docks. A large, solemn crowd was waiting at the wharf to meet us. All shops and businesses in the town had been closed, and flags had been lowered to half-mast. At one o'clock our silent procession moved up the hill to the cathedral, where Reverend Walker conducted a service, and then the casket was lowered into the ground. I had ordered a cross placed on three stone risers for my dear husband's grave. The inscription to John Rae reads:

They that wait upon the Lord
shall renew their strength

TO THE REVERED MEMORY OF HER
BELOVED HUSBAND
THIS MONUMENT IS ERECTED BY
CATHARINE J.A. RAE

Emily and I later sold the house in Addison Gardens and moved to Chislehurst, Kent, because no matter how hard I tried, it was too painful for me to walk from one room into another and not find him there. Even so, I never stopped missing the man who had been my closest companion.

In 1906, a letter addressed to me arrived in the post from the Norwegian explorer Roald Amundsen. He had just succeeded in becoming the first person to sail the elusive link in the Northwest Passage, by navigating the channel of young ice John had spotted from the western shore of the Boothia Peninsula fifty-two years earlier. Mr. Amundsen wrote that, inspired by John, he had chosen to live and travel with the Esquimaux in the Canadian Arctic with a view to being the first person to complete the route in his schooner, the *Gjoa*.

I was gratified to read Mr. Amundsen's words of praise for my dear John. The man I married had indeed been an extraordinary explorer, yet in my opinion he was so much more: an honest man with a true heart, and the best husband and partner any woman could ever hope for. As I had told him in Westminster Abbey all those years ago when we looked at the bust of Sir John Franklin, John Rae would forever be a hero.

AUTHOR'S NOTE

In researching and writing *Finding John Rae*, I made the decision to be as accurate as possible in my biographical account of Rae and with the historical characters who were known to have played a part in his life. I could not help wondering, however, whether Rae, who had spent so much of his life in the Arctic, had ever enjoyed contact with the Inuit after he returned from his explorations in the north with the Hudson's Bay Company. There was no mention of such a thing in the historical records, but the absence of information should not mean that it didn't happen. It is well known that Rae returned to the Orkneys every year to sail, shoot, fish and visit with his many friends in the area, sometimes accompanied by his wife Kate. It is satisfying to imagine that a Hudson's Bay Company ship brought an Inuit visitor from the Arctic to spend time with him. I think he would have liked that very much.

SUGGESTED FURTHER READING

Beattie, Owen & John Geiger. (1987). *Frozen in Time: The Fate of the Franklin Expedition*. United Kingdom: Bloomsbury Publishing.

Berton, Pierre. (1988). *The Arctic Grail: The Quest for the North West Passage and the North Pole, 1818–1909*. Toronto: Viking.

Bunyan, Ian, Jenni Calder, Dale Idiens & Bryce Wilson. (1993). *No Ordinary Journey: John Rae, Arctic Explorer, 1813–1893*. Edinburgh, Montreal & Kingston: National Museums of Scotland & McGill-Queen's University Press.

Delgado, James P. (1999). *Across the Top of the World: The Quest for the Northwest Passage*. Vancouver/Toronto: Douglas & McIntyre.

Heddle, Iris E. (2005). *Roughing It: The Story of John Rae as a Boy*. Kirkwall: Orkney Islands Council.

Keenleyside, Anne, Margaret Bertulli & Henry C. Fricke. (1997). *The Final Days of the Franklin Expedition: New Skeletal Evidence*. Arctic Institute of North America.

McGoogan, Ken. (2001). *Fatal Passage: The Story of John Rae, the Arctic Hero Time Forgot*. New York: Carroll & Graf Publishers.

McGoogan, Ken. (2005). *Lady Franklin's Revenge: A True Story of Ambition, Obsession and the Remaking of Arctic History*. Toronto: HarperCollins.

Newman, Peter C. (1985). *Company of Adventurers*. Toronto: Viking Canada.

Potter, Russell A. (2016). *Finding Franklin: The Untold Story of a 165-Year Search*. Kingston: McGill-Queen's University Press.

Rae, John. (1850). *Narrative of an Expedition to the Shores of the Arctic Sea in 1846 and 1847*. London: T&W Boone.

Rae, John. (2012). *The Arctic Journals of John Rae by John Rae*. Selected and Introduced by Ken McGoogan. Victoria: Touchwood Editions.

Richards, R.L. (1985). *Dr. John Rae*. Whitby, U.K.: Caedmon.

Varga, Darrell. (2012). *John Walker's Passage*. Toronto: University of Toronto Press.

Walker, John. (2008). *Passage*. Ottawa: National Film Board of Canada.

Wiebe, Rudy. (1995). *A Discovery of Strangers*. Toronto: Vintage Canada.

Wilson, John. (2003). *Discovering the Arctic: The Story of John Rae*. Toronto: Napoleon Publishing.

Woodman, David C. (1991). *Unravelling the Franklin Mystery: Inuit Testimony*. Kingston: McGill-Queen's University Press.

ABOUT THE AUTHOR

Alice Jane Hamilton is the great-great granddaughter of John Rae's sister, Marion Sibbald Rae. Marion, her husband John Hamilton and their ten children emigrated from Stromness, Orkney, Scotland, to Hamilton, Canada West (later named Ontario), in 1856. Long interested in her famous relative, Hamilton has spent many years researching the life of John Rae. She holds an Honours B.A. in English and Japanese Studies from McMaster University and a M.A. in Modern Literatures from Birkbeck College, University of London, United Kingdom. She has taught Communications, Visual Analysis and Canadian Literature at Georgian College in Barrie, Ontario. A keen historian, she has written articles for contributions to CBC Radio (*Fresh Air* and *Morningside*), as well as various news publications, including the *Globe and Mail*, the *Toronto Star* and the *National Post*. Hamilton lives with her husband in the small town of Penetanguishene, on Georgian Bay, from which John Franklin left by canoe in 1825 on his second overland journey to the Arctic, down the Mackenzie River.